Contents

S0-DRD-835

By matching up the guides at the edge of this page with the marks opposite them along the edge of the book, you can quickly turn to the unit containing the material you want.

Reference Manual

For the Office

7th Edition

Clifford R. House
President Emeritus
Cincinnati Technical College

Kathie Sigler
Dean for Administration and Professor
Miami-Dade Community College

K46
PUBLISHED BY
SOUTH-WESTERN PUBLISHING CO.
CINCINNATI   WEST CHICAGO, IL   CARROLLTON, TX   LIVERMORE, CA

ISBN: 0-538-11460-6
Library of Congress Catalog Card Number: 87-72808

2 3 4 5 6 7 8 9 10 11 12 13 14 K 1 0 9 8 7 6 5 4 3 2 1 0 9

Printed in the United States of America

Preface

Reference Manual for the Office, Seventh Edition, is a useful reference for people engaged in office work and an effective text for those *preparing* for office work. Those who work at writing, whether their efforts are creative or routine, will find the manual an easily accessible storehouse of valuable information. The revised and expanded *Study Guides* are particularly helpful for those who wish to evaluate their specific abilities or measure their improvement after study and practice.

While the seventh edition retains the important fundamentals of the first six editions, it has been revised and expanded to reflect the profound changes brought to the office workplace by computers, word processors, and other technological innovations.

All units that were retained in the seventh edition have been revised and expanded. New units or sections have been added in reference to spelling, editing, transcription, keyboarding, information processing, and filing.

Many of the changes are based on comprehensive surveys administered to representative users: students, teachers, and persons employed in offices. Suggestions from users are responsible for the retention of the spiral binding, the more intensive use of color and graphics, the detailed outline of contents at the front of the book, and the expanded index.

Reference Manual for the Office is used as a text or supplementary text in communication skills classes and a wide variety of business education classes, including office education and office procedures courses. The text and study guides are frequently used together in vocational education and adult education programs. This combination is particularly useful in cooperative education and other work-related programs in which a concentrated, short-term effort or review is required. Those who are studying to improve their office skills on their own or studying with a minimum of supervision and guidance will find the manual and study guides arranged logically for self-directed study and review.

UNIT

1   **Grammar.** Expanded. Includes all the conventions most students and writers of business documents find useful. Simplified rules. Additional examples. The section on eliminating bias in writing has been expanded.

2   **Punctuation.** Sentence patterns are used whenever possible; second-color printing emphasizes and clarifies the patterns. Quick reference chart containing the twenty-two frequently used conventions; referenced to text for detailed explanations. Spacing charts for all punctuation marks show spacing before and after each mark for keyboarding. Complete section on compound words.

3   **Capitalization.** Updated to include current preferences. Additional examples per user suggestions.

4   **Abbreviations.** New list of over five hundred commonly used business abbreviations.

Word Division. Expanded. Emphasizes current trend of eliminating or minimizing word division.

Spelling. Succinct treatment of useful rules, word roots, prefixes, and suffixes. List of English words misspelled most frequently.

7   **Numbers and Symbols.** Single, condensed table outlining conventions for writing numbers. Detailed information for writing numbers in formal style, ordinary text, informal style, functional writing, running text, and technical material. Employment of different styles within the same document.

8   **Information Processing.** Defines information processing, computer information processing, and word processing. Describes word processing: authorship, keyboarding, handwritten input, dictating, transcribing, proofreading, editing, software features, spelling checkers, thesauri, formatting, and hardware. Explains spreadsheets—and provides a complete example of how a spreadsheet works. Describes data base systems, integrated applications, and specialized applications. Provides an extensive glossary of information processing terms, identifying those used exclusively or extensively in word processing.

9   **Keyboarding Basics.** Provides information on centering, tabulation, proofreading, corrections, and the like, on conventional typewriters, electronic typewriters, word processors and microcomputers.

10   **Letters, Memos, Envelopes.** Revised and expanded. Additional examples.

11   **Reports and Manuscripts.** Revised and expanded. Additional examples.

12   **Mail, Telephone, Wire Service.** Updated to include the increased use of automated equipment, the proliferation of private messenger and mailing services, and the expansion of electronic communication.

13   **Filing.** Standard treatment in a new unit based on questionnaire response from teachers and students.

14   **Getting the Job—Getting Ahead.** Identifying employment opportunities; applying for a job; getting ahead on the job.

15   **References.** Provides information regarding almanacs, biographies, dictionaries, directories, encyclopedias, geographical materials, mail service information, publications in print, shipping information, spellers, thesauri, travel information, and word division manuals.

Please remember that recognized authorities do not always agree on matters of style, grammar, punctuation, and the like. When consensus does exist, it is reflected in this manual. When preferences differ, this manual reflects the dominant opinion—and any acceptable alternatives.

The authors would like to express their thanks to the many teachers, students, and others who have suggested improvements. Those suggestions are always taken seriously, and many of them are incorporated in this new edition.

CLIFFORD R. HOUSE

KATHIE SIGLER

Paragraph Index

Numbers refer to paragraph numbers

Unit I

Grammar

Understand:
- The way words relate to each other in sentences
- How communication is improved through the correct use of grammar

Acquire:
- The ability to recognize incorrect grammatical usage
- The ability to identify parts of speech

Be Prepared To:
- Identify and correct frequent grammatical errors
- Apply grammatical rules in business writing

The skills employers want most are basic academic skills—the ability to read, write, communicate, compute, and reason. This unit will focus on language usage by providing guidelines for identifying and using parts of speech.

You should be familiar with the major parts of speech—nouns, pronouns, adjectives, verbs, adverbs, prepositions, and conjunctions. These are the categories used to identify the part each word plays within a sentence. Some words can be used both as nouns and as verbs. Compare the uses of *mix* in the following sentences:

Noun: The *mix* of ingredients was just right. (subject)
Cassie wanted to use the correct *mix*. (object)
Verb: Please *mix* the ingredients thoroughly.

When a word plays a different role in a sentence, it may change form.

Noun: The *gratitude* of the students was obvious.
Verb: It *gratified* her to do so well on the exam.
Adjective: They reported it was a *gratifying* visit.

The dictionary is a great source of information; each word, or entry, is followed by the pronunciation guide which is followed immediately by the word's part of speech.

NOUNS

100

The most frequently used words are **nouns**. Nouns identify persons, places, things, or ideas.

Persons: Ms. Anabel Farinas, secretaries, Pat
Places: Detroit, Bayside, classroom

Things: Golden Gate Bridge, manual, mirror
Ideas: ethics, morality, justice

101 Common Nouns and Proper Nouns

There are two kinds of nouns, common nouns and proper nouns. A **common noun** names any one of a group or an entire group of persons, places, things, or ideas and is not capitalized. A **proper noun** names a particular person, place, thing, or idea and is always capitalized.

Common Nouns	Proper Nouns
teacher	Mr. Holst, Dr. Charles Klingensmith
country	United States of America, Cuba
company	Jeff Brezner Consultants, Inc. Thompson's Office Supplies
speech	"I Have a Dream"

102 Singular Nouns and Plural Nouns

Nouns referring to one person, place, thing, or idea are **singular**; Nouns referring to two or more persons, places, things, or ideas are **plural**.

Singular Nouns	Plural Nouns
book	books
woman	women
operating room	operating rooms
worker	workers
bench	benches
life	lives

NOTE: The plurals of nouns are usually formed by adding *s* (boys, rooms, workers). Some nouns, however, form the plural according to different guidelines (women, benches, lives). Consult your dictionary if you are unsure of the correct plural form of any noun.

103 Noun as the Subject

The word or word group about which the sentence is written is the **subject**. A noun, a pronoun, or a phrase or clause used as a noun may be the subject of a sentence. Noun subjects may be singular or plural.

A singular subject requires a singular verb.

> *Jose Mateo is* the best choice for the excellence award.
> *He drives* carefully since the accident.
> The *nurse was graduated* today with honors.

A plural or compound subject requires a plural verb.

> *Jose Mateo and Sheldon Lurie are* the best choices for the excellence awards. (two nouns combined)
> *They drive* carefully since the accident. (plural pronoun)
> The *nurses were graduated* today with honors. (plural noun)

104   Noun as the Object

The word or word group that receives the action of a transitive verb or verb form is the **object**. A noun, a pronoun, or a phrase or clause used as a noun may be the object in a sentence. The noun object may be singular or plural without changing the form of the verb providing the action.

104.1   Direct object — Answers the question of *who* or *what* in receiving the action of a transitive verb.

> Rick Lambright passed his CPA *examination!*

104.2   Indirect object — Receives the action of a transitive verb indirectly. When preceded by a preposition such as *to* or *for* it also functions as the **object of a preposition.** (Also see ¶142.)

> They sent the CPA scores *to Rick Lambright.* (*Rick Lambright* is the object of the preposition *to* and the indirect object of the sentence.)
>
> The school board presented the trophies *to her winning team.* (*Team* is the object of the preposition *to.*)
>
> Zoily gave *Cary* the new plans. (*Plans* is the direct object; *Cary* is the indirect object.)

104.3   Complement — Explains, further defines, or completes the description of the noun subject or object.

> Renee Betancourt Carpenter was named the new *dean.* (*Dean* further describes *Renee Betancourt Carpenter.*)
>
> They found the play *charming.* (*Charming* explains how the play was perceived and describes the word *play.*)

105   Nouns Ending in *S*

Some nouns ending in *s* are always singular, others are always plural, and still others may be either singular or plural depending upon their meaning. If you are unsure of the correct usage, consult your dictionary for further information about those nouns that are only singular or only plural.

105.1   Singular — Requires singular verb.

consensus	process	mumps	dress
summons	distress	mistress	news

> The *summons was* delivered to Janet Marie Cassidy.
> "*Mumps is* a dangerous illness for adults," stressed Dr. Tena Frank.

105.2   Plural — Requires plural verb.

savings	liabilities	profits	specifics
losings	thanks	credentials	grounds

> Cary Shookoff's *profits* for the year *were* unexpectedly high.
> The *grounds were* beautifully landscaped by The Good Earth Nursery.

NOTE: The following words are always plural and require a plural verb, *unless* they are used with "pair of."

shears	(plural verb required)
pair of shears	(singular verb required)
slacks	(plural verb required)
pair of slacks	(singular verb required)
pliers	(plural verb required)
pair of pliers	(singular verb required)
eyeglasses	(plural verb required)
pair of eyeglasses	(singular verb required)

The *eyeglasses were* found after the party.
A *pair of eyeglasses was* found after the party.

105.3   **Nouns: Same form for singular and plural.** Some nouns (not all of them ending in *s*) have the same form in both singular and plural usage. The correct verb form to be used depends upon the number of the noun (that is, Does the noun represent one thing or represent two or more?).

series	species	headquarters	corps
deer	sheep	chassis	moose
gross			means

The next *World Series is* scheduled to begin here. (one series)
Three opera series are funded this year by the endowment. (three series)

A *moose runs* across the forest. (one moose)
The *moose run* in many directions as the tiger approaches. (two or more moose)

106   # Plurals of Foreign Nouns

Foreign words used as nouns are harder to identify as singular or plural because they are not as familiar. Also, there is often more than one way to indicate the plural form. Check your dictionary when you are uncertain.

Singular—
   The *memorandum is* ready for duplicating.

Plural—
   The *memorandums are* ready for duplicating. (preferred)
   or
   The *memoranda are* ready for duplicating.

107   # Nouns Ending in -*ICS*

Nouns ending in -*ics* may be written with a singular or plural verb, depending upon the meaning of the noun.

civics	statistics	ethics
metaphysics	economics	linguistics
acrobatics	tactics	athletics

When identifying a science, an art, a body of knowledge, or a course of study, such nouns are considered singular and require a singular verb:

Acrobatics is a strenuous class taught by Diane Trapp.
Linguistics is her speciality.

When referring to physical activities or qualities, such nouns are considered plural.

The *ethics* of their decision *are* questionable.
New *statistics point* to a poor voter turnout.
Calisthenics are good for my mother's sore knee.

108 Compound Nouns

A **compound noun** is formed when two or more words are combined and used as a single noun. Compound nouns are sometimes hyphenated:

(s)	sister-in-law	middle-of-the-roader	sun-god
(pl)	sisters-in-law	middle-of-the-roaders	sun-gods

sometimes combined and written as one word:

(s)	pacemaker	downtown	photocopy
(pl)	pacemakers	(singular only)	photocopies

sometimes written as two or more words:

(s)	delivery room	secretary of state	left guard
(pl)	delivery rooms	secretaries of state	left guards

Since compound nouns are written in a variety of ways, it is always a good idea to consult a dictionary for the exact spelling. If the compound noun is not in the dictionary, it should be written as two separate words. When a compound noun is part of a company name, however, always follow the style shown on the company's letterhead.

109 Compound Nouns Ending in *Man/Men*

For information on compound nouns containing the word *man* or *men* see ¶142.1.

110 Collective Nouns

When a common noun indicates an entire group of persons, places, or things it is called a **collective noun.** Examples of collective nouns include team, group, department, organization, class, crowd, herd, staff, management, union, public, and majority.

110.1 Members acting together. If the members of the group are represented as *acting together,* the collective noun should be used with a singular verb.

The *group wants* to endorse Senator Carrie Meek.
The *majority is* in favor of a change.
    (**NOTE:** *The* precedes the collective *majority* used singularly.)
The *herd wanders* toward the watering spot at high noon.

110.2   **Members acting individually or a fraction acting separately from the whole.** If the members of the group are represented as acting *separately,* the collective noun should be used with a plural verb.

> The *group are* writing letters, driving voters, and speaking on behalf of Senator Meek.
> A *majority* of the members *are* coming tonight.
> > (**NOTE:** A precedes the collective *majority* used as a plural.)
> The *herd are* lying, walking, eating, and drinking in the pasture.

110.3   **Members acting together with later reference to members acting independently.** A group may be seen as involved in one activity, yet may be shown subsequently as members acting independently. Pronouns must agree with the proper antecedents (see ¶119). If you are referring to the group as a whole, the pronoun is plural. (Except for collectives which use the pronoun *it.*) If you are referring separately to the individuals in the group, the pronoun is singular.

> **Group acting together.**
> The *fish were* swimming furiously upstream, trying to reach *their* traditional spot for laying eggs.
> *Michigan's senators want* the legislation passed immediately. *They* want to provide *their* constituents with tax relief as soon as possible.
> The *herd drives* on through the snowstorm until *it* loses *its* way.

> **Group acting independently.**
> The *deer were* running from the big cat. *Each* feared for *his* or *her* fawn.
> The *department votes* today. *Each person wants* the election to be fair.
> I hope your *family is* coming for the holidays. *Every one* of them *is* very important to me.

111   # Geographic Locations

Geographic locations should be considered as singular and used with a singular verb when referring to one location, even though their form may seem plural.

> The *United States of America is* my home.
> *Massachusetts was* the site selected for the national convention.
> The *Canary Islands has been* their favorite hideaway.
> **But:** (all of) *The Hawaiian Islands have* something different to offer. (Reference is now made to the separate islands, thus a plural form with a plural verb.)

112   # Money, Quantities, and Time

When reference is made to one total amount of money, one quantity, or a single period of time, the form is singular (s) and a singular verb is used. When the reference is to more than one amount of money, quantity, or time period, the form is plural (pl), and a plural verb should be used.

(s)	*Her $180,000 was* the fourth prize in the sweepstakes.
(pl)	*One hundred, eighty-thousand dollars were* awarded as prizes. (Each person got one dollar.)
(s)	*Five loaves of nutbread was* her contribution to the dinner.
(pl)	*Twelve cars were* unsold at the end of the year.
(s)	*Nine months is* a long time to wait for the new baby.
(pl)	*Three hours have* passed since you last called.

113 Names of Companies and Other Organizations

Company and organization names are usually written as singular with a singular verb. However, when it is important to stress the individuals within the organization, the plural form should be used with the plural verb.

> *International Business Machines (IBM) is* a leader within the computer industry. *It continues* to keep pace with rapid changes in technology. (stressing the entire organization)
>
> *Holly McMeekin & Associates have* aided greatly in the sale of my property. *They were* always there when I had a question. (stressing individuals within the organization)

NOTE: Remember to be consistent in the agreement between company name, verb used, *and* later pronouns used for reference to the company.

114 Possessive Nouns

Possessive nouns use an apostrophe to indicate ownership. They may be either singular or plural and require corresponding verb forms.

114.1 Singular possessive noun—Requires singular verb (add 's or ' to noun—see ¶201.3).

> *Dr. Suzanne Richter's name was* placed in nomination.
> *Mary Winters' flight* to New Mexico *was* delayed due to weather.

114.2 Plural possessive noun—Requires plural verb (add ' to end of noun).

> The *students' scores* on the SAT *are* much improved.
> My *employees' presents are* to be delivered today.

115 Publications

Magazine and book titles are considered singular (and require a singular verb), even though they contain plural nouns.

> *Ladies Home Journal arrives* at my Aunt Leota's every month.
> Danielle Steel's *Secrets was* on the best-seller list for weeks.

116   References to Fractional Amounts

When fractional amounts such as:

$$\left.\begin{array}{l}\text{one-fourth}\\ \text{one-half}\\ \text{one-eighth}\\ \text{two-thirds}\end{array}\right\}\quad\text{followed by } of$$

or fractional portions such as:

may be
preceded
by a or
the
$$\left\{\begin{array}{l}\text{fraction}\\ \text{half}\\ \text{part}\\ \text{percentage}\\ \text{piece}\\ \text{portion}\end{array}\right\}\quad\text{followed by } of$$

are used, reference is singular, and a singular verb is required *if a singular noun follows or is indicated.*

> *One-fourth of* the blueprint *was* eliminated.
> *A percentage of* the painting *is* now complete.
> Only *a fraction of* the work *has* been done.

Reference is plural, and a plural verb is required *if a plural noun follows or is indicated.*

> *At least two-thirds of* the doctor's appointments *have* been rescheduled.
> *Half of* the group *have* registered for the examination. (Members of the group acting separately. See ¶110.2.)
> *Part of* the teachers *are* in favor of the issue.

117   References to "The Number" or "A Number"

The expression *the number* in a sentence refers to one specific number and is thus singular and requires a singular verb.

> *The number of custom homes* here *has* increased the value of our home.

However, the expression *a number* refers to many possible numbers. Thus, it is plural and requires a plural verb.

> *A number of employees have* used up all of their sick leave. (See also ¶110, 110.2, 110.3.)

118   References to "One of"

The expression *one of* or *one of the,* not followed by a descriptive phrase, is considered singular (refers to only *one* person or *one* thing) and requires a singular verb because the subject is *one* — **not** the object of the preposition *of.*

> *One of* them *is* going to win the nomination.
> *One of* the guests *was* the 100th visitor to the park.
> *One of* his papers *has been* accepted for publication.
> *One of* us *is* to be ready for questions.

If a descriptive phrase follows *one of* or *one of the,* you must decide if the phrase modifies just the subject, *one,* or if it modifies the object of the prepositional phrase which follows the *one.*

> She has always been one of *those who excel* at everything they do. (*Those* is the subject of *who excel* — because all of those excel, **not** just the *one.*)
> Dr. Geri Ostrow is *the only one* of those graduates *who is* working with multiple personality disorder. (Refers to the *one* person, **not** all of those graduates.)
> *The only one of the things* at the garage sale I want *is* the exercycle. (Refers to *one* thing.)

NOTE: Both *the* and *only* are required to change the meaning to singular. In the following example without both words, the meaning remains plural and requires the plural verb.

> Dr. Geri Ostrow is *only one of those graduates who are* working with multiple personality disorder. (Refers to many graduates.)

PRONOUNS

119 Pronouns are "Shorthand" for Nouns

When a noun has been identified previously, or is understood, the shorter pronoun may be used in place of the noun.

> The *councilors* agreed that *they* wanted Eileen Cunningham as *their* vice president.

Using the pronoun sounds better and is less awkward than repeating the noun.

> The *councilors* agreed that the *councilors* wanted Eileen Cunningham as the *councilors'* vice president.

The pronouns *they* and *their* replaced the noun *councilors.* The noun which a pronoun replaces is called its **antecedent** (meaning "coming before"). Pronouns must agree in person, number, and gender with the antecedent they replace. The antecedents are shown all in capital letters in the following examples:

> Dr. Kenneth Stringer read the laboratory REPORTS, put *them* in an ENVELOPE, and slid *it* into his briefcase.
> The Certified Professional Secretary EXAMINATIONS are given quarterly; *they* last two days; and *they* are considered very thorough.

120 Personal Pronouns

Personal pronouns are those pronouns that change form to indicate person. You can write or speak from three points of view. In the *first person* you talk about yourself or about a group of which you are a member. In the *second person* you talk about the person(s) to whom you are speaking, and in the *third person* you speak of anyone or anything else.

First Person Singular	First Person Plural
I, me, my, mine	we, our, ours

This is *my* new dress.
Our performance evaluation reveals areas where improvement is needed.

Second Person Singular	Second Person Plural
you, your, yours	you, your, yours

Your check-in at the conference is scheduled for noon.
You all have a chance to aid in the presentation.

Third Person Singular	Third Person Plural
he, him, his, she, her,	they, them, their, theirs
hers, it, its	

Her new car is red.
Pass out the tickets to *them,* please.

The pronoun *we* is often used instead of *I* by some who wish to avoid calling attention to themselves. However, *we* should only be used by a representative speaking on behalf of an organization, a group, another person, and the like; *I* should be used when representing a personal position or opinion.

> *I* feel it is time for us to consider a major reorganization. (a personal opinion)
> *We* shall approve your mortgage application when *we* have received all of the necessary credit approvals. (speaking on behalf of the mortgage company)

121 Indefinite Pronouns

When pronouns do not refer to a specific person, place, or thing or refer generally to a part of/portion of something, they are known as **indefinite pronouns.**

Singular:	another, anybody, anyone, anything, each, either, every, everybody, everyone, everything, much, neither, no one, nobody, nothing, one, someone, somebody, something
Plural:	both, few, many, several, others
Singular and Plural:	all, any, more, most, none, some

Singular indefinite pronouns require the use of a singular verb.

> *Each* of the reports *has its* own summary.
> (Note the agreement between *each* and *its* — both singular.)
> *Each one has* a best way to avoid confrontation.
> (Note the avoidance of the generic use of the pronouns *his* and *her.*)
> **Avoid:**   Each one has his own best way to avoid confrontation. (See ¶142.2.)

Plural indefinite pronouns require the use of a plural verb.

> *Both are* in charge of the construction crew.
> *Many* of the Sisters of St. John the Baptist *have* completed *their* doctoral degrees.

Indefinite pronouns that may be singular or plural, depending upon the noun they refer to, require a corresponding singular or plural verb.

Plural— *All* of the members *have* paid *their* annual dues. (*All* refers to
members.)

Singular— *All* of the term paper *is* complete. *It is* due tomorrow. (*All* refers to
paper.)

Since indefinite pronouns usually indicate the third person, pronouns referring to such antecedents should also be written in the third person.

Most husbands want *their* wives to be successful.

However, first or second person is used when the group referred to includes a first or second person pronoun.

Most of us want *our* wives to be successful.

Compound Pronouns

122

When *-self* (singular) or *-selves* (plural) is added to a pronoun, a **compound pronoun** is created. Use compound pronouns that employ *-self* or
-selves only in the same sentence as the noun or pronoun they modify.

	Singular	**Plural**
First Person:	myself	ourselves
Second Person:	yourself	yourselves
Third Person:	himself, herself, itself	themselves

Compound pronouns can further emphasize the noun or pronoun already
indicated.

The *students themselves* want to teach the class.
I shall call Dr. McCabe *myself* to discuss this issue.

Compound pronouns can direct the action of the verb back to the subject. When these pronouns perform this function they are called **reflexive
pronouns.**

She has convinced *herself* that she will get the job.
They have satisfied *themselves* that the verdict is just.

The following compound pronouns (which are also indefinite pronouns)
are always singular and require a singular verb:

anybody	anyone *or* any one	anything
everybody	everyone *or* every one	everything
nobody	no one	nothing
somebody	someone *or* some one	something

Everybody is required to register in order to vote.
Something strange *was* happening to the phone connection.

Any one, every one, and *some one* are written as two separate words
only when followed by *of* or when any one of a group or a number of
things is implied.

Every one of them was on time.

But: *Everyone* was on time. (Everybody was on time.)

When two of these compound pronouns are joined (by *and*) as the subject of a sentence, the verb is still singular.

Anybody and everybody is due a second chance.

When *each* or *every* is used **in front of** two or more subjects joined by *and,* the verb is still singular.

Each customer and employee *was* evacuated when the fire was discovered.

However, when *each* **follows** a plural subject, the verb should be plural.

The managers *each have* high hopes for the sales promotion.

123 Nominative, Objective, and Possessive Case of Pronouns

Not only do pronouns change form to indicate person, they also change form to indicate their function in a sentence. This pronoun function is identified as one of three cases: nominative, objective, or possessive.

123.1 The nominative case. The **nominative case** of the pronoun is used when the pronoun is the subject of the sentence (what the sentence is about) or when the pronoun is the complement of the sentence (completing or adding meaning to the verb—such as a predicate nominative [the object of a linking verb—is, am, was, were, be, been, being, seem, appear, become, thought]).

> **Nominative Pronouns:**   I, we, you, he, she, it, they, who, that, whoever, which, what

As the subject:

> *She* (**not** her) has been elected president of the Michigan Osteopathic Physicians.
> *They* (**not** them) are reviewing the production schedule.
> Jose and *she* (**not** her) had a wonderful party last night.

As the complement:

> The one with the green striped shirt might be *he* (**not** him).
> Dr. Padron said he was the one *who* (**not** whom) took the personnel reports.

123.2 The objective case. The **objective case** of the pronoun is used when the pronoun is the object (direct or indirect) of a transitive verb (the action of the verb is directed at the pronoun),

> *or*

when the pronoun is the object of a preposition (part of the prepositional phrase),

> *or*

when the pronoun is the subject or object (for exception see 125) of an **infinitive** (verb form preceded by *to*).

Objective Pronouns: me, us, you, him, her, it, them, whom, that, whomever, which, what

As the object of the verb:

Eduardo gave Suzanne and me (**not** I) help with the billing.

As the object of a preposition:

A complete physical was recommended for *him* (**not** he).

As the subject or object of an infinitive:

The director asked *her* (**not** she) to apply. (*Her* is the subject of *to apply*.)
Did Dr. Richter ask Lila Mae to consult *them* (**not** they)? (*Them* is the object of *to consult.*)

123.3 **The possessive case.** The **possessive case** of the pronoun is used when the pronoun indicates possession. When the **possessive pronoun** precedes the noun it modifies (or describes), use *my, our, your, his, her, its,* or *their.* When the possessive pronoun is separated from the noun it modifies, use *mine, ours, yours, his, hers, its,* or *theirs.*

My instruments are right here. (preceding noun)
The instruments on the cart are *mine.* (separated from noun)

Use the possessive form of the pronoun immediately before a **gerund** (a verb form ending in *ing* and functioning as a noun) or *before* a **participle** (a verb form ending in *ing* that may show tense or be used as an adjective) functioning as an adjective.

His leaving so soon was quite a surprise. (gerund)
Jan told me of *your winning* bet. (participle)

Sometimes possessive pronouns are confused with similar sounding **contractions** (shortened words in which the apostrophe indicates omitted letters). Avoid this mistake.

Possessive Pronouns	Contractions
whose	who's (who is)
your	you're (you are)
its	it's (it is)
their	they're (they are)
theirs	there's (there is)

124 # Pronoun Following "Than" or "As"

When a pronoun is used in a comparison following *than* or *as,* mentally fill in missing words to determine correct case (nominative or objective).

Penny is not paid as much as she. (paid as much as she *is paid*)
The first contestant ran faster than I. (than I *ran*)
Louis rated you higher than him. (than *Louis rated* him)

125 Pronouns Used With "To Be"

Use the objective form of the pronoun when the pronoun is the subject of, and precedes, the infinitive (see ¶135) *to be*.

> We need *him* to be here.
> Mr. Wilfredo Colon wants *them* to be neat.
> *Whom* do you want to be elected?

Use the objective form of the pronoun when *to be* has a subject (not preceded by a linking verb) and is followed by the pronoun.

> *Whom* do you want to be *me* in the play?
> The students mistook the teacher to be *me*.

Use the nominative form of the pronoun when *to be* has no subject and is followed by the pronoun.

> The guilty party was thought to be *I*.
> The doctor was thought to be *he*.

NOTE: While these examples are grammatically correct, it is clearer to say:

> They thought *I* was the guilty party.
> She thought *he* was the doctor.

126 Interrogative and Relative Pronouns

Interrogative pronouns are used to ask questions. **Relative pronouns** are used to make reference to a noun in the main clause of a sentence. The same pronouns may be used as interrogative or relative pronouns and may be either singular or plural.

> **(Interrogative — singular)**
> *Who* is coming?
> To *whom* is the letter addressed?

> **(Interrogative — plural)**
> *Who* are coming?
> To *whom* are the letters addressed?

> **(Relative — singular)**
> Laura Wilson was the one *who* typed the report. (Relative, referring to *one*.)
> Kandy Bentley-Baker, *whom* I worked with at North Campus, is now working at the New World School of the Performing Arts.

> **(Relative — plural)**
> Laura Wilson and Gloria Anasagasti were the ones *who* typed the report.
> Kandy Bentley-Baker and Richard Janaro, both of *whom* I worked with at North Campus, are now working at the New World School of the Performing Arts.

NOTE: *Who* and *whoever* are in the nominative case, while *whom* and *whomever* are in the objective case. To avoid confusion, reword the sentence to try *he, she, I, we,* or *they* to test the correct use of *who* or *whoever*; reword to try *him, her, me, us,* or *them* to test the correct use of *whom* or *whomever*. See ¶126.1 and 126.2.

126.1   Who/whoever.

Who is the next President? (*She* is the next President.)
Send the papers to *whoever* can process our application.
(*He* can process our application. The nominative case is used because *whoever* is the subject of *can process*; the entire phrase is the object of the preposition *to*.)
Carrie is the one *who* we think will do the best job.
(We think *she* [Carrie] will do the best job.)
The applications were sent to *whoever* they thought would be interested in the position.
(They thought *she* would be interested in the position.)

126.2   Whom/whomever.

The chairperson asked *whomever* to apply for the first chair.
(The chairperson asked *them* to apply for the first chair.)
To *whom* was the report directed? (The report was directed to *him*.)
They will welcome *whomever*. (They will welcome *us*.)

126.3   **Who.** Use *who* when reference is made to an individual person or individual group:

King Arthur is the one *who* lead the Knights of the Round Table.
The knights constitute the group *who* accomplished many feats.

126.4   **That.** Use *that* when reference is made to a class, species, or kind of person or group:

That is the kind of employee I should like to hire.

or when referring to places, objects, or animals:

This church is the one *that* I attended as a child.

or to introduce an essential clause: (See ¶206.15.)

The purple hat, *that* one on the shelf, is the one my mother wanted.

126.5   **Which.** Use *which* when reference is made to places, objects, and animals:

Which horse won the first prize?

or to introduce a nonessential clause: (See ¶206.15.)

The phone call, *which* I received today, was from my son.

VERBS

127

The most common sentence errors occur through the incorrect use of verbs. Therefore, an understanding of the way verbs are used within a sentence can improve your ability to communicate effectively and accurately.

In order for a sentence to be complete, it must contain both a subject and a verb. While nouns and pronouns can be the subject of the sentence providing the action (or the object [of the sentence] being acted upon) it is the **verb** that provides the action. The verb indicates what the subject does or is, or what is happening to it.

127.1   ## Verbs make statements (or suppositions — see ¶134.3).

The building directory *is* now complete.
Dr. Patrick Gettings *will be* our next vice president.

127.2   ## Verbs give commands.

Answer the call, please. (The subject *you* is understood.)
Remain in the office until I return.

127.3   ## Verbs ask questions.

Who *will attend* the secretarial convention?
Is this your briefcase?

128   # Active/Passive Verbs

If the subject of the sentence is completing the action of the sentence (that is, directing the action toward an object), the verb is said to be in the **active voice.**

128.1   ## Active voice:

Dr. Coppolechia *diagnosed* the illness.
The insurance agent *mailed* the pictures of the accident.
(The subjects, *Dr. Coppolechia* and *the insurance agent,* performed the action indicated by the verb.)

If the subject of the sentence is being acted upon, the verb is said to be in the **passive voice.**

128.2   ## Passive voice:

The report *was delivered* by courier.
Mario *was interviewed* last week.
(The subjects, *report* and *Mario,* received the action indicated by the verb.)

The passive form of the verb is appropriate when the emphasis of the sentence is on the receiver of the action of the verb or when the person or thing performing the action is not important. In **all** other cases active verb form should be used.

Weak Use of Passive Voice:
It has been requested by the manager that a full refund be sent to you immediately.

Stronger Use of Active Voice:
The manager requested a full refund be sent to you immediately.

129

Subject/Verb Agreement

One of the most common grammatical problems is subject/verb agreement. The subject and verb in the same sentence should agree. A singular
subject (one) requires a singular verb. A plural subject (more than one) requires a plural verb.

Singular Subject/Verb:
The plan *is* (**not** are) almost complete.
He *is* (**not** are) the new receptionist.

Plural Subject/Verb:
Three women *were* (**not** was) in the waiting room.
The technicians *are* (**not** is) taking golf lessons.

A compound subject (two subjects used together) requires a plural verb.
(For exception see ¶122.)

Compound Subject/Plural Verb:
Bill and Gloria *have been* (**not** has been) treated for poison ivy.

When a group is the subject of a sentence and acts collectively with a
single purpose, a singular verb is used. See ¶110.

Group Acting Together/Singular Verb:
The committee *recommends* (**not** recommend) a complete reorganization of
the Vicente Insurance Center.

When the members of a group act independently as many different persons completing the same action, a plural verb is used.

Group Acting Independently/Plural Verb:
The staff *are* (**not** is) at their desks.

130

Helping Verbs

Helping verbs are joined to other verbs to "help" indicate voice (active/
passive) or tense (where in time the action takes place—see ¶131). The
tense indicated by a helping verb shows whether something *was* happening (past progressive), *had* happened (past perfect), *had been* happening (past perfect progressive), *is* happening (present progressive), *has*
happened (present perfect), *has been* happening (present perfect progressive), *will* happen (future), *will be* happening (future progressive), *will
have* happened (future perfect), or *will have been* happening (future perfect progressive). Common helping verbs include the following:

are	might ⎱
can	might be ⎬ *Might* indicates
can be	might have ⎬ what *was* possible
can have	might have been ⎰
could	must
could be	must be
could have	must have
could have been	must have been
do (present emphatic tense)	shall
did (past emphatic tense)	shall be
had	shall have
had been	shall have been
has	should
has been	should be
have	should have
have been	should have been
is	will
May indicates action still in question or still possible ⎧ may	will be
may be	will have
may have	will have been
may have been ⎭	would
	would be
	would have
	would have been

131 ## Verb Tense

Verbs also tell time. The tense of the verb indicates the time of the event. Refer to Table 1-1 for assistance with each of the six most common verb tenses: past, past perfect, present, present perfect, future, and future perfect. Depending upon the "time" of what you are writing about, select the appropriate verb tense. Note the use of the helping verbs in all of the "perfect" tenses.

TABLE 1-1
Verb Tense

	Past	Past Perfect	Present	Present Perfect	Future	Future Perfect
Time	started and completed in past	started and completed in past before some other past action	now	action started in past, continuing in present	will happen in future	will be completed in future
Form	regular verbs* add "d" or "ed" to base form	*had* + past participle	base form (third person singular adds "s")	*have* or *has* + past participle	*shall* or *will* + base form**	*shall* or *will* + *have* + past participle**
Examples	I ordered you ordered he/she/it ordered	I had ordered you had ordered he/she/it had ordered	I order you order he/she/it orders	I have ordered you have ordered he/she/it has ordered	I shall order you will order he/she/it will order	I shall have ordered you will have ordered he/she/it will have ordered
	we ordered you ordered they ordered	we had ordered you had ordered they had ordered	we order you order they order	we have ordered you have ordered they have ordered	we shall order you will order they will order	we shall have ordered you will have ordered they will have ordered

***Note:** For irregular verbs, consult your dictionary for past and past participle verb forms.
****Note:** *Shall* is used with the first person, and *will* is used with the second and third persons. However, to express anger or other strong emotion, use *will* with first person and *shall* with second and third.

Regular/Irregular Verbs

All **regular** verbs form their various tenses in the same way as the example shown in Table 1-1 (page 19). However, **irregular** verbs vary in form for present, past, future, and past participle verb forms. Always consult your dictionary for assistance, as the principal parts of all irregular verbs are listed. If such parts are not shown, the verb is regular.

Common Irregular Verbs

Present	Past	Past Participle
am, are, is	was, were	been
become	became	become
begin	began	begun
bring	brought	brought
buy	bought	bought
choose	chose	chosen
come	came	come
do	did	done
drive	drove	driven
fall	fell	fallen
get	got	gotten/got
give	gave	given
go	went	gone
grow	grew	grown
know	knew	known
leave	left	left
lay	laid	laid (to place)
lie	lay	lain (to rest)
make	made	made
pay	paid	paid
run	ran	run
see	saw	seen
spring	sprang	sprung
take	took	taken
write	wrote	written

133 Verb Contraction

A verb contraction is constructed by combining a verb and an adverb, eliminating one or more letters, and replacing the eliminated letter or letters with an apostrophe. See ¶201.29.

would not	wouldn't
is not	isn't
could not	couldn't

Peter Fire *couldn't* find our office.

134 Verb Mood

The **verb mood** (or mode) indicates the manner of the action of the verb. The action of the verb can be in the indicative, imperative, or subjunctive mood.

134.1 Indicative mood. States a fact or asks a question.

This diamond ring *is* pretty.
Do you *think* this diamond ring is pretty?

134.2 Imperative mood. Makes a request or gives a command.

Please *call* me back this afternoon.
Come here immediately!

134.3 Subjunctive mood. Used with clauses of:

Necessity —

It is important that Ray Fernandez *be consulted*.

Wishing —

I wish Polly Burk *could preside* at this meeting.

Demand —

The marchers demanded their needs *be heard*.

Conditions which are improbable, doubtful, or contrary to fact —

If I *were* you (**but** I am not), I *would* apologize.
If you *had* your masters degree (**but** you do not), you *would* get the promotion.
He acted as if he *were* in charge. (**but** he was not in charge)
She conducted herself as though she *were* already divorced. (**but** she was not yet divorced)

135 Verb Infinitives

The infinitive form occurs when the verb (usually first person singular) is preceded by *to*.

to come	to purchase	to return

When two or more verb infinitives are used together, the preceding *to* may be omitted for the second and subsequent infinitives.

> At the closing of our house, we must remember *to read* everything first, *sign* all required papers, *pay* the attorneys involved, and *secure* the buyers' checks.
> *Sign, pay,* and *secure* are infinitives with *to* omitted.

When the infinitive follows a verb such as feel, hear, help, let, need, and see, the *to* is usually omitted.

> Please *let* me *come* to your Lotus seminar. (**not** to come)
> Would you please *help* Wade Harris *copy* the minutes of the last meeting. (**not** to copy)

Avoid "splitting an infinitive" by inserting an adverb between the *to* and the verb; instead, place the adverb before or after the infinitive for clearer meaning.

> My employer wanted me to proofread the letter carefully.
> **Not:** My employer wanted me to carefully proofread the letter.

136 Gerunds

The **gerund** is a verb form that ends in *ing* and is used as a noun. Gerunds may be used as subjects or objects.

> *Studying* hard is the only way to get good grades. (subject of the sentence)
> He went to the laundry room to do his *washing*. (object of the infinitive *to do*)

ADJECTIVES

137

Adjectives are words used to describe or add additional information about nouns and pronouns. **Descriptive adjectives** add information such as which one, how many, what kind, what size.

> The *little* spot on the patient's X ray was discovered by the *alert* radiologist.
> *Thirteen* students arrived at the *square* building in the middle of the *Calle Ocho* Festival.

138 Definite/Indefinite Adjectives

A noun preceded by *the* indicates a specific person, place, or thing; therefore, *the* is referred to as a **definite adjective** or **definite article.**

Use of *a* or *an* indicates no specific person, place, or thing; thus they are referred to as **indefinite adjectives** or **indefinite articles.** Remember to use *an* before all words beginning with a vowel (a, e, i, o, and short u) and also before all words that sound as though they begin with a vowel (such as *hour*). Before all other words, use *a.*

Definite:	*The* student came in for several placement tests.
Indefinite:	*An* individual must study hard in order to pass these accounting courses.
	A local citizens group is supporting a strong police presence in *an* area with *a* high crime rate.

139   Pronouns as Adjectives

Pronouns may be used as adjectives to modify nouns:

> *Her* score was higher than *his* score.
> *This* research paper on computers has many examples of *those* errors.

ADVERBS

140

Adjectives modify nouns; **adverbs** modify verbs. Adverbs can also modify adjectives or other adverbs. Adverbs answer the questions when, where, how, how much. Many adverbs end in *ly,* making them easy to identify.

when:	Susie *now* knows the entire family history.
	Ginny's purchase requisition will be ready *soon.*
how:	Lift the monitor *slowly* onto the desk.
	Sidney *carefully* prepared the buffet items.
where:	The essential background work will be completed *there.*
how much:	They complained *vehemently* about the visiting hours.

141   Comparisons Using Adverbs and Adjectives

Adverbs and adjectives can be used to compare one person or thing with other persons or things. When there is a comparison between two persons or things, the **comparative degree** is used. The **superlative degree** is used when comparisons are made among three or more persons or things. Table 1-2 (page 24) provides a quick reference for using adverbs and adjectives in comparisons.

141.1   Comparative degree—Comparing only two.

> Who is *older,* Pidge Burk or Larry King?
> This one is *less costly* than the last.
> She was *more diligent* in her work than Billy.

141.2   Superlative degree—Comparing more than two.

> Who is the *oldest* of the group?
> This one is the *least costly* of the lot.
> She was the *most diligent* in her work.

ELIMINATING BIAS IN WRITING

142

All individuals are entitled to written materials which present members of both sexes, different ethnic groups, and all races with equal respect, dignity, and balance. To accomplish this, all written material should emphasize the potential of each individual and group. Today's writers are making a real effort to eliminate many of the biases that were common in the past. As you become aware of discriminatory practices in writing, you will find that there are many ways to avoid such bias.

TABLE 1-2

Comparisons with Adjectives/Adverbs

	Base Form	Comparative Degree (comparing two persons or things)	Superlative Degree (comparing three or more persons or things)
One-Syllable Words	old nice	add "er" to base form* older nicer	add "est" to base form* oldest nicest
Two-Syllable Words	happy	add "er" to base form* or use *more* or *less* before base form happier more happy less happy	add "est" to base form* or use *most* or *least* before base form happiest most happy least happy
Words of More Than Two Syllables	intelligent	add *more* or *less* before base form more intelligent less intelligent	add *most* or *least* before base form most intelligent least intelligent

*****Note:** There are some minor spelling changes in some words.
Note: A few one-syllable words are written with *more* or *less* added to the base form in the comparative degree and *most* or *least* added to the base form in the superlative degree.

142.1 **Sexual identifiers in compound nouns.** Compound nouns very often contain the words *man* or *men* and have been used traditionally to refer to men and women alike. Such use is now considered discriminatory when applied to women or to groups of which women are a part. The U.S. Department of Labor helped to lead the way in the use of unbiased language with their 1975 publication, *Job Title Revisions to Eliminate Sex- and Age- Referent Language from the Dictionary of Occupational Titles*. The latest issue of the *Dictionary of Occupational Titles* (DOT) has been revised to eliminate **all** sexual identifiers.

Some alternative choices for traditionally used compound nouns (and some adjectives and verbs) are listed below. For additional assistance, consult the DOT.

Avoid	Use Instead
man, men, mankind	people, person(s), individual(s), human being(s), human race, humanity, women and men, human(s)
businessman(men)	business executive(s), business person(s), manager(s), merchant(s)
congressman(men)	congressional representative(s), member(s) of congress
chairman(men)	chairperson(s), chair(s), department head(s), moderator(s), group leader(s)
salesman(men)	sales agent(s), salespeople, salesperson(s), sales representative(s), sales force
workman(men)	worker(s)
postman(men), mailman(men)	postal clerk(s), mail carrier(s)
repairman(men)	repairer(s)
foreman(men)	supervisor(s)
spokesman(men)	spokesperson(s)
maid	house worker, housecleaner
manned	staffed
manhandle	maltreat
manhood, manliness	maturity
manly	courageous, honorable
manhole	street utility cover

In addition, use substitutes for the following words which unnecessarily identify gender:

Avoid	Use Instead
housewife	homemaker
poetess	poet
usherette	usher
co-ed	student
sculptress	sculptor
lady (or female) doctor	doctor
male nurse	nurse

142.2   ## Sexual identifiers in generic pronouns.
The generic pronouns *he, his,* or *him* have often been used to indicate any member of a group, male or female. This practice is now avoided by many who think that it is unfair to use *he, his,* or *him* when referring to a group that is not all male. (**NOTE:** When the generic pronouns *they* or *their* are used, the sex of group members is not indicated, and therefore such usage is acceptable.) Ways to avoid this bias include the following:

Eliminate the pronoun.

> **Avoid:**   Each student is responsible for *his* materials.
> **Use:**   Each student is responsible for personal materials.

Change from singular to plural.

> **Use:**   All students are responsible for *their* own materials.

Use words which do not indicate gender. (you, one, person, individual, all)

> **Avoid:**   A student must determine *her* own college major.
> **Use:**   Each individual must determine a college major.

Use job titles instead of the pronoun.

> **Avoid:**   *She* should be able to transcribe confidential information accurately.
> **Use:**   The executive secretary should be able to transcribe confidential information accurately.

Change the pronoun to an article or eliminate the pronoun.

> **Avoid:**   The doctor uses *his* patient charts to summarize *his* treatment decisions.
> **Use:**   The doctor uses patient charts to summarize the treatment decisions.

Add names to eliminate generic usage.

> **Avoid:**   The office manager announced *her* engagement.
> **Use:**   The office manager, Georgianna Stringer, announced her engagement.

Change from active to passive voice.

> **Avoid:**　*She* should inform the supervisor immediately of any emergency.
>
> **Use:**　The supervisor should be informed immediately of any emergency.

Repeat the noun instead of using the pronoun.

> **Avoid:**　If the visitor has a question concerning the appointment, *she* can check with the receptionist.
>
> **Use:**　If the visitor has a question concerning the appointment, *the visitor* can check with the receptionist.

If the methods mentioned above fail, use both pronouns. Do this as a last resort since including both the male and female pronouns is awkward.

> **Avoid:**　A legal secretary's goal is to complete *his* legal secretarial program.
>
> **Use:**　A legal secretary's goal is to complete *his or her* legal secretarial program.

142.3

Sexual identifiers in bibliographies. A recent trend is to eliminate sexual identifiers in published bibliographies by using author initials instead of first names.

Lamb, M. M. *Word Studies.* Cincinnati: South-Western Publishing Co., 1971.

142.4

Age identifiers. The latest DOT edition also eliminates implied age bias in occupational titles.

Avoid	Use Instead
stock boy	stock clerk
busboy	dining room attendant
curb girl	curb attendant

REFERENCES

U.S. Department of Labor. *Job Title Revisions to Eliminate Sex- and Age-Referent Language from the Dictionary of Occupational Titles,* 3rd ed. Washington, D.C.: U.S. Government Printing Office, 1975.

COMMONLY MISUSED WORDS

143

Words that serve both as adverbs and adjectives are often confused. Also, similar-sounding nouns and verbs are often confused with adjectives and adverbs. Use the following guide to avoid misuse of these similar words:

Accede/	The committee members *acceded* to all of our recommendations. (agreed to)
Exceed	Remember not to *exceed* the speed limit. (go beyond)

Accept/	Please *accept* our sincere regrets. (receive, approve — verb)
Except	Everyone was present, *except* Armando Ferrer. (with the exclusion of — preposition)
Access/	Patrick was trying to *access* the data bank. (get into — verb; admission — noun)
Excess	The *excess* food was taken to the children's center. (surplus — adjective; state of surplus — noun)
Adopt/	Karen and Craig McMeekin will *adopt* a son. (choose — verb)
Adept/	Roberta and Bill Stokes were both *adept* at learning data processing terminology. (highly skilled — adjective)
Adapt	The personnel department will *adapt* this form to fit the purchasing department's new requirements. (adjust — verb)
Adverse/	Her recommendations caused an unexpected *adverse* reaction. (contrary)
Averse	Dr. Maria Hernandez was *averse* to that kind of action. (disinclined, showing dislike)
Advice/	Their *advice* was to continue the project. (recommendation — noun)
Advise	The school attorney *advised* the board member, Mr. Martin Fine, that there was no conflict of interest. (provide counsel — verb)
Affect/	Maureen O'Hara's example began to *affect* Isabel's performance. (to influence, change — verb)
Effect	The *effect* of the test results was a major change in design. (result — noun)
	Rocio Lamadriz wanted to *effect* a rapid change. (bring about — verb)
Aloud/	Pam Stringer read the background information *aloud* to her students. (out loud)
Allowed	Children are not *allowed* to enter the Paella cooking area. (permitted)
Almost/	We are *almost* ready to begin. (nearly)
All Most	You are *all most* welcome to our home. (each one very welcome)
Already/	Have they left the grounds *already*? (before an understood time)
All Ready	Scotty and Holly are *all ready* to go home now. (completely prepared)

Alright/	*Alright* is not considered grammatically acceptable — do **not** use. (**NOTE:** Just as there is no word *alwrong* there is no word *alright*.)
All Right	We were relieved to hear that they were *all right*. (satisfactory, certainly)
Altogether/	The results of the survey were *altogether* too good to be true. (entirely)
All Together	The students were *all together* in the auditorium. (all in a group)
Always/	Angel Valdes is *always* looking for new parking solutions. (at all times)
All Ways	Geoff has driven *all ways* to his office to determine the shortest route. (every possible choice)
Among/	They always enjoy being *among* famous politicians. (*Among* is used with three or more persons or things when no close relationship is indicated.)
Between	The choice is *between* Bart and Rebecca for chief of staff. (*Between* is used with two persons or things; or with terms such as treaty, agreement, or discussion.)
Anyone/	Has *anyone* seen the budget printout? (anybody)
Any One	*Any one* of these courses will satisfy the requirements. (any particular item or person in a group)
Anytime/	Bart Powell was available *anytime* I had a question. (whenever)
Any Time	Did you provide a copy of this report to him at *any time* in the past? (any particular time over a period — always two words as the object of a preposition)
Anyway/	*Anyway*, I didn't win the drawing. (in any event)
Any Way	I shall be happy to be of assistance in *any way* I may help. (by any method)
Appraise/	Our new house was *appraised* at $250,000. (value)
Apprise	She promised to *apprise* the board of the results. (inform)
Assure/	Nora Murrell made it a point to *assure* Linda Pagliaro that all purchasing rules were followed. (convince)
Ensure/	To *ensure* prompt arrival, please send via overnight delivery. (make certain)
Insure	Nelson wanted to *insure* his new car before driving it off the lot. (protect against loss)

Awhile/	Kamala had to wait *awhile* to see him. (one word when used as an adverb)
A While	The patient has been gone for *a while*. (two words when used as a noun)
Badly/	This accident victim is *badly* in need of help. (very much — adverb)
Bad	It looks *bad* for our budget reports to be late. (After sensory verbs [look, smell, sound], the adjective *bad* is correct.)
Besides/	*Besides* my television, the thieves took the stereo and my new computer. (in addition to)
Beside	He stood *beside* me during the baby's birth. (next to)
Between/Among	See Among/Between
Both/	*Both* of the little ones said, "Mine." (two considered together)
Each	*Each* wanted to be first in line. (individuals considered separately)
Bring/	*Bring* the final totals to me. (to the speaker or the spot where spoken [*here*])
Take	*Take* the final totals to Frank Meistrell. (away from the speaker or the spot where spoken [*there*])
Can/	Jose *can* complete his doctorate this year. (ability, power)
May	*May* Sally enter the Senate hearings early? (permission, possibility)
Capitol/	The signing of the new education bill will take place in the *Capitol* Building at noon. (*Capitol* is used to mean the buildings used by the Congress and by state legislatures.)
Capital	The *capital* of Colorado is Denver. (*Capital* is used to mean a seat of government; a term in finance, accounting, and architecture; chief and first-rate; capital letter; and capital punishment.)
Come/	Please *come* to my office this afternoon. (to the speaker or the spot where spoken [*here*])
Go	Please *go* to Dr. Brookner's meeting tomorrow. (away from the speaker or the spot where spoken [*there*])
Command/	It was a *command* performance. (ordered — adjective; to order — verb)
Commend	Sophie Schrager was *commended* on her performance at Columbia University. (praise, recommend — verb)

Comments/	The speaker's *comments* were meaningful to the graduates. (remarks)
Commence	The graduation ceremonies will *commence* at 9:00 a.m. (begin)
Comprise/	The New Music America Festival *comprises* many individual performances. (embraces)
Compose	Joseph Celli *composed* the music for the "Escalator" performance. (create music)
	The mathematics department was *composed* of many creative individuals. (the whole made up of)
	Esther wanted to *compose* herself before confronting the new problem. (calm)
Contest/	The typing *contest* was held in Room 1561. (competition)
Context	The *context* of the sentence will help you determine the meaning of the word. (surrounding or interrelated material or conditions)
Cooperation/	The *cooperation* between the departments was much improved. (common effort)
Corporation	Bernard Fils-Aime signed the papers to formalize the new *corporation*. (an association of persons)
Currently/	The temperature is *currently* 75°. (at the present time)
Presently	The class is reading now, but the bell will ring for them to leave *presently*. (in the near future)
Decease/	The *deceased* was her neighbor. (dead person, death)
Disease	Her *disease* was diagnosed as a skin infection. (illness)
Deference/	In *deference* to your opinion, I shall reconsider. (yielding, respect)
Difference	The *difference* between the two texts was significant. (state of being unlike)
Each/Both	See Both/Each
Effect/Affect	See Affect/Effect
Eminent/	She was an *eminent* member of the community. (prominent)
Imminent	The arrival of the hurricane to the seaside community was *imminent*. (threatening to occur)
Ensure/Insure/ Assure	See Assure/Ensure/Insure
Everyday/	This is becoming an *everyday* problem with him. (routine, daily)

Every Day	*Every day* we can delay will make our position stronger. (each day)
Everyone/	Will *everyone* be coming to the meeting? (everybody)
Every One	*Every one* of them had a full physical. (each one)
Ex-/	*Ex-* used to mean *former* is **not** considered standard or formal usage.
Former	Charles Rogers is a *former* president of the faculty senate. (any officer before the current one)
Exceed/Accede	See Accede/Exceed
Except/Accept	See Accept/Except
Excess/Access	See Access/Excess
Farther/Further	See Further/Farther
Fewer/Less	See Less/Fewer
Formerly/	She was *formerly* the telecommunications consultant. (previously, before)
Formally	Rob Stevens was *formally* accepted as a member of the International Children's Foundation Board after initiation. (in a formal manner)
Forward/	Come *forward* a little into the light so that I can see your new uniform. (toward the front, progressive)
Foreword	In the *foreword* of the book, an authority mentions the author's years of careful research. (prefatory comments most often by someone other than the author)
Fourth/	It was the *fourth* time I tried to reach the accounting department. (after third)
Forth	From that day *forth,* she was never the same. (forward, onward in time)
Further/	His statement could not be *further* from the truth. (additional; greater distance in time or quantity)
Farther	Your therapist's office is *farther* than I thought. (actual distance)
Go/Come	See Come/Go
Good/Well	See Well/Good
Imminent/Eminent	See Eminent/Imminent
Imply/	Sally Buxton *implied* she did not want to leave the campus. (suggested)
Infer	I *infer* from your comments that we shall not be going to Argentina. (assume)

Incite/	The demonstrators were trying to *incite* the crowd to action. (arouse, provoke)
Insight	Arnold Fleisch demonstrated excellent *insight* into the problems experienced in the science lab. (understanding)
Indifferent/	Jay Freeman was not *indifferent* to the concerns of the classified staff personnel. (uncaring)
In Different	We each came to the same conclusion *in different* ways. (separate, other)
Insure/Ensure/ Assure	See Assure/Ensure/Insure
Irregardless/ Regardless	Do **not** use—double negative; use *regardless*. The telephones will be installed today, *regardless* of the electrical storm. (heedless, in spite of)
Its/	While the manuscript is finished, we are well aware of *its* typographical errors. (possessive pronoun)
It's	*It's* a big challenge for Noreen Humphreys. (contraction of *it is*)
Latest/	This is the *latest* announcement about cholesterol. (most recent)
Last	Carmen McCrink was the *last* one to arrive for the Arts Council meeting. (final)
Latter/	Dr. Karen Paiva and Dr. J. Terrence Kelly were the two contestants; the *latter* was the winner. (second of two)
Later	Enjoy yourself; it's *later* than you think. (after the usual or proper time)
Learn/	I want to *learn* to use the computer. (acquire knowledge)
Teach	She loved to *teach* Lotus 123. (impart knowledge to others)
Leave/	*Leave* the keys on my desk. (depart, abandon, move away)
Let	*Let* Security open the doors to the auditorium. (permit)
Leased/	Al Schlazer *leased* a condominium near the Omni Shopping Mall. (rented)
Least	Arriving on time was the *least* of our worries today. (smallest)
Less/	Our debt was *less* in those days. (We owed $2,100 then; we owe $4,800 now. [refers to quantity/ amount])

Fewer	Our debts were *fewer* in those days. (We had 10 debts then; we have 18 now. [refers to number *or* that which can be counted])
Libel/	The author was sued for *libel* after the book was published. (injury through written or printed statements)
Liable	The hospital is *liable* for the patient's care. (responsible)
Lose/	The development team did not want to *lose* a minute during the delicate negotiations. (suffer a loss)
Loose	The connection was *loose,* and the video reception was affected. (not secure)
May/Can	See Can/May
Maybe/	*Maybe* we should call if the equipment doesn't arrive soon. (possibly — adverb)
May Be	Your concerns *may be* different in the morning. (verb)
New/	We filled our wing of the research center with *new* furniture. (fresh, unused)
Knew	She *knew* Dr. Joan Schaeffer before taking the professor's class. (acquainted with)
Past/	In *past* negotiations, the union responded more quickly. (previous time — adjective, noun, adverb, preposition)
Passed	To my surprise, I *passed* the legal terminology test. (proceeded beyond — verb)
Percent/	Over 50 *percent* of our students are Hispanic. (use when accompanied by a number)
Percentage	A small *percentage* of our personnel still need to complete their withholding forms. (use when not directly accompanied by a number)
Persecute/	Teenagers often feel their parents are trying to *persecute* them. (annoy, harass)
Prosecute	Victoria Sigler was selected to *prosecute* the murder suspect. (to legally take to trial, to pursue until finished)
Personnel/	The *personnel* in your department seem very enthusiastic. (employees)
Personal	My decision to leave my position was a very *personal* one. (private)
Precede/	Your announcements will *precede* the speech. (come before)

Proceed	Please *proceed* with the meeting. (advance)
Presently/Currently	See Currently/Presently
Principle/	It wasn't the decision that was made; rather, it was the *principle* of the matter that was important to Dr. Ileana Gonzalez. (basic truth)
Principal	Mr. Craig Worthington was the very popular *principal* of the school. (chief official, capital sum of money)
Quiet/	It was a *quiet* day at the office. (still, hushed)
Quite	This is not *quite* what I was looking for. (completely, exactly)
Raise/	Would you please *raise* that corner of the table. (cause to lift up)
Rise	The sun will *rise* tomorrow at 6:25 a.m. (ascend, move upward by itself)
Really/	Are you *really* going to support Social Security reform? (actually, truly — adverb)
Real	Dr. Sarah Turbett was a *real* friend. (true, actual — adjective)
Regardless/ **Irregardless**	See Irregardless/Regardless
Respectfully/	The entire situation was handled *respectfully*. (with regard for, in deference to)
Respectively	The first, second, and third prizes will go to Carl Bethel, Shirley Gribble, and Glenn Thompson, *respectively*. (in the order given)
Sometimes/	*Sometimes* it is hard to understand written insurance reports. (now and then)
Sometime/	*Sometime* later this week, we shall schedule an important staff meeting. (at an unspecified time)
Some Time	It was *some time* before the director returned from the presentation. (a period of time)
Sum/	What is the *sum* of all your travel expenses? (total)
Some	*Some* of the audience began to leave the fringe benefits briefing. (part, a portion of)
Surely/	*Surely* you don't want to quit now? (certainly, confidently — adverb)
Sure	I am *sure* you can learn these data processing abbreviations. (certain — adjective)
Take/Bring	See Bring/Take
Teach/Learn	See Learn/Teach

Then/	Wait until the vehicle stops; *then* you can get out safely. (at that time — adverb)
Than	My performance rating is higher now *than* it was when I first started to work here. (as compared to — conjunction)
There/	Write it *there* on the check requisition. (in that place)
Their	*Their* interest was in *their* friend's mental health. (possessive pronoun)
To/	Come *to* the cafeteria with me. (preposition)
Too/	Ricky wants to come, *too.* (also)
Two	*Two* lab managers were assigned to the same unit. (number following *one*)
Week/	This *week* we have a vacation from school to celebrate the Fourth of July. (seven successive days — noun)
Weak	He was too *weak* to climb any farther. (not strong — adjective)
Well/	Ann is *well* enough to join Karen at the game. (fortunate, healthy — adjective; or rightly — adverb)
Good	The chili smells *good.* (attractive, bountiful, wholesome — adjective)
Whether/	*Whether* or not we vote, our issue still cannot win. (function word indicating alternatives)
Weather	The *weather* remained sunny during our entire conference. (state of the atmosphere)

PREPOSITIONS

144

Prepositions are connectors. They connect or show the relationship of a noun or pronoun to another word in a sentence in what is referred to as a **prepositional phrase.**

> The technician moved carefully *between* the hospital beds.

In this example, the preposition *between* shows the relationship between *the technician* (the subject) and the *beds,* the object of the preposition. When pronouns are used as the object of a preposition, they must be in the objective case (see ¶123.2).

> Yolanda placed a call *to her insurance agent.*
> Greg searched high and low *for the records.*
> Please write the telephone number *for me.*

FREQUENTLY USED PREPOSITIONS

about	from
above	in
across	into
after	like
against	of
among	off
around	on
at	over
before	past
behind	round
below	since
beside	through
between	to
by	under
down	until
during	up
except	upon
for	with
	within
	without

CONJUNCTIONS

145

Conjunctions are words used to connect two words, phrases, or clauses. **Coordinating conjunctions** connect words, phrases, or clauses that are equal in rank or stature. Common forms are *and, but, for, or, nor,* and *yet.*

> Dr. Eduardo J. Padron *and* Dr. Roberto Hernandez were honored at the banquet.
>
> The secretaries like their jobs, *but* they want to continue taking additional classes.

Correlative conjunctions are pairs of words that connect two like words, phrases, or clauses. Common forms are *either/or, neither/nor, both/and, not/but, whether/or (not), not only/but (also).*

> *Either* Dr. Vicente *or* his assistant will perform the routine review in the morning.
>
> *Neither* Lourdes *nor* I remembered the appointment yesterday.

Unit II   Punctuation

2

Understand:
- How consistent punctuation improves clarity and facilitates understanding
- The functions of each punctuation mark

Acquire:
- The ability to punctuate routine business correspondence
- Knowledge of some of the more obscure punctuation conventions

Be Prepared To:
- Punctuate sample sentences designed to build and test your knowledge of punctuation
- Recognize the incorrect application of punctuation marks

APOSTROPHE

201 The apostrophe is used to create possessive forms of certain nouns and some indefinite pronouns. It is also used as a single quotation mark. In functional writing (tables, statistical reports, and the like) it is used as a symbol for feet and minutes. Other applications are more obscure but equally useful.

Possession

201.1 **Kinds of possession.** The apostrophe is used to indicate four major kinds of possession.

Owning:	the childrens' toys
	the owner's records
Having:	the renter's apartment
	the borrowers' books
Creating:	the composer's music
	the authors' books
Measuring:	a year's work
	ten dollars' worth
	a stone's throw

201.2 **Indicating possessive relationships.** There are three ways to indicate possessive relationships.

1. An apostrophe.

Harry's book   Marcia's papers

2. A prepositional phrase.

$$\text{the parts } {\{of\} \atop \{in\} \atop \{for\}} \text{ the automobile}$$

the breeze *from* the ocean

3. The noun as a modifier.

the automobile parts
the ocean breeze

Quick Reference for Creating Possessive Forms

201.3

Apostrophe or *apostrophe s?* Refer to this chart when you know that an *apostrophe* or *an apostrophe s* is required to create a possessive form, but you do not know which is required.

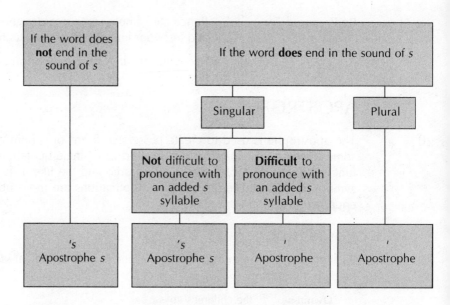

201.4 **Possessive forms in brief.** Refer to this chart for a capsule explanation of each possessive form; refer to the paragraphs indicated for more details.

SEE ¶	TO CREATE POSSESSIVE FORMS	ADD OR USE	EXAMPLES
201.5	Nouns not ending in the sound of s.	's	Marvin's bicycle the dog's tail

201.6a	Singular nouns ending in the sound of *s* (if adding *s* sound does *not* make pronunciation awkward).	's	the prince's sword the princess's veil Ralph Ross's roses the spitz's tail
201.6b	Singular nouns ending in the sound of *s* (if adding *s* sound *does* make pronunciation awkward).	'	Ulysses' coat Jane Withers' pictures
201.7	Plural nouns ending in the sound of *s*.	'	the members' votes the bosses' desks
201.8 201.9 201.10	Appositives (noun or noun substitute beside another noun or noun substitute to explain or identify it).	Use of phrase	**Not:** Henry the plumber's shop **But:** the shop of Henry the plumber
201.11	Compound nouns.	' or 's added to final word element	the ne'er-do-wells' gathering her brother-in-law's money
201.12	Gerunds (*ing* form of a verb that functions as a noun).	' or 's added to gerund's modifier	Wilma's walking Stanley's drinking
201.13	Understood nouns.	' or 's added to understood noun's modifier	at the Barnaby's (home) to the doctor's (office)
201.14	For possessive forms of nouns other than those representing people, animals, organizations, geographic locations, time, value, distance, and celestial bodies.	Prepositional phrase or noun as modifier	the transistors in the TV the handle of the hammer the TV transistors the hammer handle
201.15	Expressions suggesting personification.	' or 's	Age's resignation the Four Winds' names
201.16	Personal pronouns and the relative pronoun *who*.	Special forms	**Pronoun** **Possessive Form** he his who whose

201.17	Indefinite pronouns with regular possessive forms.	' or 's	someone's contribution the others' collection
201.18	Indefinite pronouns without regular possessive forms.	Preposi- tional phrase	the problems of a few the achievements of some (**Not** a few's or some's)
201.19	Abbreviations, singular.	's	the M.B.A.'s analysis
201.20	Abbreviations, plural.	'	the M.B.A.s' desks
201.21	Personal names ending with abbreviations or numbers.	' or 's	James Thannes, Jr.'s book the Roy Wallace IIIs' children
201.22	Joint possession, all possessors identified by name.	' or 's to final name	Wilton and Smedley's office Melanie and May's cat Plato and Epictetus' idea
201.23	Joint possession, possessor identified by pronoun.	possessive forms of nouns or pronouns	Barry's and her farm His and Celia's station wagon
201.24	Separate possession.	possessive forms of nouns or pronouns	Elsa's and John's teeth His and her books
201.25	Organizational names end-ing with an abbreviation, prepositional phrase, or number. (See ¶201.28.)	' or 's	National Music Assn.'s offices Association of CEOs' offices Association of Musicians' bus Society of 55's newspaper
201.26	Organizational names containing a possessive form. (See ¶201.28.)	' or 's	National Yeoman's Association American Women's Association
201.27	Organizational names containing a word that could be a possessive form or a plural. (Presume that it is plural. See ¶201.28.)	No apostrophe	Air Line Pilots Association National Consumers League
201.28	Regardless of conventions in ¶201.25, 201.26, and 201.27, write the name as it is used by the organization itself.	As preferred by the organiza- tion	National Science Teachers Association United Seamen's Service

Possessive Forms

Nouns

201.5 **Nouns not ending in the sound of s.** Form the possessive of a noun not ending in the sound of s by adding *apostrophe s*.

Singular:	Melba's eggs	the supplier's invoice
	Versailles's palace	the singer's voice
	the child's toy	the woman's book
Plural:	the children's toys	the women's books

201.6 **Singular nouns ending in the sound of s.** Form the possessive of a *singular* noun ending in the sound of s in one of two ways.

a. If adding *apostrophe s* does not make the word difficult to pronounce, do so.

Mavis's pet lizard   Fairfax's history
Independence's main street   Roger Adams's garage

b. If adding *apostrophe s* makes the word difficult to pronounce, add an apostrophe only.

Sophocles' tragedies   Gena Schlessings' car
Manassas' city hall   Ulysses' return

201.7 **Plural nouns ending in the sound of s.** Form the possessive of a *plural* noun ending in the sound of s by adding an *apostrophe*.

the girls' toys   the trustees' guardianship
the boys' toys   the ladies' social events

201.8 **Appositives defined.** An **appositive** is a noun (or a group of words serving as a noun) used beside another noun to explain or identify it.

Cambridge, *Massachusetts*   John Turner *the teacher*
My only first cousin, Mary Winslow

201.9 **Possessive forms of appositives.** Create the possessive form of an appositive by adding an *apostrophe* or *apostrophe s*.

Awkward: Cambridge, Massachusetts' center
Awkward: John Turner the teacher's lecture
Unclear: My only first cousin, Mary Winslow's garden

See ¶201.10 for the use of prepositional phrases to indicate possession.

See ¶206.23 for the use of commas with appositives.

201.10 **Awkward possessive appositives.** Avoid the awkwardness of using the apostrophe to create the possessive form of an appositive by using a prepositional phrase instead.

the center of Cambridge, Massachusetts
the lecture of John Turner the teacher
the garden of Mary Winslow, my only first cousin

201.11 **Compound nouns.** A **compound noun** consists of two or more words combined or used together to serve as a single noun. Apply the *apostrophe* or *apostrophe s* to the final word element.

the go-betweens' negotiations   my sister-in-law's gossip
the attorney general's opinion   the castaway's footprint

201.12 **Gerunds.** A **gerund** is the *ing* form of a verb serving as a noun. Apply the *apostrophe* or *apostrophe s* to the noun or indefinite pronoun modifying the gerund.

the children's talking   John's acting   someone's screaming

201.13 **Understood (omitted) nouns.** Apply the *apostrophe* or *apostrophe s* to the noun or pronoun modifying the understood (omitted) noun.

Take the papers to the attorney's. (office)
We spent the evening at the Haleys'. (home)

201.14 **When to use the possessive forms of nouns.** Generally, possessive forms are restricted to nouns representing the following:

people	animals	organizations	geographic locations
time	value	distance	celestial bodies

"Possession" by inanimate beings other than those listed above is indicated by using a prepositional phrase, or by using the noun as a modifier.

Not: the automobile's parts
        {*of*}
But: parts {*for*} the automobile (A prepositional phrase.)
        {*in*}
Or: the automobile parts (Using the noun as a modifier.)

201.15 **Personification.** Expressions suggesting **personification** (the giving of human qualities to places, things, or ideas) may be stated in the possessive form.

Time's toll   Youth's impatience

See ¶320.5 for capitalization and personification.

Pronouns

201.16 **Personal pronouns and the relative pronoun *who*.** Certain pronouns have special possessive forms that eliminate the use of the apostrophe.

Pronoun	Possessive	Pronoun	Possessive
I	my, mine	we	our, ours
you	your, yours	they	their, theirs
she	her, hers	it	its
he	his	who	whose

201.17 **Indefinite pronouns with regular possessive forms.** Some indefinite pronouns have regular possessive forms requiring the use of *apostrophe s*.

Indefinite Pronoun	Possessive Form
another	another's ideas
everybody	everybody's papers
one	one's possessions
others	the others' property

201.18 **Indefinite pronouns without regular possessive forms.** Some indefinite pronouns have no regular possessive forms; therefore, prepositional phrases are used to form the possessive.

Pronoun	Possessive	Pronoun	Possessive
all	of all	few	of few / of a few
each	of each		
several	of several	many	of many

Abbreviations

201.19 **Singular possessives of abbreviations.** The singular possessive of an abbreviation is formed by adding *apostrophe s* to the abbreviation.

the CPA's desk   the CEO's office
IBM's computers   station WNOG's signal

201.20 **Plural possessives of abbreviations.** The plural possessive of an abbreviation is created by adding an apostrophe to the plural form of the abbreviation.

the CPAs' desks   the CEOs' offices

201.21 **Abbreviations or numbers following personal names.** Possessive forms of personal names ending with abbreviations or numbers follow this general rule:

Singular Add *Apostrophe s*	Plural Add *Apostrophe*
Harold Williams, Jr.'s report	the Harold Williams, Jrs.' home
Gerald Anderson III's class	the Gerald Anderson IIIs' children

See ¶206.55 for use of the comma in transposed names.

Joint and Separate Possession

201.22 **Joint possession, all possessors identified by name.** If all possessors are identified by name, add *apostrophe* or *apostrophe s* to the final name only.

Sheila and Eddie's car   Plato and Socrates' philosophies

201.23 **Joint possession, possessor identified by pronoun.** If one or more possessors are identified by a pronoun, use the possessive form of each name or pronoun.

Jan's and her apartment   his and Anthony's arrangement

201.24 **Separate possession.** To indicate separate possession, use the possessive form of each name or pronoun.

Nancy's and Jan's homes   Juan's and my motorcycles

Organizational Names

201.25 **Possessive forms of organizational names ending with an abbreviation, a prepositional phrase, or a number.** The possessive form of an organizational name that ends with an abbreviation, a prepositional phrase, or a number is created by adding *apostrophe* or *apostrophe s*. See ¶201.28 with respect to using an organization's adopted style for writing its name.

> South-Western Publishing Co.'s book
> Bank of New York's deposits
> Society of Manufacturing Engineers' report
> Engine Number 9's crew

201.26 **Organizational names containing a possessive form.** If an organizational name contains a word that is obviously a possessive form, use an *apostrophe* or *apostrophe s*. See ¶201.28 with respect to using an organization's adopted style for writing its name.

> Henry's Haircutters   *Woman's Day*
> National Women's Christian Temperance Union

201.27 **Organizational names containing a form that could be either a possessive or a regular plural.** If an organizational name contains a word that could be either a possessive form or the regular (ending in *s*) plural of a descriptive word, presume that it is the regular plural—and do not use an apostrophe. See ¶201.28 with respect to using an organization's adopted style for writing its name.

> Girls Clubs of America   American Collectors Association
> Screen Actors Guild   Circus Fans Association of America

201.28 **Organization's adopted style of name.** While ¶201.25, 201.26, and 201.27 reflect prevailing practices, most organizations adopt a single style that they use and prefer. You should employ these preferred styles when you are aware of them.

Contractions and Possessives

201.29 **Confusion of pronoun contractions and possessive pronouns.** Do not confuse pronoun contractions with possessive pronouns.

Pronoun Contractions	Possessive Pronouns
it's (it is)	its (belonging to it)
they're (they are)	their (belonging to them)
who's (who is)	whose (belonging to whom)
you're (you are)	your (belonging to you)

Other Uses of the Apostrophe

201.30 **Replacing omitted characters.** When the *apostrophe* is used to replace omitted characters, it is placed at the exact point of the omission.

Contractions

I (woul)d	I'd
could n(o)t	couldn't
should n(o)t	shouldn't
o(f the) clock	o'clock

Numbers

The spirit of '76   '80 was a good year

201.31 **Words used as words rather than for their meaning.** Words used as words rather than for their meaning may be identified with apostrophes when their plural forms are used. See ¶217.2 for use of the underscore or italics to identify words used as words rather than for their meaning.

Paint the *the*'s and *and*'s to finish the poster.

201.32 **In functional writing (tables, bills, technical papers, and the like).** In tables, bills, technical papers, and other functional writing, the apostrophe may be used as a symbol for feet or minutes.

23 feet, four inches: 23' 4"   8 minutes, 22 seconds: 8' 22"

201.33 **As a single quotation mark.** The apostrophe may be used as a single quotation mark within standard quotation marks.

Gracie said, "The story 'Miss Wimple's Garden' is one of my favorites."

NOTE: If another level is needed, use regular quotation marks again.

Wilbur said, "Gracie said, 'The story "Miss Wimple's Garden" is one of my favorites.' "

201.34 **Plural forms of symbols.** The apostrophe may be used to create plural forms of symbols.

With apostrophes:	*'s	&'s	%'s	$'s	@'s	?'s
Also acceptable:	*s	&s	%s	$s	@s	?s

201.35 **Plural forms of numbers.** The apostrophe may be used to create the plural forms of numbers.

With apostrophes:	6's	8's	12's	100's	1000's
Preferable (except where confusion may result):	6s	8s	12s	100s	1000s

201.36 **Plural forms of lowercase letters.** The apostrophe is used to form the plurals of lowercase letters.

With apostrophes:	a's	b's	c's	d's	e's	f's
***Not* acceptable:**	as	bs	cs	ds	es	fs

201.37 **Plural forms of capital letters.** The apostrophe may be used to form the plurals of capital letters.

With apostrophes (acceptable):	A's	B's	C's	D's	E's	F's
Preferable:	As*	Bs	Cs	Ds	Es	Fs

*Unless it can be confused with the word *As*.

The Apostrophe with Other Punctuation

The apostrophe is treated as part of the word; no punctuation separates it from other parts (letters) of the word.

> The pool is the Monteras'. It is a large...
> The house is the Andrews', but they are...
> The file is the owners'; they will expect...

Spacing with the Apostrophe

	Before	After
Ending a word, abbreviation, etc., within a sentence	0	1
Other apostrophes	0	0

202

ASTERISK

Footnotes

202.1   **Footnotes.** The asterisk may be used to refer the reader to one or more footnotes at the bottom of a page.

The asterisk refers the reader to a footnote that will be found lower on the page. The asterisk is inserted immediately after the sentence, clause, phrase, word, etc., to which the footnote pertains.*_ _A pair of asterisks, typed with no intervening spaces, identifies the second footnote on the page.**_ _A trio of asterisks, typed with no intervening spaces,***_identifies the third footnote on the page.

———

*In the text, the asterisk follows any other punctuation mark without intervening space. An asterisk precedes the footnote it identifies without intervening space. (In this model, the underline is used to illustrate a space.)

**Insertion of the asterisk does not alter the conventions for spacing:

a. Leave two spaces after the end of a sentence.*_ _ If the sentence ends with a question mark or exclamation mark, spacing is the same—two spaces following the asterisk.

b. Leave one space between words. Count the asterisk as part of the word it follows.

c. Following a comma,*_leave one space after the asterisk.

***If more than three footnotes appear on a page, most writers use other symbols in addition to asterisks or numbered footnotes instead of asterisks. See ¶1112 for numbered footnotes.

202.2   **Footnotes following tables and other illustrations.** A table, diagram, chart, or the like, may require a footnote to identify its source, or footnotes to comment on its specific parts, or both.

Asterisks may be used to footnote an illustration requiring no more than three footnotes. The system described in the preceding model is used, except that the footnote references are incorporated into the illustration and the footnotes appear immediately below the illustration instead of at the bottom of the page. The following list illustrates footnoting with asterisks; numbered footnotes are discussed in ¶1112.

EARLY PRESIDENTS OF THE UNITED STATES

George Washington*
John Adams**
Thomas Jefferson*
James Madison*
James Monroe*
John Quincy Adams**
Andrew Jackson
Martin Van Buren
William Henry Harrison*
John Tyler*

---

*Born in Virginia
**Born in Massachusetts

Unprintable Words

202.3   **Omission of unprintable words.** Asterisks are used to indicate the omission of unprintable words. A group of three asterisks without intervening spaces may be substituted for each unprintable word, or each letter in the unprintable word may be represented by an asterisk.

He was called a *** and a ***.
She was called a ***** and a ****.

Spacing with the Asterisk

	Before	After
Following a word, abbreviation, or another punctuation mark within a sentence	0	1
At the end of a sentence	0	2
Beginning a footnote. See ¶202.1, 202.2.	0-2	0
Substituted for an unprintable word within a sentence	1	1
Substituted for an unprintable word at the end of a sentence	1	0

203   BRACE

203.1   In law documents.

The brace is used to join two or more related items. The related items are usually in the same column. Braces are used frequently in law documents.

Most computers and some typewriters have small braces, one character in height. These may be "stacked" to form a larger brace. If no braces are available, parentheses or brackets may be "stacked" in the same manner. Braces may also be drawn freehand, or with a plastic template. The latter method produces the better results.

Law Document,
Braces: _____ }
                        }   as to _____
         _____ }

Law Document,
Parentheses: _____)
)   as to _____
         _____)

Law Document,
Brackets: _____]
                        ]   as to _____
         _____]

Law Document,
Template: _____
                        }   as to _____
         _____

203.2   Grouping data in illustrations.

A brace may be used to group data in tables and in other illustrations.

$$\text{Daily Highs}\begin{cases} \text{Su} & 92 \\ \text{M} & 87 \\ \text{Tu} & 90 \\ \text{W} & 89 \\ \text{Th} & 87 \\ \text{F} & 81 \\ \text{Sa} & 88 \end{cases} \qquad \text{Sizes}\begin{cases} 30 \\ 32 \\ 34 \\ 36 \\ 38 \\ 40 \\ 42 \end{cases}\$18.88$$

203.3   In mathematical statements.

In mathematical statements, braces are used to enclose brackets which, in turn, enclose parentheses. The order is as follows:

$$\{[(\ )]\}$$
$$2\{3 + [9 - (3 + 2)]\} = 14$$

204   BRACKETS

204.1   Writer's comments.

Brackets are used to identify comments or observations inserted in quoted material by the writer.

The driver said, "It [the truck] will not start."
"That was a heart-rendering [sic] experience."

NOTE: The word *sic* means *thus* or *so*. It tells the reader that, even though there is something unusual—possibly incorrect—about the preceding part of the quotation, it is reproduced exactly (*thus* or *so*) as it appeared in the original.

204.2 **Notes on pronunciation.** Brackets may be used to insert notes on pronunciation.

Ulysses [yù lis' ēz] Esau [ē' (,)só]

204.3 **Parenthetical expression within a parenthetical expression.** A parenthetical expression within another parenthetical expression may be set off by brackets.

(All the members [seventeen of them] remained seated.)

204.4 **Making and drawing brackets.** Although most computer and word processor keyboards include brackets, many typewriter keyboards do not. Brackets can be made in one of three ways:

Typing Diagonals and Underscores	Drawing Freehand or with a Ruler	Drawing with a Plastic Template
[sic]	[sic]	[sic]

Spacing with Brackets

	Before	After
Opening Bracket		
Within a sentence	1	0
Immediately preceding a separate sentence	2	0
Immediately preceding another punctuation mark	1	0
Closing Bracket		
Following a parenthetical element within a sentence	0	1
Following normal end-of-sentence punctuation	0	2
Followed by another punctuation mark	0	0

See ¶203.3 for the use of brackets in mathematical statements.

205 # COLON

Introduction: Explanation

205.1 **Introduction: explanation.** A colon identifies a relationship in which an introductory expression (preceding the colon) introduces an explanatory or illustrative expression (following the colon).

[Introduction] [:] [Explanation or Illustration]

205.2 **Introductory expression.** An introductory expression preceding a colon should conform to these conventions:

a. The introductory expression should have a subject and predicate.

[Subject and Predicate]	[:]	[Explanation or Illustration]
These *stops are* on the list	:	Cincinnati, Dayton, and Toledo.

b. The introductory expression should cause the reader to anticipate the explanation or illustration that will follow the colon.

[Anticipatory Expression]	[:]	[Explanation or Illustration]
The following ingredients should be mixed dry	:	sugar, salt, flour, and baking powder.

c. The introductory expression should be near the colon. Intervening words should not distract the reader from the relationship identified by the colon.

Not: The following paint is needed because the customers have changed their minds about the colors to be used in the living room and kitchen: 3 gallons 1327 Moss Green, 5 quarts 1186 Daffodil Yellow, and 2 gallons 1288 Off-White Trim.

But: The customers have changed their minds about the colors to be used in the living room and the kitchen. Consequently, the following paint is needed: 3 gallons 1327 Moss Green, 5 quarts 1186 Daffodil Yellow, and 2 gallons 1288 Off-White Trim.

d. The introductory expression should not end with a verb or preposition. (Unless the items that follow are listed on separate lines.)

[Introductory Expression]	[No Verb] [No] [prepo-] [sition]	[:]	[Explanation or Illustration]

Not:

The price	includes	:	delivery, padding, installation, and a one-year guarantee on the carpet and installation.

Not:

The package consists	of	:	the three-piece living room suite, the seven-piece dining room suite, and the five-piece bedroom suite.

But:

[Introductory Expression]	[Verb or] [Prepo-] [sition]	[Explanation or Illustration]
The price	includes	delivery, padding, installation, and a one-year guarantee on the carpet and installation.

Or:

The package consists	of	the three-piece living room suite, the seven-piece dining room suite, and the five-piece bedroom suite.

Exception: The listed items appear on separate lines.

The price includes:
  Delivery
  Padding
  Installation
  One-year guarantee on the
    carpet and installation

The package consists of:
  Three-piece living room suite
  Seven-piece dining room suite
  Five-piece bedroom suite

e. The introductory expression may imply — rather than state — that something will follow.

[Implied Introduction]	[:]	[Explanation or Illustration]
The cause was obvious	:	it had rained two inches in two hours.

205.3

Explanatory or illustrative expression. An explanatory or illustrative expression follows a colon.

a. The expression following a colon may consist of one or more sentences.

[Introduction]	[:]	[Explanatory Sentence(s)]
These are the facts of the case	:	The book belonged to Sherwood. Sherwood lent the book to Rainier. The book was stolen from Rainier.

b. The expression following a colon may consist of one or more clauses.

[Introduction]	[:]	[Explanatory Clause(s)]
My opinion remains the same	:	the book still belongs to Sherwood.

c. The expression following a colon may consist of one or more words.

[Introduction]	[:]	[Explanatory Word(s)]
One word is the key to this case	:	stolen.

d. The expression following a colon may consist of the items on a list.

[Introduction]	[:]	[Explanatory List]
These officers will be elected at the next meeting:		

  President
  Vice President
  Secretary
  Treasurer

e. The expression following a colon may consist of a quotation.

[Introduction]	[:]	[Quotation]
Samuel Goldwyn said	:	"A verbal contract isn't worth the paper it's written on."

205.4

When the second independent clause does not explain the first. Use a semicolon to separate equally important independent clauses when the second clause does not explain or illustrate the first.

[Independent Clause]	[;]	[Independent Clause]
It rained yesterday	;	it will rain today.

205.5 **Independent clauses linked by a transitional expression.** Use a semicolon to separate independent clauses linked by a transitional expression (some of which are shown below). See ¶216.4.

[Independent Clause]	[;] [however] [,]	[Independent Clause]
	[furthermore]	
	[indeed]	
They arrived on time	; indeed ,	they were early.

A comma is required after most transitional expressions. A few transitional expressions (thus, so that, yet, hence, and then) require no hesitation in thought or speech and, therefore, require no comma.

The scouts were prepared	; thus	they did well.

Capitalization after the Colon

205.6 **First word after a colon.** The first word after a colon *must* be capitalized if the conventions described in Unit 3 apply to it.

Here is the answer: I must run and hide.
The following have been selected: USA, USSR, and UK.
I have just read *The New Year: The Birth of Science.*

205.7 **Proper nouns and proper adjectives.** After a colon, capitalize each proper noun and each proper adjective (adjective made from a proper noun — see ¶303).

The following have been elected: Marcia, Edward, and Tillie.
The task can be described in one word: Herculean.

205.8 **Quoted sentence.** After a colon, capitalize the first word in a quoted sentence.

The guide explained: "You can see the valley from here."

205.9 **Explanatory independent clause is dominant element.** If the element after the colon is an independent clause that is the dominant or most general element in the sentence, capitalize its first word.

This is the reason: Southbound traffic is heavy. (The element following the colon is an independent clause; it is the dominant element in the sentence; its first word is capitalized.)

Southbound traffic is twice as heavy: that is the reason. (The element following the colon is an independent clause; it is not dominant; its first word is not capitalized.)

This is the reason: southbound traffic. (The element following the colon is dominant, but it is not an independent clause; its first word is not capitalized.)

205.10 **Two or more sentences following a colon.** If two or more sentences (punctuated by periods) follow a colon, the first word of each sentence is capitalized.

The tree should stay: It will grow fast. We need the shade.
Not: The tree should stay: It will grow fast; we need the shade.
Not: The tree should stay: It will grow fast, and we need the shade.

205.11 **List following a colon.** After a colon, capitalize the first word on each line of a line-by-line list.

The following items were displayed:

Watches
Clocks
Lamps
Radios

NOTE: This convention is not altered by the use of item numbers, quantities, prices, or the like.

1.	Watches	3 Watches	1.	3 Watches
2.	Clocks	8 Clocks	2.	8 Clocks
3.	Lamps	4 Lamps	3.	4 Lamps
4.	Radios	5 Radios	4.	5 Radios

Other Uses of the Colon

205.12 **Literary references.** The colon is used in literary references to:

a. Separate title and subtitle.

Diet: A Key to Good Health

b. Separate volume number and page number in footnotes and bibliographies.

Volume 11, pages 123 and 124.   11:123–124.

c. Separate city of publication and name of publisher in footnotes and bibliographies.

Cincinnati: South-Western Publishing Co.

NOTE: See ¶1110–1112 for bibliography and footnote styles.

205.13 **Biblical references.** A biblical reference may be written with a colon.

Proverbs 4:7 refers to chapter 4, verse 7 of the Book of Proverbs.

205.14 **Ratios or proportions.** A colon may be used to express ratios or proportions.

The differential has a ratio of 1.8:1.   *Or*
The differential has a ratio of 1.8 to 1.   *Or*
The differential has a ratio of 1.8-to-1.

Spacing with the Colon

	Before	After
In normal use within a sentence	0	2
Time of day, reference initials, ratios	0	0

206 COMMA

Separating Main Clauses

206.1 **Independent clauses linked by a coordinating conjunction.** In a compound sentence, a comma is used to separate independent clauses linked by a coordinating conjunction.

[Independent Clause]	[,] [and]	[Independent Clause]
	[but]	
	[or]	
	[for]	
	[nor]	
	[yet]	
It is a very difficult task	, but	we must do our best.
This is the place to camp	, and	now is the time to stop.

NOTE: Do not separate a coordinating conjunction from the clause it precedes.

Not:	The game may start on time	, but,	we shall not be there.
But:	The game may start on time	, but	we shall not be there.

206.2 **Short compound sentences.** If both clauses of a compound sentence are short, the comma between them *may* be omitted.

[Independent Clause]	[and]	[Independent Clause]
	[but]	
	[or]	
	[for]	
	[nor]	
	[yet]	
The price is high	and	the service is poor.
The driver is here	but	the truck will not start.

206.3 **Compound sentence with three or more independent clauses.** If a compound sentence consists of three or more independent clauses, punctuate it as you would any series.

[Independent Clause] [,]	[Independent Clause] [,]	[and] [Independent Clause]
		[but]
		[or]
		[nor]
Some were awake ,	some were asleep ,	and some were missing.

206.4 **Simple sentence with compound predicate.** A simple sentence with a compound predicate must **not** have a comma between the two predicates. Do not confuse this form with that of a compound sentence. See ¶206.1 for examples of compound sentences.

[Subject]	[Predicate]	[and]	[Predicate]
		[but]	
		[or]	
		[for]	
		[nor]	
		[yet]	
Marion	ran	and	jumped.

> **Not:**   Marion ran, and jumped.

No matter how long the two predicates, a comma is **not** used unless there is a specific reason for its use:

> Marion ran quickly across the wet grass and jumped clumsily into the rear seat of the moving car.

206.5

Simple sentence with compound subject. A simple sentence with a compound subject must **not** have a comma between the two subjects.

[Subject]	[and]	[Subject]	[Predicate]
Girls	and	boys	spoke.

> **Not:**   Girls, and boys spoke.

206.6

Comma splice. If the independent clauses of a compound sentence are not joined by a coordinating conjunction (and, but, or, for, nor, yet) a comma should **not** be used to separate the independent clauses.

> **Not:**   The goats were grazing on the cliff, they were not afraid of falling. (This error is called a **comma splice.**)

But:

[Independent Clause]	. [;]	[Independent Clause]
The goats were standing on the cliff	;	they were not afraid of falling.

Or:

[Independent Clause]	[.]	[Independent Clause]	[.]
The goats were standing on the cliff	.	They were not afraid of falling	.

After Introductory Elements

General convention. Commas are used after an introductory element if that element is one of the following:

[Participial or Infinitive Phrase]	[,]	[Independent Clause] See ¶206.7
[Dependent Clause]		See ¶206.8.
[Long Prepositional Phrase]		See ¶206.9.
[Independent Comment]		See ¶206.10.
[Mild Interjection]		See ¶206.11.
[Word(s) in Direct Address]		See ¶206.12.

206.7

Introductory participial or infinitive phrase. Use a comma after an introductory participial or infinitive phrase.

[Participial Phrase]	[,]	[Independent Clause]
Having gotten lost in my own thoughts	,	I drove past my freeway exit.

[Infinitive Phrase]	[,]	[Independent Clause]
To see the town	,	I drove to the top of nearby Mount Pleasant.

206.8

Introductory dependent clause. Use a comma after an introductory dependent clause.

[Dependent Clause]	[,]	[Independent Clause]
If the tractor stalls again	,	we shall not finish the job today.
As I turned the last corner	,	I saw the ambulance parked at the curb.

206.9 **Long prepositional phrase.** Use a comma after a long introductory prepositional phrase.

[Long Prepositional Phrase]	[,]	[Independent Clause]
In order to meet the minimum requirements	,	take one tablet each day.
Until the matter is settled	,	there is nothing more we can do.

If the introductory prepositional phrase is short, or if there is no break in thought or speech, the comma may be omitted.

[Short Prepositional Phrase]	[Independent Clause]
After the game	the real fun began.
Until it rains	the grass will be brown and dry.

206.10 **Introductory independent comment.** Use a comma after an introductory independent comment.

[Independent Comment]	[,]	[Independent Clause]
In my opinion	,	the machine will never pay for itself.
If I have my way	,	we will not make the purchase.

206.11 **Introductory mild interjection.** Use a comma after an introductory mild interjection.

[Mild Interjection]	[,]	[Independent Clause]
Oh	,	to be back in St. Louis.
Well	,	food is really a necessity.

206.12 **Direct address.** Use a comma after an introductory word or words in direct address.

[Word or Words in Direct Address]	[,]	[Independent Clause]
George	,	will you please come here.
Ladies and gentlemen	,	it is time for the show to begin.

206.13 **Introducing second clause.** A transitional expression or independent comment introducing the second clause in a compound sentence should be treated as though it were introducing a sentence. The clauses are separated by a semicolon; the coordinating conjunction (and, but, or, nor, yet, for) is omitted.

[Independent Clause]	[;]	Transitional Expression or Independent Comment	[,]	[Independent Clause]
I was at the job site on time	;	however	,	the others were not.
We have seen the end of an era	;	in my opinion	,	those days will never return.

Parenthetical (Nonessential) Elements

Identifying Nonessential Elements

206.14   **Parenthetical element defined.** A **parenthetical element** is an explanatory word, phrase, or clause that is part of the sentence, but is independent of the basic structure and meaning of the sentence.

A **parenthetical element** is also called a **nonessential element:** it is not essential to the structure or meaning of the sentence.

206.15   **Essential and nonessential elements.** The following characteristics are helpful in identifying essential and nonessential sentence elements:

     a.   Nonessential elements are parenthetical. If you place parentheses around the element, does the sentence retain its meaning? Is it still properly constructed? If so, the element is nonessential.

     b.   If you delete the element in question, does the remainder of the sentence stand alone as a properly constructed sentence? Does it retain its meaning? If so, the element is nonessential.

     c.   Does the element interrupt the flow of thought expressed by the remainder of the sentence? If so, the element is nonessential.

206.16   **Essential elements.** An element that is essential to the meaning or structure of the sentence is not set off with commas.

> The ship *Norway* is one of the largest cruise liners.
> (Naming the ship is essential to the meaning of the sentence.)
> The house *at the end of the lane* will soon be for sale.
> (Identifying the house is essential to the meaning of the sentence.)

Introductory Nonessential Elements

206.17   **Introductory independent comments.** An independent comment usually expresses the writer's opinion about the sentence or the subject with which the sentence deals.

[Nonessential Independent Comment]	[,]	[Independent Clause]
In my opinion	,	the new bridge will be inadequate.
Without a doubt	,	that was the best game of the year.

206.18   **Introductory transitional expressions.** A transitional expression reminds the reader of the context within which the sentence occurs. It may cause the reader to reflect on ideas previously expressed, or anticipate thoughts yet to be expressed, or both.

[Transitional Expression]	[,]	[Independent Clause]
Furthermore	,	there have been no other indications of dishonesty.
Consequently	,	we allowed two weeks for completion.

206.19   **Introductory direct address.** The sentence may be addressed to an individual or group.

[Introductory Direct Address]	[,]	[Main Clause]
Maurice	,	this is your hat.
Girls	,	it's time to get out of the pool.

Nonessential Elements Interrupting a Sentence

206.20 **Interrupting independent comment.** Independent comment may occur within the sentence.

The problem, *as I see it,* is our lack of liquid assets.

206.21 **Interrupting transitional expressions.** A transitional element may interrupt the sentence.

That simple fact, *however,* will soon be accepted by everyone.

206.22 **Interrupting direct address.** Direct address may occur as an interruption to the flow of the sentence.

Take the report, *Benny,* and correct all the errors we have found.

206.23 **Nonessential and essential appositives.** **Appositives** are nouns or noun phrases that identify the immediately preceding noun.

Nonessential appositives *are* set off with commas.

Essential appositives are *not* set off with commas.

Nonessential: John Wayne, *the actor,* played in many Westerns.
Essential: John Wayne *the actor* was a tall man; John Wayne *the baker* is a short man.

206.24 **Contrasting expressions.** Parenthetical expressions inserted for contrast are set off by commas.

The gulls, *not the sandpipers,* were making the noise.
His lips, *but not his eyes,* were smiling.

206.25 **Individual words.** Individual words may be set off with commas to give those words additional emphasis.

She smiled, *artificially,* and removed the card from the envelope.

206.26 **Interrupting phrases.** Interrupting (nonessential) phrases are set off with commas.

The captain, *sweeping the crew with his eyes,* turned on his heel and disappeared down the passageway.
Their leader, *putting on a great show of indifference,* turned to face me.

206.27 **Phrases that do not interrupt.** Essential phrases are not set off with commas.

The students *sitting in the last row* cannot hear the lecturer.
Our efforts *to raise the money* have been successful.
The car *with the red leather upholstery* won the prize.

206.28 **Interrupting clauses.** Nonessential (interrupting) clauses are set off with commas.

You can return your ballot by mail or, *if you plan to attend the meeting,* cast your vote in person.
The chief, *who appreciates a well-told tale,* listened to the entire story.

206.29 **Clauses that do not interrupt.** Essential clauses are not set off by commas.

> The server *who expects a tip* should please the diner.
> The ship *that had just returned to port* was nearly deserted.

Nonessential Elements Ending a Sentence

206.30 **Independent comment.** Independent comment may occur at the end of the sentence.

> That is the worst performance we have ever given, *in my opinion.*

206.31 **Transitional expressions.** Transitional expressions may be written at the end of the sentence.

> The rain does not hurt the rhubarb, *as a rule.*

206.32 **Direct address.** Direct address may occur at the end of the sentence.

> Turn the lights off when you leave, *Willie.*

206.33 **Contrasting expressions.** Parenthetical expressions may be used for contrast at the end of a sentence.

> The disturbance was caused by the workers, *not the students.*
> They stopped at Palmdale and Pasadena, *but not Pismo Beach.*

206.34 **Individual words.** An individual word may be set off with a comma at the end of a sentence to give that word additional emphasis.

> She faced him squarely and smiled, *artificially.*

206.35 **Nonessential phrases.** A nonessential phrase may be set off with a comma at the end of a sentence.

> The captain turned on his heel and disappeared down the passageway, *sweeping the crew with his eyes as he went.*
> Their leader turned to face me, *putting on a great show of indifference as he spoke.*

206.36 **Essential phrases.** An essential phrase at the end of a sentence is not set off with a comma.

> The best seats are not in the back row *of the theater.*
> This is the third time they have been late *for the show.*

206.37 **Nonessential clauses.** A nonessential clause at the end of a sentence is set off with a comma.

> You can return your ballot by mail, *if you prefer.*
> The glove was given to detective Hardwig, *who had searched for it the day before.*

206.38 **Essential clauses.** An essential clause at the end of a sentence is not set off by a comma.

> You can return your ballot by mail *if you do not attend the meeting.*
> The glove was given to the detective *who had searched for it the day before.*

Words in a Series
Items in a Series

206.39   **Basic convention.** When a sentence contains items in a series, use a comma after each item in the series except the last.

$$\begin{bmatrix} \text{Remainder of} \\ \text{Sentence} \end{bmatrix} \quad \begin{bmatrix} \text{Item} \\ a \end{bmatrix} \quad [,] \quad \begin{bmatrix} \text{Item} \\ b \end{bmatrix} \quad [,] \quad \begin{matrix} \text{[and]} \\ \text{[or]} \\ \text{[nor]} \end{matrix} \quad \begin{bmatrix} \text{Item} \\ c \end{bmatrix} \quad \begin{bmatrix} \text{Remainder of} \\ \text{Sentence} \end{bmatrix}$$

We ordered   bacon   ,   eggs   ,   and   toast   for breakfast.

206.40   **After the last item in a series.** Add a comma after the last item in a series [Item c] only if there is a specific reason for doing so.

>   Abe, Bill, and Carissa, each running for the plane, failed to see the
>   ticket agent.
> **But:**   Abe, Bill, and Carissa ran for the plane and failed to see the ticket
>   agent.

206.41   **Comma after the next-to-last item in a series.** Use a comma after the next-to-last item in a series [Item b] to avoid confusion.

> **Not:**   Move the cars tagged with the following colors: red, yellow and
>   black, green, brown and tan. *(Four or five cars?)*

206.42   **Series of two items.** Do not use a comma between two words that constitute a series.

> The tray contains nothing but nuts and bolts.

206.43   **When the items in a series are connected by *or, nor, and,* or *but.*** Do not use commas to separate items in a series when those items are connected by *or, nor, and,* or *but.*

> The tray contains nuts and bolts and washers.

206.44   **Series ending with *and so forth, and so on,* etc.** When a series ends with an expression such as *etc., and so forth,* or *and so on,* that ending expression is preceded by a comma. The ending expression is also followed by a comma — unless it falls at the end of a sentence.

> The tray of nuts, bolts, washers, etc., was not sorted.*
> The tray contained unsorted nuts, bolts, washers, etc.
> ***NOTE:**   The use of *etc.* in midtext should be avoided.

206.45   **Preference in organization names.** Regardless of the conventions that may seem to apply, write the name of an organization as the name is written by those representing the organization.

> Florea, Hafner and Olinger Co.   Wegman, Patton, and Levitz, Inc.
> Gulf + Western Industries, Inc.   Chapman Horn and Gilvert Co.

Adjectives Preceding a Noun

206.46   **More than two adjectives preceding a noun.** When more than two adjectives precede a noun, use a comma after each adjective that could correctly be followed by the word *and.* See, also, ¶206.48.

It was a long (and) hot (and) humid day.
It was a long, hot, humid day.

206.47 **Two adjectives preceding a noun.** When two consecutive adjectives precede a noun, separate the two adjectives with a comma. See, also, ¶206.48.

It was a vast, quiet lake that seemed at peace with itself.

NOTE: ¶206.47 is a refinement of ¶206.43. If the *and* is actually used, the comma is not.

It was a vast and quiet lake that seemed at peace with itself.

206.48 **Modification patterns.** When two or more adjectives precede a noun, any one of several modification patterns may exist.

a. The preceding adjectives may each modify the noun. In this case, use a comma after each adjective except the last. Notice that the word *and* can be substituted for all the commas. See ¶206.46.

[Remainder of Sentence]	[adjective]	[,]	[adjective]	[,]	[adjective]	[noun]
They were a	carefree	,	silly	,	giddy	group.

b. The noun and the adjective immediately preceding it may be so closely related that they express a single idea. In this case, the other adjectives in the series may modify that single idea.

Notice that the word *and* can be substituted for the commas in each case—and that *and* **cannot** be inserted between the other adjectives (*hot* and *summer; old* and *county*). See ¶206.46.

[Remainder of Sentence]	[adjective]	[,]	[adjective]	[adjective + noun]
It was a	long	,	hot	summer day.
We approached the	dreary	,	old	county jail.

c. More than two words may be required to express the combined idea.

Notice that the word *and* **cannot** be inserted after any of the adjectives; no commas are used. See ¶206.46.

[Remainder of Sentence]	[adjective]	[adjective]	[adjective]	[noun]
We approached the	old	county	jail	building.
They planned a	surprise	happy	birthday	party.

Repeated and Omitted Words

206.49 **Repeated words.** Words repeated for emphasis are separated by commas.

No, no, that is not what I meant at all.
That picture is very, very old.

206.50 **Repeated verbs.** Use a comma to separate repeated verbs—those that are identical and next to each other.

> When you work, work hard; when you play, play hard.

206.51 **Repetitive words omitted.** The comma may be used to replace repetitious words that are easily perceived.

> The good oranges are on top; the bad, on the bottom.
> **NOTE:** The comma replaces the repetitious words *oranges are*.

206.52 **Omission of *that*.** Omission of the conjunction *that* can create a definite pause in the sentence. A comma should be inserted to mark that pause.

> The problem is, neither part is machined within tolerances. (pause)
> Lynn felt the program would succeed. (no pause)

Conventional Formats

206.53 **Personal names.** A comma should be used to set off an abbreviation (but **not** a number) following a personal name.

> Jacinto Montez, Jr.   C. D. Rutherford III
> Wallace Rindgate, CPA   Jose P. Lozano, Sr.

NOTE: However, each person's name should be written as that person prefers.

> Thomas Wentling, III, Esq.   Walter Tidwell Jr.

206.54 **Personal names in sentences.** An abbreviation following a personal name in a sentence is set off with two commas.

> Wallace Rindgate, CPA, will chair the panel.

If the name is normally written without a comma, no comma is used before or after the abbreviation or number—unless the sentence structure otherwise calls for a comma.

> Walter Tidwell III will be the next person to leave.
> In the case of Walter Tidwell III, we can make an exception.

206.55 **Transposed names.** When a name is written last-name-first, the transposed portion is set off with commas.

> Lewandowski, Stanley B., Jr.   Sasser, John M., III
> Monroe, Edward R.   Valentine, Richard D., Esq.

The Comma with Other Punctuation

Dash, ¶207.14–207.17.
Parentheses, ¶212.8–212.17.
Quotation mark, ¶215.34.

Spacing with the Comma

	Before	After
In normal use within a sentence............................	0	1
Followed by a closing quotation mark......................	0	0
In a number...	0	0

DASH

207 The dash can be used to indicate a sudden break in thought — and to place emphasis on the expression following that break. Although parenthetical expressions may be set off by parentheses (they are spoken in a whisper, not emphasized) or with commas (indicating that they are spoken in normal conversational tones), parenthetical expressions set off by dashes are spoken in a loud voice — or shouted!

The Dash Indicating Interruptions

207.1 **Sharp break in thought.** Use a dash to set off an abrupt break in thought at the end of a sentence — and a pair of dashes to set off a sudden break in thought within a sentence.

> I can help you do the job right — but only if you will listen.
> Face the target — the one slightly to the right — before you lower the rifle.

207.2 **Sentence broken off.** A dash may be used to indicate that a sentence has been broken.

> You can go through Cambridge and Zanesville and then —   However, there is a better way.

NOTE: If the **broken-off** sentence is a statement, the dash is followed by two spaces. (The two spaces are left *only* if what follows is a complete sentence.) No other punctuation is necessary.

207.3 **Question broken off.** A dash may be used to indicate that a question has been broken off. The dash is followed by a question mark; the question mark is followed by two spaces.

> Is there time for me to — ?   No, I see that there is not.

207.4 **Exclamation broken off.** A dash may be used to indicate that an exclamation has been broken off. The dash is followed by an exclamation mark; the exclamation mark is followed by two spaces.

> I can't believe that you would — !   But I guess I shouldn't be surprised.

The Dash Indicating Emphasis

207.5 **Emphasizing a single word.** The dash may be used to emphasize a single word.

> Money—that is their only interest!
> They are interested in one thing—money—above all else!
> There is only one thing in which they are interested—money!

207.6   **Restatement.** The dash and a restated thought may be used for emphasis.

> That was a good game—as good as any we have seen this season.
> There were four of them—yes, four of them—standing there doing nothing.

207.7   **Hesitation or stammering.** The dash is used to indicate hesitation in speech or stammering.

> I like the red—no, the blue one, or— I'll take the black one.

207.8   **Summary.** A dash may be used to emphasize the summary of ideas expressed earlier in the sentence.

> Poverty, hunger, suffering, greed, corruption—all were painfully apparent.
>
> **But:**   Poverty, hunger, suffering, greed, and corruption were painfully apparent. (A dash should not be used if the summarizing word [all] is not the subject of the sentence.)

207.9   **Appositive.** A dash may be used to set off an appositive when an emphatic break is desired.

> They realized that Harry Farnsworth—the plumber—had been called to fix the wiring.
> The person called to fix the wiring was Harry Farnsworth—the plumber.

207.10   **Quotation.** A dash may be used before the source of a quotation.

> Certitude is not the test of certainty.
>   —Oliver Wendell Holmes, Jr.

The Dash with Other Punctuation

207.11   **Before an opening dash and after a closing dash.** Do not use additional punctuation to indicate the break in thought before an opening dash or after a closing dash (For exception, see ¶207.2–207.4).

> **Not:**   The car was moving slowly,—but erratically.
> **Not:**   The car moved slowly—but erratically,—down the road.
> **But:**   The car was moving slowly—but erratically.
> **Or:**   The car moved slowly—but erratically—down the road.

Colon

207.12   **Dash instead of a colon.** When an emphatic but informal break is desired, use a dash instead of a colon to introduce an explanatory element.

> At the carnival last year, a small child won the prize—a pumpkin.

207.13   Colon instead of a dash. A colon may be used instead of a closing dash if the subsequent explanatory expression otherwise merits the use of a colon. Do *not* use both the colon and the dash to close the expression.

> This is the prize—the top prize of the contest: a new convertible.

Comma

207.14   Dash emphasizing the second independent clause in a compound sentence. A dash may be used instead of a comma before the coordinating conjunction in a compound sentence; this form provides a stronger break and greater emphasis on the *second* independent clause.

> The storm is severe—but it is not a hurricane.

207.15   Dashes setting off a nonessential element for emphasis. A nonessential element that requires special emphasis may be set off with dashes instead of commas.

> That is the reason—the real reason—for the change.
> They talked about the real reason for the change—greed.

207.16   Dashes setting off a nonessential element containing commas. When a nonessential element contains commas, the sentence can sometimes be improved by setting off the nonessential element with dashes instead of commas.

> Only a few people remember—Anna, Beth, and Clarence are among them—how dark those days really were.

207.17   Dash conflicting with a comma. When a closing dash conflicts with a comma, retain the dash and eliminate the comma.

> You say that the car is economical—and dependable—but it is neither.
> **Not:**   You say that the car is economical—and dependable—, but it is neither.
> **Not:**   You say that the car is economical—and dependable,—but it is neither.

Parentheses

207.18   Dashes instead of parentheses. When strong emphasis is desired, use dashes instead of parentheses to set off a parenthetical element.

> The last of the old cars—a Model T Ford—was moved from the museum.

207.19   Dash conflicting with a parenthesis. When a closing dash conflicts with a closing parenthesis, the closing parenthesis prevails.

> Use a darker color (green would be my first choice—it blends well with the other colors) on the bottom.

Semicolon

207.20   Dash replacing a semicolon. When a strong but informal break is desired between main clauses, use a dash instead of a semicolon.

> This is the fourth time I have told you—I hope it is the last.

207.21   **Dash conflicting with a semicolon.** When a closing dash and a semicolon separating the clauses of a compound sentence fall at the same point, the semicolon prevails.

> Read the book — the one I recommended previously; it will explain the concept better than I can.

Declarative Statement, Question, or Exclamation

207.22   **Declarative statement.** A declarative statement set off with dashes within a sentence is not followed by a period.

> Our group — we are identified by our green caps — will go first.

207.23   **Question.** A question set off with dashes within a sentence is followed by a question mark placed just before the closing dash.

> The reference book — is it an encyclopedia? — is not on the shelf.

207.24   **Exclamation.** An exclamation set off with dashes within a sentence is followed by an exclamation mark placed just before the closing dash.

> The reference book — it is an encyclopedia! — is back on the shelf.

End-of-Sentence Punctuation

207.25   **Dash conflicting with period, question mark, or exclamation mark.** When a closing dash falls at the end of a sentence, the regular end-of-sentence punctuation takes precedence.

> That is what we need — a vacation!
> **Not:**   That is what we need — a vacation — !

Spacing with the Dash

	Before	After
In normal use	0	0
Following a broken-off statement	0	2
Following the question mark at the end of a broken-off question	0	2
Following the exclamation mark at the end of a broken-off exclamation	0	2

208   # DIAGONAL (SLANT, SLASH, SOLIDUS, STROKE, VIRGULE)

208.1   **Indicating choice.** The diagonal may be used to indicate alternatives.

> This model may be ordered with radial tires and/or hub caps.
> (See note at ¶208.2.)

208.2 **Abbreviations.** The diagonal is used in several abbreviated forms.

> w/buttons with buttons   B/L bill of lading
> miles/hour miles per hour   c/o care of
> **NOTE:** These uses are usually confined to functional writing (tables, forms, informal memos, and the like).

208.3 **Dates and seasons.** The diagonal may be used (instead of a hyphen) between years to indicate that the years are successive — or, in the same manner, to indicate a single season spanning two calendar years. **NOTE:** This usage is for informal writing only.

> 1776/77   377/376 B.C.   the 1966/67 season

208.4 **Quoted poetry.** Lines of poetry quoted within a sentence or paragraph may be separated from one another by diagonals. Space before and after the diagonal. If more than two lines of poetry are quoted, space the lines as they are in the original poem — or single space and start all lines of the poem five spaces to the right of the left margin.

> I think the exact lines were, "A crimson finger, drawn across the sky / To sweep the land where western ridges lie, . . ."

Spacing with the Diagonal

	Before	After
Separating two lines (no more) of poetry quoted within a sentence	1	1
All other uses	0	0

209 # ELLIPSIS MARKS

Indicating Omissions

209.1 **Indicating an omitted word or words.** Ellipsis marks may be used to indicate the omission of a word or words within a sentence, usually a sentence that is quoted.

> The mayor, a large woman with a booming voice, led the parade.
> The mayor, a large woman . . . , led the parade.
> The mayor . . . led the parade.

209.2 **Beginning a quoted sentence.** Ellipsis marks may be used to indicate an omission at the beginning of a quoted sentence.

> **Original:** In these parts, one's word is as good as one's bond.
> **Quoted:** In the author's hometown, ". . . one's word is as good as one's bond."

209.3 **At the end of a sentence.** Three ellipsis marks are used to indicate the omission of a word or words at the end of a sentence; the original end-of-sentence punctuation is retained after the ellipsis marks.

The swamp is the lowest spot in the county, and a real problem.
The swamp is the lowest spot in the county. . . .

Is the swamp the lowest spot in the county, and a real problem?
Is the swamp the lowest spot in the county . . . ?

The swamp is the lowest spot in the county, and a real problem!
The swamp is the lowest spot in the county . . . !

209.4　**At the end of a paragraph.** Ellipsis marks at the end of a paragraph may indicate the omission of the end of a sentence if the end punctuation **follows** the marks. If the end-of-sentence punctuation **precedes** the ellipsis marks, a sentence, several sentences, a paragraph, or several paragraphs have been omitted.

Ellipsis Marks Not Used

209.5　**Short quotations.** A short quotation that is obviously a sentence fragment does not require ellipsis marks.

The author cited the "high cost of not reading."

209.6　**Run-in quotation of a complete sentence.** When a sentence is quoted as part of another longer sentence, ellipsis marks are not necessary.

The second sentence on page 22 reads, "This phenomenon has been observed by at least a dozen scientists over a period of twelve years."

209.7　**Displayed quotations.** Ellipsis marks are not required before or after a displayed quotation that is set in a panel. Quoted material displayed in this fashion is sometimes called an **extract**.

Quoted material may be set in five spaces from the left margin and single spaced (preferred), or set in five spaces from the left *and right* margins and single spaced. No beginning or ending ellipsis marks are required in this format except between two inset paragraphs where an omission is made, or if the quoted material begins in midsentence. Material omitted in the middle of a quotation would, of course, be indicated by ellipsis marks. **No** external quotation marks are used in an extract.

Informal Use of Ellipsis Marks

209.8　**Connecting loosely related ideas.** Ellipsis marks are sometimes used to connect loosely related ideas—particularly in advertising material.

Put away a little money . . . every week . . . at United Trust, and . . . before you know it . . . a little will be a lot!

209.9　**Introducing display lines in a list.** Ellipsis marks may be used to introduce a list of items or to introduce the individual items in a list.

Buy at Glitz and get . . .　　　　　Buy at Glitz and get
　low prices　　　　　　　　　　　. . . low prices
　instant financing　　　　　　　　. . . instant financing
　factory service　　　　　　　　　. . . factory service

Ellipsis Marks with Other Punctuation

209.10 **Omission within a sentence.** Omit punctuation before or after ellipsis marks within a sentence unless it is required for clarity or correct form in the condensed sentence.

> **Original:**   They came; they saw; they bought; and they left very little.
> **Condensed:** They came; . . . they bought; and they left very little.

> **Original:**   The cup, the cup, of course that was the missing clue.
> **Condensed:** The cup . . . was the missing clue.

209.11 **Omission at the end of a sentence.** The end-of-sentence punctuation follows the ellipsis marks. See ¶209.3.

209.12 **Omission at the end of a paragraph.** The conventions for omissions at the end of a sentence do not apply to omissions at the end of a paragraph as noted earlier. See ¶209.4.

Spacing with Ellipsis Marks

	Before	After
Within a sentence	1	1
Following an opening quotation mark	0	1
Preceding a closing quotation mark	1	0
Following end-of-sentence punctuation	1	2

NOTE: Write the ellipsis mark by entering ._._.
 (_ = Strike space bar.)

EXCLAMATION MARK

210 The exclamation mark is useful in those rare instances in which truly strong feeling should be expressed. The effect of the exclamation mark is enhanced by using it infrequently — and appropriately.

210.1 **Expressing surprise, enthusiasm, disbelief, and other strong emotions.** Use an exclamation mark after an appropriate element of a sentence — or at the end of a sentence — to express strong feeling.

> **Dissent:**   I cannot agree(!) with that point of view or with anything else the speaker said.

NOTE: If the exclamation mark falls at a point at which there is not a natural break in the sentence, enclose the exclamation mark in parentheses. Since this creates a forced break in the flow of the sentence, it is frequently better to place the exclamation mark at the end of the sentence.

> **Irony:**   Another offer of a "free vacation!"
> **Amusement:** Look at the nose on that clown!
> **Resignation:** Well, you can't win them all!
> **Surprise:**   Oh! I didn't know you were standing there.

Disbelief: Huge! I can't believe the size of this auditorium.
Enthusiasm: What a performance!
**Other strong
  feeling:**   Leave that alone!

210.2 **Following *Oh*.** *Oh* may be used as either a strong or a mild exclamation. As a *strong* exclamation, it is followed by an exclamation mark; as a *mild* exclamation, it is followed by a comma. In both cases, it is capitalized only when it begins a sentence or stands alone.

Oh! What a beautiful sight.
Oh, I think I shall stay home this evening.
I tried to tell you, but—oh, what's the use.

210.3 **Following *O*.** *O* is an indicator of direct address. It says, "I am directing this to you." *O* is not followed by any punctuation unless it is called for by the structure of the sentence. *O* is capitalized regardless of its position in the sentence.

O Lord, why me?   Why me, O Lord?
When I said, "O," I did not mean "oh."

210.4 **Following elliptical sentences.** Exclamation marks are frequently used at the ends of elliptical sentences—short expressions that are used as sentences.

Full Sentence: You hurry! You hurry! You hurry! The show is about to begin.
Elliptical: Hurry! Hurry! Hurry! The show is about to begin.

The Exclamation Mark with Other Punctuation

Dash, ¶207.24–207.25.
Parentheses, ¶212.9, 212.11, 212.13, 212.17.
Quotation marks, ¶215.38.

Spacing with the Exclamation Mark

	Before	After
Ending a sentence	0	2
Enclosed in parentheses	0	0
Closing parenthesis after an exclamation mark	0	1
Within a sentence, followed immediately by another punctuation mark	0	0
Within a sentence, not followed immediately by another punctuation mark	0	0

HYPHEN

211 The use of hyphens in compound forms is covered in this section. See Unit 5 for the use of hyphens in word division.

Compound Words

211.1 **Definition.** A **compound word** is a combination of words expressing a single concept. A compound word may be written open (window shade), hyphenated (window-shop), or solid (windowsill).

When a word combination is first coined, writers tend to use a hyphen to separate its components. If the compound becomes a permanent and frequently used form, the hyphen is usually dropped and the compound written solid.

Even though this process may take many years, there is enough change in compound words to make it advisable for the writer who is unsure of a compound form to use the latest edition of a reliable dictionary. Compound forms in this unit are consistent with those shown in the 1987 printing of *Webster's Ninth New Collegiate Dictionary,* published by Merriam-Webster, Springfield, Massachusetts.

211.2 **Prefixes.** Certain prefixes are frequently combined with a variety of words to produce forms that are compound in every respect — except that they consist of a prefix and word rather than two words. These forms are frequently treated as compounds — as they are in this reference manual.

cooperate   *anti*climax   *quasi*-judicial   *pseudo*science

211.3 **Standard compound forms.** The conventions for writing compound nouns are so varied and without pattern that it is almost accurate to say that each compound word is its own rule. Even the most useful descriptions of those conventions contain many exceptions. Current standard forms are shown in any good, up-to-date dictionary. If one of the following conventional forms does not match the one about which you are in doubt, look it up in your dictionary.

211.4 **Temporary compound forms.** In addition to the standard dictionary forms, a writer may use a temporary compound form as an adjective preceding a noun — or may coin a temporary compound form for a special purpose. A news reporter might write about a *quasi-official* meeting; a science fiction writer might write about a *pseudogalaxy* that is wholly imaginary.

211.5 **Compound nouns and verb phrases.** Do not confuse a compound noun and a verb phrase:

Compound Nouns	Verb Phrases
a big *get-together*	to *get together* after class
a *holdup* at the store	to *hold up* the store
a complete *sellout*	to *sell out* the stock
a little *runaway*	to *run away* from home

211.6 **Gerund and its object.** A gerund is the *ing* form of a verb functioning as a noun. Certain compounds are formed by combining the gerund and its object — in transposed order.

[object] [gerund]
house painting
distance running
car washing

211.7   **Dual job titles.** When a person holds two positions simultaneously, a job title may be fashioned by joining two appropriate job titles with a hyphen.

[noun] [-] [noun]
architect - contractor
producer - director
secretary - treasurer

211.8   **Numbers.** In spelling out numbers, join *one* through *nine* to the base number (*twenty, thirty . . . ninety*) with a hyphen.

seventy-two dollars and twenty-three cents
four thousand, two hundred sixty-three dollars and forty-nine cents

211.9   **Fractions.** To spell out a fraction, connect the numerator and denominator with a hyphen—unless one of them already contains a hyphen.

[numerator] [-] [denominator]
three - fourths
twelve and   seven - eighths

But: Twenty-two thousandths   thirteen thirty-seconds
thirty-seven sixty-fourths

211.10   *Master* **plus noun compounds.** Most standard compounds beginning with *master* are written open. All temporary compound forms beginning with *master* should be written open.

[master] [noun]
master   teacher
master   gunner
master   bedroom

Temporary compounds: master manager   master printer

But: master-at-arms   mastermind   masterpiece

211.11   *Quasi* **plus noun compounds.** Compound nouns beginning with *quasi* are written open; temporary compound nouns beginning with *quasi* should also be written open.

[quasi] [noun]
quasi   contract
quasi   corporation

See ¶211.28 for adjectival compounds containing *quasi*.

211.12   *Self* **plus noun compounds.** Many compound nouns are formed using *self* as the first element. Virtually all standard compound nouns

beginning with *self* are hyphenated; temporary compound nouns beginning with *self* should also be hyphenated.

        [self] [-] [noun]
        self   - image
        self   - esteem
        self   - revelation

But: selfish, selfless

See ¶211.29 for adjectival compounds containing *self*.

211.13   *Semi* **plus noun compounds.** A few compound nouns are written
with *semi* as the first element. Nearly all *semi* plus noun compounds are
written solid. Most *semi* compounds are used as adjectives. See ¶211.30
for adjectival compounds containing *semi*.

        [semi][noun]
          semicircle
          semidesert
          semidome

211.14   *Vice* **plus noun compounds.** Compounds formed using *vice* as
the first element are hyphenated, written open, and written solid. The
standard *vice* forms are listed below. Temporary *vice* forms should be
hyphenated: vice-chairperson, vice-manager, and the like.

vice admiral	vicegerency	vice president	vicereine
vice-chancellor	vicegerent	viceregal	viceroy
vice-consul	vice presidency	vice-regent	viceroyalty
	viceroyship		

211.15   **Descriptive phrases.** Certain descriptive phrases are used as nouns.
Hyphens are used between their words to indicate clearly that the phrase
conveys a single concept.

        Johnny-come-lately   stay-at-home
        stick-in-the-mud   stick-to-itiveness

211.16   **Nouns beginning with *grand*.** Compound nouns that designate
relatives and begin with *grand* are written solid.

[grand][noun]	grandfather	grandnephew
grandaunt	grandmother	grandniece
granddaughter	grandson	granduncle

211.17   **Nouns beginning with *great*.** Compound nouns that designate
relatives and begin with *great* are hyphenated.

[great] [-] [noun]	great-grandfather	great-nephew
great - aunt	great-grandmother	great-niece
great - granddaughter	great-grandson	great-uncle

211.18   **In-laws.** Compound nouns designating *in-laws* are hyphenated.

[noun] [-] [in] [-] [law]	mother-in-law
brother - in - law	sister-in-law
daughter - in - law	son-in-law
father - in - law	

211.19 **Compound nouns ending in *ache*.** Compound nouns ending in *ache* are written solid.

[noun][ache]		
	backache	stomachache
earache	headache	toothache

211.20 **Compound nouns ending in *book*.** Many compound nouns ending in *book* are written solid; others are written open.

[noun][book]	[noun] [book]
textbook	comic book
notebook	reference book
checkbook	account book

All temporary compound forms ending in *book* are written open.

coupon book	illustration book	registration book

211.21 **Compound nouns ending in *elect*.** Compound nouns ending in *elect* are hyphenated—unless the name of the office itself consists of more than one word. Temporary compounds should follow the same convention.

[office] [-] [elect]	senator-elect
president - elect	vice president elect

Compound Adjectives

211.22 **Hyphenated compound adjective before a noun.** Generally, a hyphen is used to join two or more words functioning as a single adjective before a noun.

[word] [-] [word]	[noun]
well - known	person
tax - free	bond
soft - spoken	farmer
love - hate	relationship

[word] [-] [word] [-] [word]	[noun]
holier - than - thou	attitude
cloak - and - dagger	plot

[word] [-] [word] [-] [word] [-] [word]	[noun]
Sunday - go - to - meeting	clothes
seat - of - the - pants	decision

211.23 **After a noun.** When the words in a compound adjective are used after a noun (not as a compound adjective) hyphens are not used to join them unless the words make up a permanent hyphenated compound.

a person who is well known
a bond that is tax free
a farmer who is soft spoken
a relationship consisting of love and hate
an attitude that you are holier than I
clothes to wear to Sunday meeting
a decision made by the seat of the pants

211.24   **Adverb ending in *ly* before a noun.** When the first word of a compound adjective is an adverb ending in *ly,* hyphens are not used to join the elements of the compound.

[adverb] [ending in *ly*]	[word]	[noun]
gently	running	brook
heavily	traveled	road
rapidly	increasing	prices
newly	constructed	street

211.25   ***All-* compounds as adjectives.** Adjectival *all-* compounds are hyphenated whether they precede or follow the noun.

[all] [-] [word]	all-American
all - embracing	all-or-nothing
all - inclusive	all-purpose

211.26   ***Cross-* compounds as adjectives.** Adjectival *cross-* compounds are generally hyphenated.

[cross] [-] [word]	cross-sectional
cross - country	cross-eyed
cross - county	cross-legged
	cross-referenced

Except:	crossbred	cross multiplied
	crosscourt	crosstown
	crosscut	crosstree
	crosshatched	

211.27   ***Half-* compounds as adjectives.** Adjectival *half-* compounds are hyphenated whether they precede or follow the noun.

[half] [-] [word]	half-soled
half - baked	half-timbered
half - cocked	

Adjectival *half-* compounds that are not hyphenated:

halfhearted
halftime
halftone
halfway

211.28   *Quasi-* **compounds as adjectives.** Adjectival *quasi-* compounds are hyphenated whether they precede or follow the noun. See ¶211.11 for *quasi-* compounds as nouns.

[quasi] [-] [word]   quasi-public
  quasi - judicial   quasi-legislative

211.29   *Self-* **compounds as adjectives.** Adjectival *self-* compounds are hyphenated whether they precede or follow the noun. See ¶211.12 for *self-* compounds as nouns.

[self] [-] [word]   self-educated
  self - adjusting   self-imposed
  self - incriminating   self-protective

But: selfless (selflessly, selflessness)
          selfish

211.30   **Prefixes in adjectival forms.**

a.   Adjectives formed using the following prefixes are almost always written solid:

anti	anticrime	**pro**	prodemocratic
co	cooperative	**re**	revitalized
extra	extralegal	**semi**	semipermanent
inter	interterm	**sub**	subordinate
non	nonallergic	**super**	supercharged
over	overweight	**ultra**	ultralight
post	postseason	**un**	undemocratic
pre	prewar	**under**	understated

Exceptions: The hyphen is used to distinguish between homonyms. A *recovered* couch is one that has been returned to its owner; a *re-covered* couch is one with a new cover.

A hyphen is also used if the second element of the compound form is capitalized, or if it is a number:

pro-English   under-21
inter-American   pre-1900

A hyphen may be used for clarification when the second element of a compound adjective consists of more than one word or includes a prefix.

the non-overweight members of the gym class
an anti-postseason-event group

b.   Adjective compounds using these prefixes are written with a hyphen:

	all-	all-powerful	
(When ex means past or previous)	**ex-**	ex-president	(See Unit 1 word list)
	self-	self-appointed	

Numbers in Compounds

211.31

Number and noun form a compound. When a compound is comprised of a number and a noun and that compound appears before the noun that is modified, the number is singular and the compound is hyphenated.

[number]	[-]	[noun] [noun]	
four	-	way stop	an intersection with four stops
one	-	horse town	a town with one horse
second	-	class citizen	one who is economically or culturally deprived
4	-	quart jug	a jug that holds four quarts

Exceptions:

a $12 million building	an 18 percent note
a first day cover (stamps)	firsthand information
firstborn child	a secondhand car

211.32

Other compounds with numbers. Conventions for writing compounds including numbers vary widely. Some typical patterns are as follows:

the number two person	*or*	the second in command
a class-A restaurant	*or*	a class A restaurant
8-5 odds	*or*	the odds are 8 to 5
a 50-50 chance	*or*	a fifty-fifty chance
20/20 vision	*or*	twenty-twenty vision
a 2-to-1 ratio, *or a ratio of 2 to 1, or a 2:1 ratio*		

211.33

Ranges. Use the hyphen to express numeric and alphabetic ranges.

1-20	*1* through *20*
21-99	*21* through *99*
A-E	*A* through *E*
in-inventory	*in* through *inventory* (alphabetically)

NOTE: The hyphen is usually typed solid when used to express ranges. It is frequently set off with spaces when used to express alphabetic ranges.

1-9	Ar-Bi	*or*	Ar - Bi
27-224	A-M	*or*	A - M

Other Uses of the Hyphen

211.34

Suspending hyphens. If two or more related compound forms have a common base, use suspending hyphens rather than repeating the base word.

The display included 6-, 8-, 12-, and 16-cylinder engines.
NOTE: If the suspending hyphen is not followed by a punctuation mark, it is followed by a space.
The display included 6- and 8-cylinder engines.

211.35   **Improvised words.** The hyphen may be used to form improvised words.

> an A-frame house
> an H-shaped beam   *or*   an H beam
> an I-shaped beam   *or*   an I beam
> a bad S-curve
> a U-turn sign
> a Y-shaped intersection
> an X-mark

Spacing with the Hyphen

	Before	After
In normal use (compound words, etc.)	0	0
Suspended	0	0 *or* 1
Alphabetic Ranges	0 *or* 1	0 *or* 1
Numeric Ranges...............................	0	0

212   # PARENTHESES

Enclosing Parenthetical Elements

212.1   **Parenthetical elements in general.** Parentheses, commas, and dashes are used to set off parenthetical expressions.

Parentheses lower the speaking voice to a whisper, seeming to apologize for intruding with information so nonessential.

> The golden rule (Matthew 7:12) guides their decisions.

Commas lower the reading voice, indicating that the enclosed element is nonessential.

> The golden rule, an important principle, guides them.

Dashes raise the reading voice to a shout, emphasizing the element they set off. Dashes may set off *essential* or *nonessential* expressions, but they always *emphasize*.

> **Essential:**   One principle—the golden rule—guided their decisions.
> **Nonessential:**   The ring—a gold one—was in a velvet case.

212.2   **Parenthetical elements.** A parenthetical element may be a word (or a number or some other symbol), a phrase, a clause, or a sentence.

> **Word:**   The document was printed in small (elite) type.
> **Phrase:**   The smaller type (twelve characters to the inch) is elite.
> **Clause:**   The larger type (it is called *pica*) is easier to read.
> **Sentence:** (The smaller type will allow us to get more on a page.)

212.3   **Testing parenthetical constructions.** To test a sentence containing a parenthetical expression for correctness, read the sentence without the parenthetical expression. If it stands as a complete sentence, the parentheses have probably been used correctly.

> **Incorrect:**   The last of the grapes (all of which were purple concords) in the vat.
>
> **Correct:**   The last of the grapes (all of which were purple concords) were in the vat.

212.4   **Enclosing references.** Parentheses may be used to enclose references to other pages or sections in the same document, or to other documents.

> This is not always the case. (See Watson, page 23.) In another instance (see page 33) the results were entirely different.

Parentheses Organizing Data

212.5   **Outlines.** Parentheses may be used to enclose numbers and letters in an outline, giving the outline format additional levels of organization.

> I. ----------
>> A. ----------
>>> 1. ----------
>>>> a) ----------
>>>>> (1) ----------
>>>>>> (a) ----------
>>>>>>> i) ----------

212.6   **Enumerations.** Numbers or letters organizing an enumeration may be enclosed in parentheses.

> Follow this procedure: (1) Assemble the wheels and axles. (2) Mount the axles under the body of the car. (3) Install the top, doors, and trim.

212.7   **Numeric information.** Detailed nonessential numeric information is frequently enclosed in parentheses — particularly confirming (restated) information in law documents.

> **Dates:**   The developer left the premises the same year (1972).
> **Time:**   The extension will be for thirty-one (31) days.
> **Amount:**   The check is for $24.51 (twenty-four and 51/100 dollars).
> **References:**   This activity is covered in the bylaws (see section 27, paragraph 12, page 22).

Parentheses with Other Punctuation

Opening Parenthesis

212.8   **Before an opening parenthesis.** Do not use a comma, semicolon, colon, or dash before an opening parenthesis. (See ¶212.6 for exception.)

Not:
- There were three numbers on the board, (5, 6, and 9).
- There were three numbers on the board; (5, 6, and 9).
- There were three numbers on the board: (5, 6, and 9).
- There were three numbers on the board — (5, 6, and 9).

But: There were three numbers on the board (5, 6, and 9).

Or:
- There were three numbers on the board, 5, 6, and 9.
- There were three numbers on the board; they were 5, 6, and 9.
- There were three numbers on the board: 5, 6, and 9.
- There were three numbers on the board — 5, 6, and 9.

212.9 **No punctuation after an opening parenthesis.** After an opening parenthesis:

Do not use a punctuation mark.

Do not capitalize the first word unless it begins a complete parenthetical sentence *standing alone*.

That chair (it is Chippendale) is a bargain.
That chair is a bargain. (It is Chippendale.)

Unless: The first letter following the parenthesis would be capitalized anywhere in the sentence (proper adjective, proper noun, the pronoun *I*).

That chair (I believe it is Chippendale) is a bargain.

Closing Parenthesis

212.10 **Period before a closing parenthesis.** Do not use a period before a closing parenthesis unless:

The parenthetical expression ends with an abbreviation.

The parade started on the main street (Fifth Ave.).

The entire expression stands alone as a parenthetical sentence.

The parade started on the main street. (That is Fifth Avenue.)

212.11 **Question mark or exclamation mark before a closing parenthesis.** Do not use a question mark or exclamation mark before a closing parenthesis unless the mark applies only to a parenthetical element that is part of a longer sentence, *and* is different from the punctuation mark used at the end of the sentence.

Not: Will the game (is it tomorrow?) be over by four?
But: Will the game (is it tomorrow) be over by four?
And: Will the game (it is tomorrow!) be over by four?

Not: What a game (it is tomorrow!) it will be!
But: What a game (it is tomorrow) it will be!

Exception: The entire expression stands alone as a parenthetical sentence. See ¶212.15.

(What a great day we have had!)

212.12 **No comma, semicolon, colon, or dash before a closing parenthesis.** Do not use a comma, semicolon, colon, or dash *before* a closing parenthesis.

> The book (*The Complete Computer Guide*), despite its title, is not complete.
> Run the test again (the basic diagnostic test); we must be certain of the results.
> Run the test again (the basic diagnostic test): we must be certain of the results.
> The leaves will fall—in the autumn (or fall, if you prefer)—as they always have.

212.13 **After a closing parenthesis.** When the parenthetical element ends the sentence, place the end-of-sentence punctuation after the closing parenthesis.

> We shall begin the series tomorrow (Thursday).
> Will the series begin tomorrow (Thursday)?
> The series must not begin until tomorrow (Thursday)!

Parenthetical Sentences

212.14 **Before a parenthetical sentence.** If an entire sentence is parenthetical, the previous sentence is punctuated normally: there may be a period, question mark, or exclamation mark (followed by two spaces) before the opening parenthesis.

> This may be the last day this price is available! (The new model will go on sale tomorrow.)

212.15 **Ending a parenthetical sentence.** When the entire sentence is parenthetical, use no punctuation after the closing parenthesis; place the end-of-sentence punctuation before the closing parenthesis.

> (This is a parenthetical sentence.)

Punctuation Enclosed by Parentheses

212.16 **Question mark.** A question mark within a sentence may be enclosed by parentheses to express doubt.

> The advertisement says there is a lifetime(?) guarantee.

212.17 **Exclamation mark.** An exclamation mark may be used to emphasize a word or other sentence element.

> The advertisement says there is a lifetime(!) guarantee.

Spacing with Parentheses

Opening Parenthesis	**Before**	**After**
Parenthetical expression is *not* a free-standing sentence	1	0

Opening Parenthesis	Before	After
Parenthetical expression *is* a free-standing sentence	2	0
Parenthetical matter immediately precedes a question mark or exclamation mark	0	0
Closing Parenthesis		
Following parenthetical expression within a sentence	0	1
Following normal end-of-sentence punctuation	0	2
Followed by another punctuation mark	0	0

213 PERIOD

At the End of a Sentence

213.1 **Statement.** Use a period following a statement. The sentence may be a simple statement of fact.

> There are three eggs in the basket.
> The textbook gives the answer to number eight as *false*.

The statement may affirm, assert, avow, or declare an opinion.

> The landscape is the best painting in the exhibit.
> In my opinion, the answer to number eight is *false*.

213.2 **Request.** The statement may be a request phrased as a question.

> Will you lay the book on the table.
> Will you lay the book on the table?

Both examples are punctuated correctly. The first sentence is a polite request *phrased* as a question. The person to whom it is addressed is expected to respond by *complying with the request*. The second example is a *question;* the person to whom it is addressed is expected to answer — probably *yes* or *no*.

213.3 **Command.** A mildly stated command, in which the writer does not wish to display a sense of force or urgency, may be punctuated with a period.

> Leave the dishes on the table.
> Do not walk the dog through the neighbors' yards.

More forceful commands, particularly those meant to convey a sense of urgency, may be punctuated with an exclamation mark.

> Stop where you are!
> Come out of there with your hands up!

213.4   **Indirect question.** Use a period to mark the end of an indirect question.

> He asked how so many planes can use the same runway.
> The most important question is when dinner will be served.

213.5   **Elliptical sentence.** An elliptical sentence is one in which words are omitted, but understood.

> (*you*) Stop that.   (*my answer is*) No.   (*the time is*) Now.
> Without a doubt (*what you say is true*).

Organizing Text

213.6   **Outlines.** Use a period after each number or letter that identifies a division or subdivision in an outline (except where a parenthesis or parentheses are used). See ¶212.5 for a more detailed example.

> I.   Paleolithic Artifacts
>   A.   Stone Instruments
>   1.   Axe Heads

213.7   **Run-in heading.** A period or other appropriate end-of-sentence punctuation is used after a run-in heading. A run-in heading starts at the left margin or is indented; it is the left-most item on a line of text; and, it begins a paragraph.

> **This is a run-in heading.** A run-in heading is followed (on the same line) by the text of the paragraph. The text of the paragraph does not rely on the heading for any of the meaning of the paragraph. Therefore, the first sentence of the paragraph usually repeats the thought (but not the exact words) of the heading.

213.8   **Listed items.** Listed items may be identified by letters or numbers followed by periods.

> 1.   Disks   A.   Disks
> 2.   Printer ribbons   B.   Printer ribbons
> 3.   Paper   C.   Paper

> Some of the common conventions for printing or typing enumerations are as follows:

> 1.   Leave two spaces after the period following the identifying letter or number before each item. The number or letter may be placed at the left margin, or indented. The identifying number in this item is indented.

> 2.   The text, starting with the second line, may be placed at the left margin (see item 1) or flush with the identifying number or letter. The lines in this item are placed flush with the number *2*. This illustration is the preferred arrangement.

> 3.   The second line (and subsequent lines) may also be placed flush with the first line. The contrasting styles are easily seen in these three illustrative items. In practice, these styles are *not mixed in the same enumeration.*

4. Be consistent in the use of periods at the ends of items. When a lead element is used, with or without a colon:

A. Use a period at the end of *every* line, or

B. Use a period at the end of each line that consists of one or more sentences or elliptical sentences,

or

C. Use a period at the end of the last line and commas or semicolons after the preceding lines, treating the entire enumeration as a single sentence.

Other Uses of the Period

213.9 **Decimals, abbreviations, acronyms, contractions.** Other common uses of the period are:

Decimals, see ¶715.
Abbreviations, ¶401–428.
Acronyms, ¶410.
Contractions, ¶414.

The Period with Other Punctuation

Dash ¶207.25.
Parentheses ¶212.9, 212.10, 212.13–212.15.
Quotation Marks ¶215.38.
To form an ellipsis ¶209.10–209.12.

Spacing with the Period

	Before	After
Ending a sentence	0	2
After an abbreviation within a sentence	0	1
After a number or letter indicating an enumeration	0	2
When followed by another punctuation mark (comma, closing parenthesis, closing quotation mark)	0	0
As a decimal	0	0

214 # QUESTION MARK

Direct Question

214.1 **Full sentence.** Use a question mark to indicate a direct question.

Will you be there before starting time?
Did the contractor finish the job on time?

214.2 **Elliptical sentence.** An elliptical sentence is one from which one or more understood words have been omitted.

"I removed the seal from the box," said Willis.
"Why?" asked Terry.
(The complete question is, "Why did you remove the seal from the box?")

214.3 **Question in the form of a statement.** A sentence that is phrased as a statement may be identified as a question by its context or by the fact that it is spoken with rising inflection. Such a sentence is punctuated with a question mark.

They returned your money when you asked for it?
Our flight will arrive on time?

Question as Part of a Longer Sentence

214.4 **Question at the beginning of a sentence.** A question at the beginning of a longer sentence may be followed by a question mark. Alternatively, the entire sentence may be phrased as an indirect question.

How can we make the change? is the question.
The question is how we can make the change.

214.5 **Question within a sentence.** A short question within a longer sentence may be set off with commas if it converts the longer sentence into a question. The longer sentence, having become a question, is followed by a question mark.

The sentence: It is true that the inspector has been here.
The question: It is true, is it not, that the inspector has been here?
or
It is true that the inspector has been here, is it not?

214.6 **Expression introducing question within a sentence.** A question at the end of a sentence may be introduced with a comma or a colon. The colon is preferred if the introductory element is a formal statement.

The question is, how can we solve the most important problem?
Are you sure they were asked the question: How can we solve the most important problem?

214.7 **Questions in series as a single sentence.** A series of brief questions with a common subject and predicate may be treated as a single sentence, using question marks or commas.

Shall we schedule golf? tennis? swimming?
Shall we schedule golf, tennis, swimming?

214.8 **Questions in series as separate sentences.** A series of brief questions may be *elliptical* sentences and are treated as separate sentences.

Shall we schedule golf? When? Where?

214.9   **Series of independent questions.** A series of brief questions not sharing the same subject and predicate must be treated as independent questions.

Is the match over? Did we win? Was it close?

Uncertainty or Doubt

214.10   **Expressing uncertainty or doubt.** A question mark enclosed by parentheses may be used at any appropriate point in a sentence to express uncertainty or doubt.

They were said to have married(?) in 1982.
(Expresses doubt that they were or are married.)

They were said to have married in 1982(?).
(Expresses uncertainty about the date of the marriage.)

The Question Mark with Other Punctuation

Dash, ¶207.23, 207.25
Parentheses, ¶212.9, 212.11, 212.13, 212.16.
Quotation marks, ¶215.38.

Spacing with the Question Mark

	Before	After
Ending a sentence	0	2
Enclosed in parentheses	0	0
Within a sentence; not followed directly by another punctuation mark	0	1
Within a sentence; followed directly by another punctuation mark	0	0

215   # QUOTATION MARKS

Direct and Indirect Quotations

215.1   **Direct quotation.** Quotation marks are used to enclose the exact words spoken or written.

"I think we can fix your nose," the doctor said at last.
"May I help you?" asked the clerk.

215.2   **Indirect quotation.** An indirect quotation conveys what the quoted person said, but not the exact words of the quotation. Indirect quotations *frequently* begin with *if, that, whether,* or *why.* Indirect quotations are not enclosed by quotation marks.

Denise asked if we are all going to go in the same car.
Donald replied that he did not think that was the plan.

Someone asked whether or not we are supposed to bring our own lunch.
Serge wanted to know why the travel arrangements were not made.

215.3   **Direct question.** A direct question is not necessarily a direct quotation.

The question is, has the pilot filed a flight plan?
(Direct question, not a quotation.)

The question is whether or not the pilot has filed a flight plan.
(Indirect question, not a quotation.)

Did the passenger ask whether or not the pilot has filed a flight plan?
(Direct question, indirect quotation.)

Did the passenger ask, "Has the pilot filed a flight plan?"
(Direct question, direct quotation.)

215.4   **Selective quotation.** A selective quotation contains the *exact* words of the speaker or writer, but not *all* of the words spoken or written.

The other golfer shouted "over the hill."
(The other golfer actually shouted, "Your ball went over the hill.")

See ¶209.1–209.5 for use of ellipsis marks in fragmentary quotations.

215.5   **Quoting *yes* and *no*.** Do not use quotation marks around the words yes and no unless there is a need to emphasize the fact that they are the exact words of the speaker or writer.

If the driver says yes, we should take the front seat.
It seems to me that the director enjoys saying "no."

215.6   **Well-known sayings.** Do not use quotation marks around well-known sayings, mottos, proverbs, and the like.

I suppose that we are better safe than sorry.

Quotation Marks for Emphasis

215.7   **Humor.** A play on words may be enclosed in quotation marks. Any other form of humor is usually not treated in this manner unless it is (or contains) a direct quotation.

When she saw his tools spread around the living room floor, she asked him to put his "playthings" away.

215.8   **Slang and other nonstandard expressions.** A nonstandard expression used by a writer for special effect may be enclosed in quotation marks if it is the writer's intent to call attention to the expression itself or to the fact that the expression does not represent the writer's normal style. Such usage is often pretentious and always dated (since slang words become unfashionable very quickly).

She got so involved in the totally "radical" waves that she had to "book" to reach class on time.
Yes, it is true that I think he is a "tweeb."

215.9 **Coined words.** Words that are coined by a writer for special effect usually should be placed in quotation marks.

> The appearance of the job indicates clearly that the mechanic has mastered the "takeaparts" and needs a lot of work on the "puttogethers."

215.10 **Colloquialisms.** A colloquialism is an expression suitable for informal, familiar speech rather than writing. A colloquialism may be placed in quotation marks. This form is particularly appropriate if the writer believes the colloquialism may not be understood by readers.

> This kind of heating stove is known as a "woodburner."
> An older airplane with only two landing wheels forward and a tail skid or wheel aft is called a "tail-dragger."

215.11 **Definitions.** Formal definitions may be enclosed in quotation marks. When this style is used, the word defined is printed in italics; in typewritten material, the word defined is underscored.

> A *microcomputer* is a "very small computer that employs a microprocessor to process data."

215.12 **Technical terms.** In normal text, technical terms should be introduced with definitions, using the style illustrated in ¶215.11.

> Every microcomputer has a *microprocessor,* a "computer processor made on a single semiconductor chip."

If a technical term is not to be defined, it may be enclosed by quotation marks the first time it is used.

> A "microprocessor" is the heart, or brain, of the microcomputer.

215.13 **Translations.** Foreign words are frequently translated in the manner in which English words are defined. See ¶215.11.

> It was a *lapsus linguae,* a "slip of the tongue."

215.14 **Following *marked, labeled, signed, headed,* etc.** Expressions following introductory words, such as *marked, labeled, signed, headed,* and the like, are enclosed in quotation marks.

> The notice on the bulletin board was marked "Urgent."
> The package was labeled "Fragile."
> The love letter was signed "Your Secret Admirer."
> The column was headed "Net Loss."

215.15 **Word used as a word; not for its meaning.** A word used as a word rather than for its meaning may be enclosed in quotation marks. Current usage, however, favors use of the underscore.

> Paint the "and" a little larger, and the sign will be complete.
> *or*
> Paint the and a little larger, and the sign will be complete. (preferred)

Punctuating Sentences Containing Quotations

Quotation Beginning a Sentence

215.16   **Statement at the beginning of a sentence.** When a quoted statement begins a sentence, replace the period that would normally follow the statement with a comma.

> "That is the last time I shall do your work for you," she said.
> "That will be the first item on the menu," said the chef.

215.17   **Question at the beginning of a sentence.** When a quoted question begins a sentence, retain the question mark. No comma is used; the question mark is written before the quotation mark.

> "Will you come to the ball?" he asked.
> "How can we possibly meet this deadline?" asked the boss.

215.18   **Exclamation at the beginning of a sentence.** When a quoted exclamation begins a sentence, retain the exclamation mark. No comma is used; the exclamation mark is written before the quotation mark.

> "What a day!" said the laborer as he laid down his shovel.
> "That's the last time you'll get away with this!" said Wimple.

215.19   **Word or phrase at the beginning of a sentence.** When a quoted word or phrase begins a sentence, it is followed directly by the closing quotation mark — unless the structure of the sentence requires additional punctuation before the closing quotation mark.

> "Time for Arrest" is an interesting title for the speech.
> "Time for Arrest," the title of the speech, is appropriate.

Quotation Within a Sentence

215.20   **Quotation that does not interrupt the sentence.** A quotation that does *not* interrupt the flow of the sentence is enclosed by quotation marks. If a quotation that does not interrupt the flow of the sentence was originally followed by a period, the period is dropped (unless it falls at the end of the sentence). If the quoted expression was originally followed by a question mark or an exclamation mark, it is retained.

> I do not think that "If I can" is an adequate reply.
> You must remember to say "Please" and "Thank you."
> Shouting "Hear! Hear!" is a demonstration of approval.
> Do not say "You know?" after every sen ence.

215.21   **Quotation that is an essential element.** Do not set off with commas a quotation that is an essential element of the sentence in which it is quoted.

> You may not say "It is easier said than done" after you have tried to write it.

215.22 **Quotation that is a nonessential element.** A quotation that is a nonessential element in the sentence in which it is quoted is set off by commas.

> His famous words, "Never say die," were spoken then.

Quotation at the End of a Sentence

215.23 **Introductory element such as *he said*.** When an introductory expression such as *he said* or *she said* occurs before a quotation that ends a sentence, the introductory expression is usually followed by a comma.

> Kathryn said, "Put the books away before you start the game."
> She said, "Where did you put the flowers?"

215.24 **Introductory element a formal statement.** When the introductory element is a formal statement, a colon is used before the quotation.

> She summarized her statement in this manner: "Jacob is guilty."

215.25 **Long quotations.** Quotations of more than one sentence are introduced with a colon.

> The dean then said: "A few of you made the dean's list this term. Several of you, struggling to keep afloat in a sea of Fs, are at the opposite end of the spectrum."

215.26 **Displayed quotations.** An extract, displayed in a panel (set in from the left margin) is introduced with a colon and not enclosed by quotation marks. See ¶209.7.

> This is the quotation:
>
> > Now is the time for the ablest and the best to come forward and do what their fathers and mothers did a generation ago: give what is needed and do what needs to be done. These are trying times.

Formatting and Punctuating Quotations

Quotations with Interrupting Expressions

215.27 **Interrupted by *she said, said Harry*, etc.** When a quotation is *interrupted* by an expression identifying the speaker, follow this pattern:

> "This is the third time," said Harry, "that I have told you."
> **NOTE:** The first word of the resumed quotation is *not* capitalized.

215.28 **Quotations spanning two sentences.** If a quotation with an interrupting expression spans two sentences, each sentence is punctuated separately.

> "This is the third time I have told you," said Harry. "Please see that it does not happen again."

Special Formats

215.29

Dialogue. Dialogue is writing in which two or more people are represented as conversing. Quote the expressions of each person in turn. Start a paragraph for each new expression.

> "How could you say that to me, Alice?"
> "It was the least I could do, Herb."
> "The least you . . ."
> "Yes, I wish I could have done more."

215.30

Conversation in plays, scripts, and court transcripts. In plays, scripts, and court transcripts, the name of each speaker appears before each expression. Quotation marks are not used.

> HERB: How could you say that to me, Alice?
> ALICE: It was the least I could do, Herb.
> HERB: The least you . . .
> ALICE: Yes, I wish I could have done more.

215.31

Poetry. Poetry may be quoted by reproducing the entire poem or part of the poem and crediting the author before or after the poem itself. Permission should be obtained to reproduce more than one line of a poem protected by copyright. The poem should be reproduced line for line.

> There was an Old Man with a beard,
> Who said: "It is just as I feared!
> Two owls and a hen,
> Four larks and a wren
> Have all built their nests in my beard."
> Edward Lear

Omissions in Quoted Material

See ¶ 209.1–209.12 for the use of ellipsis marks to indicate omissions.

Quotation Within a Quotation

See ¶ 201.33 for punctuating a quotation within a quotation.

Insertions in Quoted Material

See ¶ 204.1 on the use of brackets to insert explanations into quoted material.

Capitalization in Quoted Material

See ¶ 301.2 and ¶ 318 on capitalization in quoted material.

215.32   Titles underscored or enclosed by quotation marks. Major titles are underscored in typewritten text or italicized in printed text, not enclosed by quotation marks.

Italicize in Printed Text Underscore in Typewritten Text (a)	Enclose by Quotation Marks Capitalize as Shown (b)	No Italics No Quotation Marks (c)

Books and Booklets (Published)
Magazines
Newspapers
Long Poems
Collections of Shorter Poems
Plays
Operas, Oratorios
Other Long Musical Compositions
  (except when designated by form
  and a number [and/or key])
Paintings
Drawings
Statues
Other Works of Art
Movies
Musicals
	Manuscripts (Unpublished)
	Chapter and Part Titles
	Features and Articles
	Short Stories
	Essays
	Dissertations
	Theses
	Lectures
	Television Shows
	Radio Shows
	Songs
	Short Musical Compositions
		foreword
		preface
		introduction
		contents
		chapter
		appendix
		glossary
		bibliography
		index
		series
		edition
		act
		scene
		stanza
		diary
		journal
		memorandum
		sign
		motto
		symphony
		sonata
		etude
		concerto

(a) and (b) Capitalize the first and last word and all other words except
  articles (a, an, the), short conjunctions (and, as, but, for, if, not, or,
  so, yet), short prepositions (as, at, by, for, in, of, on, to, up), and the
  to in infinitives.
(c) In text, do not capitalize the words in this column unless they are
  part of a title or unless cross-referenced within the text.		

Quotation Marks with Other Punctuation

215.33   Colon. The colon is placed **outside** quotation marks.

> There was one major flaw in her definition of "taste": it reflected her own peculiar prejudices.

215.34   Comma. The comma is placed **inside** quotation marks.

215.35   Dash. The position of the dash relative to quotation marks depends on how the dash is used.

> **a.** When the quotation is part of the nonessential element set off with dashes, and the closing dash and closing quotation mark occur at the same point, the dash is placed **outside** the closing quotation mark.
>
> See if you can find the Jones manuscript—the one entitled "Seeing All There Is to See"—in that stack over there.

b. If the sentence breaks off immediately after the quotation, place the dash **outside** the closing quotation mark.

I'm not at all sure, but I think the title is "The Grass Grows Greener" —

c. If the sentence within the quotation breaks off, place the dash **inside** the closing quotation mark.

I heard her say, "To think that I can't remember — "

215.36

Parentheses. The closing parenthesis may go inside or outside the closing quotation mark.

a. When the quotation is part of the parenthetical element, place the closing parenthesis **outside** the closing quotation mark.

He has given the same speech (the one entitled "Trying Times for Trying People") more times than I can remember.

b. When the parenthetical element is part of the quotation, place the closing parenthesis **inside** the closing quotation mark.

He agreed to the wording "Paid (By Check)" until the contract was ready to sign.

215.37

Semicolon. Place a semicolon **outside** the closing quotation mark.

She said, "I truly hate the way you behave"; however, she looked as though she could have said much more.

215.38

End-of-sentence punctuation with quotation marks. Use the following patterns to resolve conflicts between end-of-sentence punctuation and quotation marks. (**NOTE:** When such a conflict arises, the stronger mark of punctuation prevails.) Use an introductory comma if the quotation does not blend into the preceding sentence elements.

Statement "statement."	We saw "Upstairs, Downstairs."
Statement "question?"	We heard "What's Love Got to do With It?"
Statement "exclamation!"	The driver shouted, "I will!"
Question "statement"?	Did you see "Upstairs, Downstairs"?
Question "question?"	Did you hear "What's Love Got to do With It?"
Question "exclamation!"	Did the driver shout, "I will!"
Exclamation "statement"!	You should see "Upstairs, Downstairs"!
Exclamation "question"!	Do hear "What's Love Got to do With It"!
Exclamation "exclamation!"	Do not shout "I will!"

Spacing with Quotation Marks

Opening Quotation Marks	**Before**	**After**
Beginning a sentence......................................	2	0
Following a colon...	2	0
Following a dash	0	0

Opening Quotation Marks	**Before**	**After**
Following an opening parenthesis.........................	0	0
All other uses...	1	0
Closing Quotation Marks		
Ending a sentence..	0	2
Immediately preceding another punctuation mark..	0	0
All other uses...	0	1

216 SEMICOLON

Semicolon Between Independent Clauses

216.1 **Coordinating conjunction replaced.** A semicolon may be used to replace the coordinating conjunction between independent clauses. (Coordinating conjunctions are *and, but, or, nor, yet,* and *for.* An *independent clause* has a subject and a verb and can stand alone as a sentence.)

> The traffic is worse and the noise is unbearable.
> The traffic is worse; the noise is unbearable.

NOTE: Do not replace a coordinating conjunction with a comma. This error is called a *comma splice* or *comma fault.*

> **Not:** The traffic is worse, the noise is unbearable.

216.2 **Closely related independent clauses.** If the independent clauses of a compound sentence are closely related, a coordinating conjunction or a semicolon will provide a sufficiently strong break.

> The tire is flat and the wheel is bent.
> The tire is flat; the wheel is bent.
> **Not:** The tire is flat, the wheel is bent. (Comma splice.)

216.3 **Independent clauses *not* related.** If the independent clauses of a compound sentence are **not** related, the elements should be re-formed into two separate sentences in order to achieve a stronger break.

> Time seemed to stand still. Neither of them wanted to be the first to speak.

216.4 **Independent clauses linked by transitional expression.** When independent clauses are linked by a transitional expression, use a semicolon to separate the clauses.

> It is well past quitting time; however, no one seems ready to quit.

The following is a partial list of transitional expressions:

besides	indeed	finally
accordingly	first	therefore

furthermore	second	thus
hence	then	meanwhile
however		yet

NOTE: Most transitional expressions are followed by a pause; the pause is indicated by a comma (furthermore, therefore, and the like). A few transitional expressions (hence, thus, so that, then, yet) are **not** followed by a pause and are, therefore, not followed by a comma. See ¶ 206.13.

216.5

Coordinating conjunction *and* transitional expression. In

a sentence containing both a coordinating conjunction **and** a transitional expression between independent clauses, use a comma before the coordinating conjunction.

> The early tour leaves at sunrise, and therefore we shall eat breakfast with the group.

216.6

Between independent clauses containing commas. A semi-

colon should be used between independent clauses if the commas separating items in series would otherwise make the sentence unclear.

> **Unclear:** I ordered lettuce, tomato, and mayonnaise, and parsley, tartar sauce, and pickle came instead.
>
> **Better:** I asked for lettuce, tomato, and mayonnaise; parsley, tartar sauce, and pickle came instead.

216.7

Conjunction, comma, semicolon, period, colon, or dash?

Each of these forms creates a break or pause of different length and intensity:

a. A conjunction between short, closely related independent clauses can cause the sentence to flow smoothly, creating virtually no pause at all.

> The water is cool and the sand is warm.

b. A comma lengthens the pause.

> The water is cool, and the sand is warm.

c. A semicolon lengthens the pause and creates contrast.

> The water is cool; the sand is warm.

d. Creating separate sentences further lengthens the pause and intensifies the contrast.

> The water is cool. The sand is warm.

e. Use the colon when the expression beginning the sentence introduces and is explained or amplified by the expression ending the sentence.

> Several consecutive cold days have brought winter conditions to the beach: the water and wind make it too cold to swim or sunbathe.

f. The dash indicates a sharp break in thought.

> We went to the beach expecting to bask and splash — but the cold water and chilly wind quickly dashed those hopes.

216.8 **Items containing commas in a series.** For additional clarity, items that contain commas and are in series may be separated by semicolons instead of commas.

> The cook promised to remove the parsley, tartar sauce, and pickle; toast, scrape, and butter the bun; and add lettuce, tomato, and mayonnaise.

The Semicolon with Other Punctuation

Dash, ¶207.20, 207.21.
Parentheses, ¶212.8, 212.9, 212.12.
Quotation marks, ¶215.37.

Spacing with the Semicolon

	Before	After
All uses	0	1

217 # UNDERSCORE OR ITALICS

Titles See ¶215.32.

The Underscore (Italics) for Emphasis

217.1 **Underscoring and italics.** Some computers and word processors can print italics directly. Characters entered in italics appear on the screen in italics; hard copies are printed in italics. Italics and the normal type face can be mixed. Virtually all typesetting processes can produce italics.

Since most typewriters and computer printers cannot produce italics both easily and well, underscoring is frequently substituted for italics. When a manuscript is printed, underscoring will automatically be converted to italics unless notations to the contrary are made.

217.2 **Words used as words rather than for their meaning.** A word referred to as a word instead of for its meaning should be underscored or printed in italics.

> Put the *It* at the top of the sign and the *hit* at the bottom.

NOTE: A word referred to as a word instead of for its meaning *may* be enclosed by quotation marks. Use of the underscore (or italics) is preferable, however. See ¶215.15.

217.3 **Definitions.** In text, the formal definition of a word should appear in this format:

[word defined]	[definition]
[underscored or in italics]	[in quotation marks]
The noun *land* means	"the solid part of the earth's surface."

A semiformal definition may be written:

> *Land* is the solid part of the earth's surface.

An informal definition may be written:

> Land is the solid part of the earth's surface.

217.4 **Foreign expressions.** Foreign expressions that have **not** become part of the English language are underscored (or printed in italics). Those that have been accepted as part of the English language are typed or printed normally.

> She spoke *ex animo* (from the heart).
> **But:** The inequalities were settled on a quid pro quo basis.

217.5 **Names of individual ships, aircraft, and the like.** The names of individual vehicles are underscored (or italicized).

> The *Sunward, Starward,* and *Seaward* are sister ships.
> The boat was named *Rosinante,* after Don Quixote's horse.

Placement of Underscoring

217.6 **In general.** Underscore the exact element to which attention is to be called—and no more. If a complete sentence is to be emphasized, underscore the entire sentence, including the end-of-sentence punctuation. (**NOTE:** Entire sentences are rarely underscored.)

> <u>He turned, looked at the stranger, and saw—himself!</u>

If a sentence element is to be emphasized, do not underscore any sentence punctuation mark that may appear before or after the element. (**NOTE:** If, however, italics are employed, the mark following would be printed in the italic typeface.)

> He turned, looked at the stranger, and saw—<u>himself</u>!

NOTE: If the underscored element contains a punctuation mark when it stands alone, the punctuation mark should be underscored.

> The book is called <u>What's in it for Me?</u>

See ¶ 217.8.

217.7 **Names.** The names of newspapers and magazines and the titles of books are underscored, but word endings added to them are not. (**NOTE:** Even if italics are used, the endings added are *not* italicized.)

> <u>Modern Maturity</u>'s circulation   the May and June <u>TV Guide</u>s

217.8 **Under punctuation.** Underscore punctuation that is part of the element being emphasized. Do not underscore end-of-sentence punctuation unless it is part of the element being emphasized. (**NOTE:** If, however, italics are employed the end-of-sentence punctuation would be printed in italic typeface, regardless.)

> Later in the season, we shall see <u>The Merchant of Venice</u> and <u>A Midsummer Night's Dream</u>.

Unit III   Capitalization

Understand:
- When capitalization should be used
- Why capitalization is important for emphasis and identity

Acquire:
- The ability to recognize incorrect capitalization
- The ability to apply capitalization rules correctly

Be Prepared To:
- Identify and correct incorrect capitalization usage
- Apply capitalization rules to documents containing no capitalization

3

300   **Capitalization** is the practice of using capital (uppercase) letters for emphasis and identification. Capitalized words demand more attention, and thus become more important within the context of the surrounding words.

301   ## Basic Capitalization Rules

301.1   **First word in a sentence.** **Always** capitalize the first word in a sentence. This indicates to the reader where a new sentence begins.

> *The* auditor needs your assistance immediately!
> *Students* often need encouragement during finals week.

301.2   **First word in a quoted sentence.** **Always** capitalize the first word of a quoted sentence.

> Evelyn said quickly, "*Please* take my seat."

301.3   **First word in expressions as sentences.** **Always** capitalize the first word of expressions used as sentences.

> *Come* here!   *Incredible!*   *Why* not?

301.4   **First word of a question within a sentence.** **Always** capitalize the first word of a formal independent question within a sentence.

> The question remains: *Why* was the scheduling not completed?

301.5   **Names of specific persons, places, or things.** **Always** capitalize the exact names of specific persons, places, or things.

101

Dr. Elizabeth Lundgren will deliver the lecture.
He had his car serviced at *Benton's Auto Mart*.
Reye's syndrome is a concern for parents with young children.

301.6 **Nicknames or created names.** Nicknames or created names that represent particular persons, places, or things are also capitalized.

Charlie	the Sunshine State	Deep South
a Cadette scout	Susie Q	Big Brother

301.7 **Common nicknames or created names.** When nicknames or created names become common, however, they are no longer capitalized as their usage applies to general categories of persons, places, or things.

india ink	french fries	manila envelope
china pattern	plaster of paris	romaine lettuce

It is important to note that since capitalization is for the purpose of emphasizing certain words, excessive use of capitalization will reduce the value of this important tool.

302 # Abbreviations

The capitalization of abbreviations generally follows the capitalization of the words being abbreviated.

United States of America	U.S.A. *or* USA
International Telephone & Telegraph	ITT
account	acct.

Abbreviations of proper nouns are generally capitalized, following the same rules as those used for unabbreviated proper nouns.

Columbia Broadcasting System   CBS

Abbreviations of common nouns are not capitalized.

each	ea.
amount	amt.

Exceptions:

eastern standard time	EST
anno Domini	A.D.
collect on delivery	COD

See Unit 4 for additional information regarding abbreviations.

303 # Adjectives

Capitalize adjectives which are derived from proper names.

Canada (n)	Canadian (adj)
Boston (n)	Bostonian (adj)

304 ## Advertising

In advertising copy, some words may be capitalized for special emphasis.

Don't miss our *Going-Out-of-Business Sale!*

305 ## Business Letters

Within a business letter, the following capitalization rules always apply:

305.1 **Date.** Capitalize the first letter of the month.

December 18, 19--

305.2 **Inside address.** Capitalize the first letter of the personal or professional titles preceding names, professional titles on a line by themselves, names of individuals, names of companies or organizations, names of streets, avenues, cities, both letters of the two-letter state abbreviation. (**NOTE:** When capitalizing several words in a title, do not capitalize articles [*the, a, an*], short prepositions [four or fewer letters], or short conjunctions [*and, as, nor, or, but*].)

Ms. Irene Canel-Petersen
Director of Research
The Duffy Manufacturing Company
2834 Avenida del Sol
Barceloneta, PR 00617-4832

Dr. Lourdes Rabade
Public Relations Division
Creative Group
2001 W. Sixty-eighth Street
Hialeah, FL 33016-1002

305.3 **Salutation.** Capitalize the first word in a business letter salutation, as well as the title and last name.

Dear Dr. Schram: Dear Ms. Thomas-Gibson
(Mixed Punctuation)   (Open Punctuation)

Ladies and Gentlemen:
(Mixed Punctuation)

305.4 **Headings.** Capitalize the first letter in attention and subject lines. (*Subject* may also be typed in all capitals.)

Attention Technician White   Subject: Welch, Reina
                                SUBJECT: Welch, Reina

305.5 **Within the body of the letter.** Follow all other capitalization rules covered in this unit.

305.6 **Complimentary close.** Capitalize only the first word in a complimentary close.

Sincerely,   Yours truly,   Sincerely yours
(Mixed Punctuation)   (Mixed Punctuation)   (Open Punctuation)

306 — Business Organizations/Institutions

Always follow the preference indicated by an organization for the capitalization of its name. The official letterhead is always a good guide.

Capitalize the specific names of associations, churches, clubs, colleges and universities (including divisions within a college or university), companies, conventions, fraternities and sororities, hospitals, independent committees and boards, institutions, libraries, schools, synagogues, and political parties.

Mt. Sinai Medical Center	Temple Beth El
Coppolechia Memorial Library	Michigan State University
Wayne County Realtors Association	Department of Duplicating
American Secretarial Association	Thornton Jewelry Designers
Variety Childrens Association	Department of Psychology
Democratic National Committee	

307 — Compass Points

307.1

North, south, east, and west. Capitalize *north*, *south*, *east*, and *west* only when they refer to specific regions, or are part of a proper name.

the South	the Midwest	the South Pole

Do **not** capitalize such words when they indicate a general direction, rather than a specific region.

He lives somewhere on the *west* side of town.

307.2

Easterner, Westerner, Southerner, and Northerner. **Always** capitalize words such as *Easterner, Westerner, Southerner,* and *Northerner.*

307.3

Eastern, western, southern, and northern. Capitalize words such as *eastern, western, southern,* and *northern* only when they refer to the region's residents, customs, political or cultural activities. When such words precede a proper name, capitalize only if they are part of the name itself.

Suzanne was always noted for her *Southern* hospitality.
The *Western* states voted as expected.
She was able to identify the *Northern* Cross (constellation).

But: The winter storm has blanketed the *eastern* states.
Mountain flowers are the prettiest in *northern* Colorado.

308 — Direct Address

308.1

Title as direct address. Capitalize any title used as a direct address.

Please give me a call, *Doctor,* when the results are available.
But: The *doctor* is not in the hospital at this moment.

308.2   **Miss, sir, or madam.** Do not capitalize terms such as *miss, sir,* or *madam* when used as a direct address.

> Yes *sir,* I shall check it out immediately.

Education

309.1   **Titles of specific courses.** Capitalize the titles of specific courses, but do not capitalize references to general academic subject areas (except languages).

| **Specific course:** | All students are required to take *Principles of Business* before graduation. |
| | A new course, *Advanced Sports Health Analysis,* will be added. |

| **General subject area:** | Nelson wants to take a course in *history*. |
| **But:** | Sharon is studying *Spanish*. (See ¶319.3.) |

309.2   **Academic degree.** When used with the name of an individual, an academic degree is capitalized. When used with the word *degree,* however, academic degrees are usually not capitalized.

| **With name:** | Victoria Sigler, *Juris Doctor,* is an excellent attorney. |
| **With degree:** | Most colleges offer both the *bachelor of science* and the *bachelor of arts* degrees. |

Government

310.1   **Government bodies.** Capitalize the names of countries and international organizations, as well as the national, state, county, city, and local bodies and agencies within them.

the United Nations	Germany
Ft. Collins School District	Department of Education
the Johnson Administration	the Utah Legislature
the Cabinet	

310.2   **Short forms of international and national bodies.** Also capitalize the short forms of international and national bodies and their major divisions when the reference is clear.

> the Court (United States Supreme Court)
> the Agency (Central Intelligence Agency)
> the House (House of Representatives)
> the State Department (Department of State)
> the Bureau (Federal Bureau of Investigation)

310.3   **Officials and titles.** Titles of international, national, and state government officials are capitalized when they immediately *precede a specific individual's name, as part of the name.* (Ambassador, Attorney

General, Chief Justice, Chief of Staff, Governor, King, Lieutenant Governor, President, Prime Minister, Prince, Princess, Queen, Secretary-General of the United Nations, Secretary of State, Vice President) These titles are **not** capitalized, however, when used to refer to an *entire class of officials.*

> *State Senator Carrie Meek* called me today about the HMO Bill.
> *President John F. Kennedy* was responsible for starting the Peace Corps.

But: Candidates for *treasurer* must have budgetary experience.

310.4 **Title in place of a personal name.** A title used *in place of* a personal name is capitalized *only* for toasts or in formal introductions, with rare exceptions.

> Ladies and gentlemen, the *President of the United States.*

310.5 **Titles following a personal name.** Titles following a personal name or used alone instead of a name are generally lowercased.

> Sis Smith, *administrative assistant,* took charge.
> The *vice president* began the meeting on time.

310.6 **Laws, treaties, bills, acts.** Laws, treaties, bills, and acts which have been formally adopted are capitalized when used with their full title but are not capitalized when the shortened forms are used in place of the full name.

Full Title	Short Form
Public Law 88-6578	the law
the Panama Canal Treaty	the treaty
Senate Bill 9758	the bill

Exception:	The Constitution of the United States of America	the Constitution

310.7 **Federal.** *Federal* should be capitalized if it is part of a proper name of a federal agency, act, or law. References to government or federal government are not capitalized unless they are part of a specific title.

> Federal Bureau of Investigation   Federal Reserve Board
> **But:** All of this is governed by *federal,* state, and local laws.
> We need to get help from the *government* officials on this.

310.8 **-Elect, former, late.** Do not capitalize words such as *-elect, former,* or *late* when they are used with titles and/or names.

> President-elect Robinson chaired the meeting.
> The *late* Russell Sigler was remembered through a scholarship fund in his name.

311 # Hyphenation

311.1 **Within a sentence.** Capitalize hyphenated words within a sentence in the same way you would capitalize those words if they stood alone.

It was *mid-April* before her condition began to improve.
The *Spanish-speaking* students are helping me learn Spanish.
It was Wade Harris' *thirty-eighth* annual Treasure Hunt.

311.2

Beginning a sentence. At the beginning of a sentence, however, remember to capitalize the first letter of the hyphenated word:

Mothers-in-law take too much abuse.
Up-to-date equipment is a must for accurate diagnosis.

311.3

Hyphenated titles. Capitalize each word except articles (*the, a, an*), short prepositions (four or fewer letters), short conjunctions (*and, as, but, nor, or*), and second elements not of equal force with the first.

Miami-Dade Community College   Slow-and-Easy Rowing Machine
Self-sustaining Reaction   Over-the-Hill Gang

312

Nouns Including Letters and Numbers

Nouns followed by letters or numbers should be capitalized, with the exception of *note, line, page, size,* and *verse.* Capitalizing the noun *paragraph* is optional.

Appendix C	line 17
Article VI	page 116
Bulletin 88	size 16
Chapter XVIII	note 3
Column 2	verse 6
Diagram 9	
Exhibit D	
Figure 79	
Paragraph 9 *or*	paragraph 9
Invoice 33-959	
Lesson 44	
Room 1515	

313

Outlines

Each item in an outline should begin with a capital letter.

  I.   Complete each item.
  II. Skip over any question demanding excess time.
  III. If all items are completed, go back to those skipped.
  IV. If time remains after all items are completed, check your answers.

  I.   Colored Pens
  II. Scissors
  III. Construction Paper
  IV. Glue

314

Persons

314.1

Names of individuals. Names of individuals should be capitalized, spelled, and spaced exactly as the person does. A name containing a prefix such as *d', da, de, del, della, di, du, l', la, le, mac, mc, o', van,* or *von* can vary in capitalization and spacing. Follow the individual's preferences.

Zoila de Zayas   Patrick W. Gettings
Maria Elena Diaz   Marilyn Gottlieb-Roberts
William Dawson, Jr.   Nadine A. von Gandia

314.2 **Titles of relatives.** Titles of relatives are capitalized when they precede a name, or when they are used in place of a name. They are not capitalized, however, when they follow a possessive pronoun, or when they simply describe a family relationship.

Mother, please come to my room.
Uncle Ken works in the assembly department.
Aunt Leota and *Aunt Sammy* visited me when I was in the Navy.

But: My *cousin* enrolled in a dietary technician program.
I have sixteen *aunts* and *uncles.*

315 ## Personal and Professional Titles

315.1 **Title preceding name.** Capitalize all formal titles when they precede a name.

Ms. Jill Gregalot   Commissioner Miller Dawkins
the* Reverend Kim Porter   President Robert McCabe

NOTE: *The* must precede *reverend* when used with a name because *reverend* is an adjective; furthermore, its use is limited to writing and introductions — it is not used in direct address.

315.2 **Titles following name.** Do not capitalize such titles when they follow the name:

Robert McCabe, president   Beverly Creely, professor

315.3 **Titles set off by commas.** Do not capitalize such titles when the personal name that follows is set off by commas (appositive).

The *vice president,* Yvonne Santa Maria, will speak later.
But: *Vice President* Yvonne Santa Maria will speak later.

315.4 **Occupational titles.** Do not capitalize occupational titles when they precede or follow personal names.

The introduction was made by *surgeon* Naim Nichar.
We had dinner at the home of Mercy Miranda, *attorney.*

But, when the occupational title is a specific job title:

Senior Editor Jocelyn LeGrand is working with me on my book.

315.5 **Titles in place of personal names.** Generally, do not capitalize official titles when they follow a personal name or are used in place of a personal name. (See ¶310.5.) (Exceptions are made for titles of high government officials — see ¶310.4.)

Annie Betancourt, *president,* will preside at the meeting.
Calling the group together was Richard Schinoff, *dean.*

NOTE: Some companies capitalize all or some of the titles of company officials. Always follow the procedures preferred by your employer, and respect the preferences of others regarding their own titles.

315.6

Doctoral degree. With the doctoral degree, use *Dr.* before the name **or** the academic abbreviation following the name, but not both.

Dr. William McNae   *or*   William McNae, D.O.

Not: Dr. William McNae, D.O.

316

Places, Things, and Ideas

316.1

Specific places, things, or ideas. Capitalize the entire titles of specific places, things, or ideas. (Do not capitalize articles, short prepositions, or short conjunctions used with these titles, however, unless they are the first word of the title.) Do **not** capitalize the short forms used in place of the full title.

Woodward Medical Center	the medical center
Jefferson Department Store	the store
Equal Rights Amendment	the amendment
Penobscot Building	the building
The Denver Post	the newspaper

316.2

City. Capitalize *city* when it is part of a proper name, or part of a created name.

Panama City   **But:**   the city of Cincinnati
the Automotive City

316.3

State. Capitalize *state* only when it follows a state name, or is part of a created name.

Colorado State   **But:**   the state of Colorado
the Sunshine State

316.4

Common words part of proper name. Capitalize words such as *the, upper, lower, west, east, north,* and *south* only when they are part of a proper name.

The Washington Post   West Virginia   Upper Peninsula

317

Pronouns

Always capitalize the pronoun *I.*

You know that *I* want to enter this contest.

All other pronouns are not capitalized unless they begin a sentence.

It was *my* computer program that was used.
Her aunt was the one wearing the black hat.

318   # Publications

318.1   **Principal words in titles.** Capitalize the principal words (and the first word after a colon or dash) in titles of publications (books, magazines, journals, pamphlets, newspapers) and other artistic works (movies, plays, songs, paintings, sculptures, poems). Titles of complete published works or complete artistic works (motion pictures, long musical compositions) are underscored, italicized, or typed in all capital letters.

Book	I find the *Physician's Desk Reference* a helpful aid.
	I find the PHYSICIAN'S DESK REFERENCE a helpful aid.
Magazine	Your first copy of *The Balance Sheet* arrived today.
	Your first copy of THE BALANCE SHEET arrived today.
Newspaper	The *Newark Star Ledger* won the award.
	The NEWARK STAR LEDGER won the award.

Symphony —— referred to by a special, given, descriptive title:
We have tickets for tonight's performance of the *Emperor Concerto* by Beethoven.

But: A classical composition referred to by type of piece [e.g., symphony] and number does **not** have its title set in italics or all capital letters nor is it underscored.
We have tickets for tonight's performance of Beethoven's Symphony no. 9 in D Minor.

318.2   **Titles of poems, songs, television/radio programs.** The titles of short poems, songs, and television/radio programs are enclosed in quotation marks.

All of the students watched "General Hospital" every afternoon.

318.3   **Capitalize each line within a poem.**

Across a Crowded Room*
Your face: My eyes wander around your face.
It's power: I shake and I'm amazed at its power.
What it does to me:
I feel strong and weak and sick and well.
I want to scream!
I want to sing:
"Some enchanted evening you will see a stranger . . ."
Your face: the magnificent power of your face.
I haven't spoken one word to you.
Yet I would walk blindfolded through Times Square,
Sleep all night in Central Park,
Fly to Siberia in the dead of winter
If I could be sure that at the end
The smile on your face
Would be for me.

—Larry Apple

*This poem was created especially for "The Biggest Book in the World: A Celebration of Words and Images by artists from New York and South Florida" as a part of the Miami Bookfair International.

319   # Religions, Races, Peoples, and Languages

319.1   ## Supreme being, persons revered. Capitalize references to a supreme being or to persons revered.

our Lord God   Buddha   Allah   Saint Luke

319.2   ## Personal pronouns in reference to supreme being. Personal pronouns used in reference to a supreme being are not capitalized, though they once were.

We can count on *his* guidance.

319.3   ## Races, peoples, tribes, languages. Capitalize all names of races, peoples, tribes, and languages.

Hispanics   Afro-Americans   Zuni Indians
French   Europeans   Orientals

320   # Time

320.1   ## Days and months. Capitalize names of days and months.

Monday   December   Wednesday   June

320.2   ## Holidays and religious days. Capitalize names of holidays and religious days.

Martin Luther King Day   Passover
Mother's Day   New Year's Eve

320.3   ## Historical events. Capitalize the names of historical events and nicknames used for historical periods.

World War I   the Great Depression

320.4   ## Decades and centuries. Do not capitalize the names of decades and centuries unless they are part of a nickname.

in the nineteen-sixties   in the forties
But: the Roaring Twenties

320.5   ## Seasons. Do not capitalize seasons of the year unless they are part of a specific title or are personified.

spring fever   fall colors   summer sunshine

But: Spring and Summer Sale
Oh beautiful *Spring,* I enjoy your days.

Unit IV   Abbreviations

Understand:
- What abbreviations are
- How abbreviations are used in business writing

Acquire:
- A vocabulary of common abbreviations
- The ability to recognize common abbreviations

Be Prepared To:
- Apply rules for abbreviation to business writing
- Recognize incorrect use of abbreviated forms

4

400   **Abbreviations** are shortened forms of words or phrases. They are used to save space and time. While a few abbreviations are permitted in general business writing (*Ms.*, *a.m.*, and the like), most are confined to illustrations within documents, such as tables and graphs, or to items internal to a company, such as computer reports, personal notetaking, and informal memos.

401   ## Basic Uses

Easily Recognized

Dr. Patrick Gettings   **instead of:**   *Doctor* Patrick Gettings

Tables and Graphs

Stock #	Weight		Stock Number	Weight
86759	280 *lbs*	**instead of:**	86759	280 *pounds*
55784	110 *lbs*		55784	118 *pounds*

Notetaking

Remem: *Pls* get *brfcse frm hm tonite.*

GENERAL GUIDELINES

402   ## When to Use

Be cautious in the use of abbreviations. Use only those abbreviations that readers will recognize. Do not sacrifice the clarity and meaning of your writing by forcing a reader to pause to try to determine the meaning of an abbreviation.

Some abbreviations are used so consistently that they are preferable to the full word or words, even in the most formal writing.

Titles and Degrees Before/After Names

Dr. Jill Mangold	Elsa Agramonte, Ph.D.
Oscar de Zayas, Jr.	Ms. Liz Samuels
Mrs. Ida Gropper	Craig McMeekin, Ed.D.

(**NOTE:** The kind of titles illustrated in this column are not for formal writing, such as engraved invitations.)

Official Part of a Company Name

C & S Paving & Equipment Rental, Inc.
Hi-Lu Corp.
Jenbar Construction Co.

Time (**NOTE:** These expressions are not for formal writing, such as engraved invitations. See ¶427.)

8:00 a.m.   1120 B.C.   10:00 p.m., PST (See ¶405, **NOTE**)

4

403   Consistency

Be consistent! Use the same form of each abbreviation throughout the same document.

Exception: When using an abbreviation for the *first time* in a document, you may wish to use the complete form followed by the abbreviation (in parentheses) for clarity. Throughout the remainder of the document, however, only the abbreviated form will be used.

> The Skill Training Improvement Program (*STIP*) has been refunded for a record ninth year. *STIP* has consistently met or exceeded its training goals.

404   References

Check a dictionary or other reference for acceptable forms of abbreviations not listed in this unit. Many references have a section on abbreviations; some of them include alphabetic lists. One caution — the correct punctuation and/or capitalization may not be indicated in the dictionary listing of the abbreviation. In such cases, follow the rules provided in this unit.

405   Preferred over Contraction

Like abbreviations, contractions are shortened forms of words or phrases. Unlike abbreviations, however, contractions contain an apostrophe to indicate where letters have been omitted. Since abbreviations are often easier to read and understand, the use of abbreviations is generally preferred to the use of contractions. **NOTE:** In formal writing the contraction *o'clock* is used rather than *a.m.* or *p.m.*

Word	Abbreviation	Contraction
national	natl.	nat'l.
association	assn.	ass'n.

Exception: Some verb and date forms have no easy abbreviation. In such cases, use the contraction.

couldn't	can't	won't	'83 (for 1983)

406   Capitalization

The capitalization of abbreviations generally follows the capitalization of the words being abbreviated.

United States of America	U.S.A. *or* USA
International Telephone & Telegraph	ITT
account	acct.

Abbreviations of proper nouns are generally capitalized, following the rules used for capitalization of unabbreviated proper nouns.

Beginner's All-purpose Symbolic Instruction Code   BASIC

Abbreviations of common nouns are not capitalized.

each	ea.
amount	amt.

Exceptions:	eastern standard time	EST
	anno Domini	A.D.
	collect on delivery	COD

407   Punctuation and Spacing

(**NOTE:** The modern trend is toward the elimination of periods in abbreviations. Some of these abbreviations without periods have passed into common usage; others have not.)

Single words: Use period at end: Dr., Ms., Chas.

But: Shortened words (not really abbreviations) use no period: memo, photo, math, 3d, steno, auto

All capitals: Use no periods, no spaces: IBM, NAACP, NBC

But:
(See ¶409.)	Academic Degrees	B.A., B.S., M.A.
(See ¶417.)	Geographic	U.S.A. (*or* USA), U.S.S.R.
(See ¶427.)	Time	B.C., A.D.

All lowercase: Use periods, no spaces: p.m., q.v., o.m.

But: (See ¶420.)   Measurement   mm, mph (*or* m.p.h.), psi

Two words: Use periods and spaces: op. cit., gr. wt.

But:
(See ¶409.)	Academic Degrees	Ed.D., Ph.D.
(See ¶416.)	Foreign Expressions	ad hoc, et al.

Within a sentence, an abbreviation is followed by one space.

Please place the AIB code immediately after the banking course description.

A mark of punctuation following an abbreviation within a sentence is placed **immediately** after the abbreviation, with no spaces between the abbreviation and the punctuation mark.

It was 2:00 *p.m.,* and Bob was not yet at the meeting.

If the abbreviation ends the sentence, two spaces follow the end-of-sentence punctuation.

The new dean was introduced as Cristina Mateo, *Ph.D.* A....
The new computer was upgraded to *640K.* The...

A question mark or exclamation mark following an abbreviation at the end of the sentence is placed immediately following the abbreviation, with no spaces between the abbreviation and the punctuation mark.

The president emphasized that the meeting would begin at exactly 2:00 *p.m.!*

408   Plurals and Possessives

The plurals of most abbreviations are formed by adding *s:*

mgr. → mgrs.	Dr. → Drs.	ave. → aves.
*MD → MDs	*DO → DOs	CPA → CPAs
*See ¶ 409.		

Some abbreviations, particularly those of weights and measurements, have the same form in the singular and plural.

ft   in   m   qt

Plurals of some single-letter abbreviations are formed by doubling the letter:

p. 105 → pp. 105–107   (referring to pages)
l. 8 →   ll.   8–10   (referring to lines)

Some abbreviations form the plural irregularly.

Mr. → Messrs. (**NOTE:** This plural abbreviation should *only* be used in addressing unmarried brothers, business partners, or members of a firm.)
Mrs. → Mmes. (**NOTE:** The use of this plural abbreviation is not considered good form.)
Ms. → Mses. or Mss. (**NOTE:** This plural is **not** standard. Since *Ms.* is not truly an abbreviation for a longer word, a plural is illogical.)
No. → Nos.

To assist in identification, lowercase letters and lowercase abbreviations with punctuation often form the plural by adding *'s.*

Changing the c's to e's   p.o.e.'s

Possession in abbreviations is indicated by adding *'s* when the abbreviation is singular, *s'* when the abbreviation is plural.

Singular	Plural
Doctor B's orders	CPAs' annual convention
U.S.A.'s treaty	DOs' residency program
RN's resume	MDs' graduation

409

Academic Degrees

Academic degrees are written with periods following the abbreviation for each word and no spaces.

B.S.	B.Ed.	B.A.	M.A.	M.Ed.	M.S.
Ph.D.	Ed.D.	M.B.A.	J.D.	D.D.	D.A.

The Certified Professional Secretary (CPS), Certified Public Accountant (CPA), Certified Financial Planner (CFP), and Chartered Life Underwriter (CLU) designations are generally written in capitals and without periods.

A total of twenty individuals passed the *CPS* examination.

When academic titles follow an individual's name, do not use titles such as Dr., Mr., Ms., Mrs., or Miss before the name.

Sis Smith, MD   *or*   Dr. Sis Smith   (**not** Dr. Sis Smith, M.D.)

Other titles which do not duplicate a degree following the name, **may** be used in front of the same name.

Dr. Irene Lipof, Professor of Social Science   *or*   Irene Lipof, Ph.D.
Vice President Bill Stokes, CPA   the Reverend Ned Glenn, D.D.

The American Medical Association and the American Osteopathic Association prefer that no periods be used in medical abbreviations. Within the medical profession, titles such as MD, DO, RN, and FACS (Fellow of American College of Surgeons) are often written without periods.

Elias Padilla, RN   James McCormick DO

410

Acronyms

A shortened, pronounceable word created by using the first letter of each of the words in a longer title is called an **acronym**. Acronyms save time and space in writing and time in speaking, especially when a title is particularly long. Note that most acronyms are written with capital letters; some common acronyms are written in lowercase letters. Spaces and punctuation marks are eliminated.

National Organization for Women	NOW
Comprehensive Employment and Training Act	CETA
College Level Examination Program	CLEP
Zone Improvement Plan	ZIP
North Atlantic Treaty Organization	NATO
Mothers Against Drunk Driving	MADD
Environmental Prototype Community of Tomorrow	EPCOT
light amplification by stimulated emission of radiation	laser

Commonly used acronyms are included in ¶428. They are followed by the designation (ac).

Note that **acronyms** are different from ordinary abbreviations, as they are pronounced as one word. The following **abbreviations**, however, are pronounced letter by letter:

IBM	YMCA	YWCA	WDW	JTPA

411 Broadcasting Stations and Systems

Radio and television broadcasting stations and broadcasting networks and systems are abbreviated in capital letters with no periods or spaces.

Detroit — WXYZ-AM   Miami — WLYF-FM   MGM Studios
       /   \
(station)   (system)   NBC   CBS   UPI News Service

412 Chemical and Mathematical Abbreviations

When using the symbols representing chemical elements and formulas, do not use periods.

Au = Gold   Ni = Nickel   Cu = Copper   Zn = Zinc

When using the symbols representing mathematical abbreviations, do not use periods.

sin = sine   cos = cosine
log = logarithm   pi = the value given to the nonending, nonrepeating
decimal

413 Compass Directions

When a compass direction is used as a **noun**, write it in full and begin with a capital; do not abbreviate.

She is from the *Midwest*.

When a compass direction is used as an **adjective**, write it out; do not abbreviate and do not capitalize.

The International Bookfair was held on the east side of the street.

NOTE: Different uses require different capitalization. For additional information, please refer to Unit 3, ¶307.

In Addresses

When a compass direction *precedes a street name*, it is generally written out.

Dr. Kenneth Stringer
114 *East* Michigan Boulevard
East Lansing, MI   48864-1401

However, when doing so would cause the inside address to be out of balance (or in tables where space is limited), it is also permissible to abbreviate a compass direction before a street name.

Ms. Bonnie McCabe   Ms. Bonnie McCabe
11621 *S.W.* 11201 Street   *or*   11621 *SW* 11201 Street
Miami, FL   33176-1260   Miami, FL   33176-1260

NOTE: For special U.S. Postal Service rules for addressing envelopes, please refer to Unit 10.

When a compass direction *follows a street name,* insert a comma to separate the street name from the abbreviation and then abbreviate in capital letters. Follow local practice in determining the spacing or use of periods. In the absence of a local preference, eliminate periods and spaces.

Mrs. Castell Bryant
6919 Liberty Street, *NE*
Philadelphia, PA   19126-6900

In Technical Material

When a compass direction is included in technical material, use all capital letters and omit all punctuation and spacing.

SSW	NE	W
(south-southwest)	(northeast)	(west)

414   Contractions

Abbreviations and contractions are both shortened forms of words and phrases; do not confuse them. When writing contractions, an apostrophe is inserted at the point where any letter or number is eliminated. See Unit 1, ¶133, and Unit 2, ¶201.30, for more information on contractions.

wouldn't	we'll	gov't.	'88

415   Dates

Days of the week and **months of the year** should be written in full. When space is limited (as in charts, tables, and the like), however, the following abbreviations are permissible:

Jan.	Feb.	Mar.	Apr.	May	June
July	Aug.	Sept.	Oct.	Nov.	Dec.
Sun.	Mon.	Tues.	Wed.	Thurs.	Fri.	Sat.

On forms or in computerized reports, it may be desirable to abbreviate days and months even further. In such cases use the following:

Ja	F	Mr	Ap	My	Je	Jl	Ag	S	O	N	D
Su		M		Tu		W		Th		F	Sa

416   Foreign Expressions (See ¶428)

417   # Geographic Abbreviations

Try to avoid geographic abbreviations, except in forms, tables, computerized reports, or when space is extremely limited. Exceptions to this rule are extremely long names such as *U.S.S.R.* (Union of Soviet Socialist Republics) and *U.S.A.* (United States of America).

NOTE: When geographic names are abbreviated in capital letters, periods (*but no spaces*) follow each letter.

United Kingdom	U.K.
New York City	N.Y.C.
Philippine Islands	P.I.
United Arab Republic	U.A.R.

State and Province Abbreviations

Table 4-1 shows the names of the states, districts, and territories of the United States; the standard abbreviations of the names; the two-letter abbreviations that are used with ZIP Codes; and the capital cities.

TABLE 4-1

State, District, and Territory Names; Abbreviations; Capitals

The following table shows the names of the states, districts, and territories of the United States; the standard abbreviations of the names; the two-letter abbreviations that are used with ZIP Codes; and the capital cities.

Name	Standard Abbreviation	Two-Letter Abbreviation	Capital
Alabama	Ala.	AL	Montgomery
Alaska	Alaska	AK	Juneau
Arizona	Ariz.	AZ	Phoenix
Arkansas	Ark.	AR	Little Rock
California	Calif.	CA	Sacramento
Colorado	Colo.	CO	Denver
Connecticut	Conn.	CT	Hartford
Delaware	Del.	DE	Dover
District of Columbia	D.C.	DC	Washington (National capital)
Florida	Fla.	FL	Tallahassee
Georgia	Ga.	GA	Atlanta
Guam	Guam	GU	Agana
Hawaii	Hawaii	HI	Honolulu
Idaho	Idaho	ID	Boise

(continued)

TABLE 4-1 *(continued)*

Name	Standard Abbreviation	Two-Letter Abbreviation	Capital
Illinois	Ill.	IL	Springfield
Indiana	Ind.	IN	Indianapolis
Iowa	Iowa	IA	Des Moines
Kansas	Kans.	KS	Topeka
Kentucky	Ky.	KY	Frankfort
Louisiana	La.	LA	Baton Rouge
Maine	Maine	ME	Augusta
Maryland	Md.	MD	Annapolis
Massachusetts	Mass.	MA	Boston
Michigan	Mich.	MI	Lansing
Minnesota	Minn.	MN	St. Paul
Mississippi	Miss.	MS	Jackson
Missouri	Mo.	MO	Jefferson City
Montana	Mont.	MT	Helena
Nebraska	Nebr.	NE	Lincoln
Nevada	Nev.	NV	Carson City
New Hampshire	N.H.	NH	Concord
New Jersey	N.J.	NJ	Trenton
New Mexico	N.Mex.	NM	Santa Fe
New York	N.Y.	NY	Albany
North Carolina	N.C.	NC	Raleigh
North Dakota	N.Dak.	ND	Bismarck
Ohio	Ohio	OH	Columbus
Oklahoma	Okla.	OK	Oklahoma City
Oregon	Oreg.	OR	Salem
Pennsylvania	Pa.	PA	Harrisburg
Puerto Rico	P.R.	PR	San Juan
Rhode Island	R.I.	RI	Providence
South Carolina	S.C.	SC	Columbia
South Dakota	S.Dak.	SD	Pierre
Tennessee	Tenn.	TN	Nashville
Texas	Tex.	TX	Austin
Utah	Utah	UT	Salt Lake City
Vermont	Vt.	VT	Montpelier
Virgin Islands	V.I.	VI	Charlotte Amalie, St. Thomas
Virginia	Va.	VA	Richmond
Washington	Wash.	WA	Olympia
West Virginia	W.Va.	WV	Charleston
Wisconsin	Wis.	WI	Madison
Wyoming	Wyo.	WY	Cheyenne

Table 4-2 shows the names of the Canadian provinces, the standard abbreviations of the names, the two-letter abbreviations of the names, and the capitals of the provinces.

TABLE 4-2

Canadian Names, Abbreviations, and Capitals

The following table shows the names of the Canadian provinces, the standard abbreviations of the names, the two-letter abbreviations of the names, and the capitals of the provinces.

Name	Standard Abbreviation	Two-Letter Abbreviation	Capital
Alberta	Alta.	AB	Edmonton
British Columbia	B.C.	BC	Victoria
Manitoba	Man.	MB	Winnipeg
New Brunswick	N.B.	NB	Fredericton
Newfoundland	Newf./Nfld.	NF	St. John's
Northwest Territories	N.W. Ter.	NT	Yellowknife
Nova Scotia	N.S.	NS	Halifax
Ontario	Ont.	ON	Toronto
Prince Edward Island	P.E.I.	PE	Charlottetown
Quebec	Que.	PQ	Quebec
Saskatchewan	Sask.	SK	Regina
Yukon Territory		YT	Whitehorse

Saint is generally abbreviated within the United States by using *St.*

St. Joseph   St. Louis   St. Thomas

Port, Point, Mount, Heights, and *Fort* are not generally abbreviated within the United States unless space is limited.

Fort Lauderdale   Cleveland Heights
East Point   Fort Meyers

Outside of the United States, however, follow local customs and preferences regarding the use of such abbreviations.

418 ## Government and International Agencies

Abbreviations for government and international agencies are generally written all in capital letters with no periods and no spaces. (Also see ¶428.)

CIA   FHA   UNICEF   OPEC   NASA

419 ## Information Processing (See ¶428)

420   Measurements

420.1   Standard form.

Standard form. Abbreviate standard units of measurement in lower-case letters. Most frequently no periods are used.

in	inch(es)*	ft	foot/feet	yd	yard(s)
sq in	square inch	mph	miles per hour	wpm	words per minute

*When using this abbreviation for *inch* within a sentence, make certain it cannot be confused with the preposition *in*. In such cases either add a period (*in.*) or spell out *inch*.

In measurements including abbreviations and numbers, a space is included between the number and abbreviation. In simple measurements, the abbreviation may be inserted at the end of a series of numbers.

34 sq ft	80 × 92 in	17 ft 3 in *or*
		17' 3" (See ¶201.32.)

In measurements including symbols, however, there are no spaces between number and symbol, or symbol and letter abbreviation.

78°F   62°C

420.2   Metric.

Metric. Abbreviate metric units of measurement with lowercase letters and no periods.

meter	m	gram	g	liter	L
square*	sq	cubic*	c	(liter uses capital *L*, to avoid confusion with the number *1*)

*These forms are used in combination with base units. For example, one *cubic* centimeter.

Metric Prefixes — Add the prefix to the basic metric units provided above.

deka	da	(×10)	hecto	h	(×100)
kilo	k	(×1000)	deci	d	(1/10)
centi	c	(1/100)	milli	m	(1/1000)

NOTE: Metric abbreviations represent both singular and plural forms.

In expressing per hour measurements with metric abbreviations, use the / to represent *per*.

60 km/hr   sixty kilometers per hour

421   Medical Abbreviations

Commonly used medical abbreviations are included in ¶428. Each one is followed by the designation (m). See note in ¶409 for preferences of medical associations.

422   Numbers (See Unit 7.)

423   ## Organizations and Groups

Many organizations and groups are best known by their abbreviated names.

IBM   WDW   AFL-CIO   NOW   UPI

The foregoing abbreviations may be used except in formal writing. In addition, many parts of organization or group names may be abbreviated.

| Co. | Company | Inc. | Incorporated | Ltd. | Limited |
| Corp. | Corporation | Mfg. | Manufacturing | Bros. | Brothers |

Always write the name of an organization or group as its members prefer. The letterhead of the organization provides a good example to follow.

424   ## Personal Names and Initials

Abbreviated forms of given names are often used in writing lists of names and in other places where space is limited; they are *never* pronounced. Nicknames are shortened forms of names that may be spoken or written (but not in formal communication).

	Abbrev. Form		**Nickname**
Richard	Rich.	*or*	Dick *or* Rick
Thomas	Thos.	*or*	Tom
Elizabeth	Eliz.	*or*	Liz
Suzanne	Suz.	*or*	Sue

NOTE: Periods are included with the abbreviation, but not following the nickname. Whenever possible, follow an individual's personal preferences in using both abbreviations and nicknames.

Initials within a name should be capitalized. Each initial is followed by a period and a space.

M. Duane Hansen   Robert J. Blood
T. M. Tachibana   M. B. Stringer

When using initials only, type all in capital letters with no periods and no spaces.

KSS   JAS
LT   for Lee Tannenbaum

But: ZEZ   for Zoila E. de Zayas

425   ## Titles

Personal — **Singular:**	Mr.	**Plural:**	Messrs. (See ¶408.)
	Mrs.		(See ¶408.)
	Ms.		(See ¶408.)
	Dr.		Drs.

NOTE: Since *Miss* (singular) and *Misses* (plural) are not abbreviations, no period is used after these titles. *Ms.* is a title commonly used in business writing wherein identification of a woman's marital status serves no purpose.

When *Saint* is part of a name, follow individual preference for writing out or abbreviating.

> Professor Delphine St. Thomas   Anabel San Lorenze
> **NOTE:** In Hispanic names *San* may represent *Saint.*

Always abbreviate *Jr.* and *Sr.* following personal names. *Esquire* may be spelled out or abbreviated (*Esq.*). These abbreviations should be used with full names. A personal title may be used *before* the full name with *Jr.* and *Sr.,* but **never** with *Esq.*

> Dr. Dale Romanik, *Sr.*   Lourdes Perez, *Esq.**

> ***NOTE:**   *Esq.* is used by lawyers within the USA. It is most correctly applied to males; however, some females now use it.

Designations such as *II, III, 2d, or 3d* follow full names. No periods or commas are used; however, if an individual wishes to use a comma, follow his preference.

> Nickson Benedico III

Professional — Professional titles should be written in full whenever possible.

> Vice President Betty Lundgren   Professor Joyce Crawford
> the Reverend Leonard Bryant   Vice Mayor Dewey Knight

When titles are long, or when space is limited, *professional titles* may be abbreviated if the full name or last name and initials are used.

> First Lieutenant Jean Stark   1st Lt. Jean Stark
> Father Lynn Forrester   Fr. Lynn Forrester

NOTE: When titles begin with *the,* do **not** abbreviate.

> The Honorable Xavier Suarez   the Reverend Harriet Spivak

426

Business Symbols (See Unit 7.)

427

Time and Time Zones

Use the abbreviations *a.m.* and *p.m.* with numerals in expressions of time.

> 4 p.m.   3:30 a.m.   8:30 p.m., EST *or*
>   8:30 p.m. (EST)

Use *o'clock* for emphasis and in formal writing, but eliminate *a.m.* and *p.m.*

>   four o'clock in the afternoon
> **Not:**   4 p.m. o'clock

The following time zones are abbreviated as indicated:

	Standard Time	Daylight Savings Time (DST)
Eastern	EST	EDT
	(eastern standard time)	(eastern daylight time)
Central	CST	CDT
Mountain	MST	MDT
Pacific	PST	PDT

428 Business Abbreviations Commonly Used

This listing contains abbreviations for common medical terms (m), governmental agencies, common academic degrees, information processing terms (IP), common English phrases, common foreign phrases (f), acronyms (ac), and time zone abbreviations.

A.A.	assoc. in arts
AAA	Amer. Automobile Assn.
AAMA	Amer. Assn. of Medical Assts.
A.A.S.	assoc. in applied science
ABA	Amer. Bankers Assn.
	Amer. Bar Assn.
ABC	Amer. Broadcasting Company
acct.	account
ACLU	Amer. Civil Liberties Union
A.D.	anno Domini
ADC	Aid to Dependent Children
addnl.	additional
ad hoc	for a particular purpose (f) Latin meaning "for this" — **not** an abbreviation, no periods
ad lib.	as desired; at pleasure (f) from Latin meaning "at will"
ADP	automatic data processing (IP)
ad. val.	
or A/V	ad valorem
ad or advt.	advertisement
AEC	Atomic Energy Comm.
AFA	Advertising Federation of America
AFB	Aid for the Blind; air force base
AFD	Association of Food Distributors
afft.	affidavit
AFL-CIO	Amer. Federation of Labor and Congress of Industrial Orgs.
AIB	Amer. Inst. of Banking
AIDS	acquired immune deficiency syndrome (ac) (m)
a.k.a.	also known as
ALGOL	algorithmic-oriented language (IP)
ALU	arithmetic and logic unit (IP)
a.m.	*ante meridiem* (before noon)
AMA	Amer. Medical Assn.

Amer.	America, American
AMS	Administration Management Society
amt.	amount
ans.	answer
ANSI	American National Standards Institute
AP *or* a/p	accounts payable
API	Amer. Petroleum Institute
APL	a programming language (IP)
approx.	approximately
APR	annual percentage rate
aq	water (m)
AR *or* a/r	accounts receivable
ARC	Amer. Red Cross
ARM	Adjustable Rate Mortgage
ARMA	Assn. of Records Mgrs. and Administrators (ac)
ASA	Amer. Stdards Assn.
	Amer. Statistical Assn.
ASAP *or* asap	as soon as possible
ASCAP	Amer. Society of Composers, Authors, and Publishers (ac)
ASCE	Amer. Society of Civil Engineers
ASCII	Amer. Standard Code for Information Interchange (ac) (IP)
ASME	Amer. Society of Mech. Engineers
assoc.	associate
assn.	association
asst.	assistant
ASTA	Amer. Society of Travel Agents (ac)
ASTD	Amer. Society of Training Directors
astd.	assorted
att.	attached
AT&T	Amer. Telephone & Telegraph
attn.	attention
atty.	attorney
A.V. *or* AV	audiovisual
ave.	avenue
avg. *or* av.	average
B.A. *or* A.B.	bachelor of arts
bal.	balance
BASIC	Beginner's All-purpose Symbolic Instruction Code (ac) (IP)
B.B.A.	bachelor of business administration
BBB	Better Business Bureau
bbl	barrel(s)
B.C.	before Christ
BCD	binary-coded decimal (IP)
B.Ed.	bachelor of education

BIA	Bureau of Indian Affairs
bid	twice a day (m)
BIOS	basic input/output system (IP)
bit	binary digit (IP)
bl	bale
B/L or BL	bill of lading
bldg.	building
blvd.	boulevard
BP	blood pressure (m)
bps	bits per second (IP)
bros.	brothers
B.S.	bachelor of science
B/S or BS	bill of sale
Btu	British thermal unit
bu	bushel(s)
bus.	business
c	centi, as prefix 1/100
c. or ca.	circa, approximately (f)
C	100 or Celsius
Ca	Calcium (m)
CA	Cancer (m)
CAB	Civil Aeronautics Board
CAD	computer-aided design (IP)
CAI	computer-assisted instruction (IP)
CAM	computer-aided manufacturing (IP)
CARE	Cooperative for Amer. Relief to Everywhere (ac)
CAT	computerized axial tomography (ac) (m)
	Computer Aided Translation (IP)
CB	Citizens Band
CBC	complete blood count (m)
CBS	Columbia Broadcasting System
cc	cubic centimeter (m)
	carbon copy
CCP	console command processor (IP)
CCU	coronary care unit (m)
CD	certificate of deposit
CDT	central daylight time
CEO	chief executive officer
cf.	confer, compare (f)
CFO	chief financial officer
cg	centigram(s)
chg.	charge
CIA	Central Intelligence Agency
c.i.f. or CIF	cost, insurance, and freight
CIM	computer input microfilm (IP)
CLU	chartered life underwriter
cm	centimeter(s)
CMOS	complementary metal-oxide semiconductor (IP)

CNS	central nervous system (m)
co.	company
c/o	care of
COBOL	common business-oriented language (ac) (IP)
COD	collect on delivery
COM	computer output microfilm (IP)
comm.	commission
cont.	continued
CORE	Congress of Racial Equality (ac)
corp.	corporation
CPA	certified public accountant
cpi	characters per inch
CP/M	Control Program for Microprocessors (IP)
cps	characters per second
CPS	certified professional secretary
CPU	central processing unit (IP)
cr.	credit
CRT	cathode-ray tube (IP)
CSC	Civil Service Commission
CST	central standard time
ctn.	carton
cu	cubic
cu cm	cubic centimeter
cu. in. *or*	
cu in	cubic inch
cwt.	hundredweight
d	deci, as prefix 1/10
da	deka, as prefix × 10
D.A.	doctor of arts
d.b.a. *or*	
DBA	doing business as
D.B.A.	doctor of business admin.
D.D.	doctor of divinity
D.D.S.	doctor of dental surgery (m)
	doctor of dental science (m)
dept.	department
dis.	discount
dist.	district
distr.	distributor
div.	division
dna	does not answer *or* does not apply
D.O. *or* DO	doctor of osteopathy (m)
DOS	disk operating system (IP)
doz. *or* dz.	dozen
DP	data processing (IP)
dr	dram, debit
Dr.	Doctor
dstn.	destination

dtd.	dated
DX	diagnosis (m)
ea *or* ea.	each
EBCDIC	Extended Binary Coded Decimal Interchange Code (IP)
EEC	European Economic Community
ECOM	electronic computer-originated mail (ac) (IP)
Ed.D.	doctor of education
EDP	electronic data processing (IP)
Ed.M.	master of education
Ed.S.	specialist in education
EDT	eastern daylight time
EEG	electroencephalogram (m)
EEOC	Equal Employment Opportunity Comm.
EENT	eye, ear, nose, and throat (m)
EFT	electronic funds transfer
e.g.	*exempli gratia* (for example) (f)
EKG	electrocardiogram (m)
enc.	enclosure
ENT	ear, nose, and throat (m)
EOF	end of file (IP)
EOM *or*	
e.o.m.	end of month
EPCOT	Environmental Prototype Community of Tomorrow (ac)
EPROM	erasable programmable read-only memory (IP)
ER	emergency room (m)
ERIC	Educational Resources Information Center (ac)
ESP	extrasensory perception
Esq.	Esquire
ESS	electronic switching system (IP)
EST	eastern standard time
et	and (f)
ETA	estimated time of arrival
et al.	*et alia* (and others) (f)
etc.	*et cetera* (and so forth) (f) — Avoid the use of *etc.* in running text.
et seq.	*et sequens* (and the following) (f)
	et sequentes (those that follow) (f)
exp.	expense
ext.	extension
F	Fahrenheit
FAO	Food and Agriculture Org. of the United Nations
FAX	facsimile transmission (ac) (IP)
FBI	Fed. Bureau of Investigation
FBLA	Future Bus. Leaders of Amer.
FCC	Fed. Communications Commission
FDA	Food and Drug Administration
FDIC	Fed. Deposit Insurance Corp.
fed.	federal

FHA	Fed. Housing Administration
FIFO	first in, first out (ac) (IP)
fl. oz.	fluid ounce
f.o.b. *or* FOB	free on board
FORTRAN	formula translation (ac) (IP)
FRB	Fed. Reserve Bank
	Fed. Reserve Board
FRS	Fed. Reserve System
frt.	freight
ft	foot, feet
FTC	Fed. Trade Commission
fwd.	forward
FY	fiscal year
FYI	for your information
g	gram(s)
gal	gallon(s)
GAO	General Accounting Office
GI	gastrointestinal (m)
GNP	gross national product
govt.	government
gr.	grain, gross
gr. wt.	gross weight
GTT	Glucose Tolerance Test (m)
GU	genitourinary (m)
gyn	gynecology (m)
h	hecto, as prefix × 100
HBO	Home Box Office
HBP	high blood pressure (m)
hdlg.	handling
hdqrs.	headquarters
HGB *or* hb	hemoglobin (m)
HMO	health maintenance org.
hr	hour(s)
HUD	Dept. of Housing and Urban Development (ac)
IABC	Intl. Assn. of Bus. Communicators
ibid.	*ibidem* (in the same place) (f)
IBM	Intl. Business Machines
IC	integrated circuit (IP)
ICC	Interstate Commerce Comm.
	Indian Claims Commission
ICU	intensive care unit (m)
ID	identification
idem	the same (f) — not an abbreviation
IDP	integrated data processing (IP)
i.e.	*id est* (that is) (f)
ILGWU	Intl. Ladies' Garment Workers' Union
IMF	Intl. Monetary Fund
in. *or* in	inch(es)

inc.	incorporated
incl.	including, inclusive
ins.	insurance
inst.	institute
int.	interest
intl.	international
inv.	invoice
invt.	inventory
I/O	input/output (IP)
IOU	I owe you
IQ	intelligence quotient
IRA	individual retirement acct. (ac)
IRS	Internal Revenue Service
IV	intravenous (m)
J.D.	doctor of jurisprudence
Jr.	junior
JTPA	Job Training Partnership Act
k	karat, kilo
K	kilobyte
kg	kilogram(s)
km	kilometer(s)
L	liter(s)
l. (ll.)	line(s)
LAN	local area network (ac) (IP)
laser	light amplification by stimulated emission of radiation (ac)
lb(s)	pound(s)
LCD	liquid crystal display screen (IP)
LIFO	last in, first out (ac) (IP)
LL.B.	bachelor of laws
loc. cit.	*loco citato* (in the place cited) (f)
LPN	licensed practical nurse (m)
LQP	letter quality printer
LS	*locus sigilli* (in place of the seal) (f)
LSI	large-scale integration (IP)
ltd.	limited
m	meter(s); milli, as prefix 1/1000
M	1,000 (symbol)
M.A. *or* A.M.	master of arts
MADD	Mothers Against Drunk Driving (ac)
max.	maximum
M.B.A. *or* MBA	master of business administration
MC	master/mistress of ceremonies
M.D. *or* MD	doctor of medicine
M.Div.	master of divinity
mdse.	merchandise
MDT	mountain daylight time

M.Ed.	master of education
memo	memorandum — not an abbreviation — shortened word
Messrs.	Misters (See ¶408 for correct usage.)
mfg.	manufacturing
mfr.	manufacturer
mg	milligram(s)
mgr.	manager
MGM	Metro-Goldwyn-Mayer
MI	myocardial infarction (m)
mi	mile
MICR	magnetic ink char. recognition (IP)
min	minute(s)
min.	minimum
MIS	management information systems (IP)
misc.	miscellaneous
ml	milliliter(s)
mm	millimeter(s)
Mmes.	plural of Madame (Best to avoid; See ¶408.)
mo	month(s)
MO	mail order; money order
modem	modulator-demodulator (IP)
mpg	miles per gallon
mph	miles per hour
Mr.	Mister
Mrs.	Mistress
Ms.	Title for woman that does not identify marital status
M.S.	master of science
Mses. *or*	
Mss.	plural of Ms. (Do **not** use; see ¶408.)
MST	mountain standard time
n/30	net in 30 days
N/A	not applicable
NAACP	Natl. Assn. for the Advancement of Colored People
NAM	Natl. Association of Manufacturers (ac)
NANA	North Amer. Newspaper Alliance (ac)
NAS	Natl. Academy of Sciences
NASA	Natl. Aeronautics and Space Administration (ac)
natl.	national
NATO	North Atlantic Treaty Org. (ac)
NBC	Natl. Broadcasting Company
NBS	Natl. Bureau of Standards
NCR	no carbon required (paper)
NEA	Natl. Education Assn.
neg	negative
NLRB	Natl. Labor Relations Board
NMA	Natl. Microfilm Assn.
No. (Nos.)	Number(s)
nol. pros.	unwilling to prosecute (f)

non seq.	it does not follow (f)
NOW	Natl. Org. for Women (ac)
NRC	Nuclear Regulatory Comm.
NSF	Natl. Science Foundation
nt. wt.	net weight
NYD	not yet diagnosed (m)
NYSE	New York Stock Exchange
OAS	Org. of Amer. States
OB/GYN	obstetrics/gynecology (m)
OCP	optical character printing (IP)
OCR	optical character recognition (IP)
o.d. *or* OD	overdraft
OK	(okay) all right
o.m.	every morning (m)
o.n.	every night (m)
op. cit.	*opere citato* (in the work cited) (f)
OPEC	Org. of Petroleum Exporting Countries (ac)
opt.	optional
OR	operating room (m)
org.	organization
orig.	original
o/s *or* OS	out of stock
OTC	over-the-counter
oz	ounce(s)
p. (pp.)	page (pages)
PA	public address
PABX	private automatic branch telephone exchange (IP)
PAP smear	Papanicolaou Smear (m)
PBS	Public Broadcasting Service
PBX	private branch exchange (IP)
pc	photocopy; personal computer
pd.	paid
PDT	Pacific daylight time
P/E	price/earnings ratio
PERT	Program Evaluation and Review Technique (ac)
PHA	Public Housing Administration
Ph.D.	doctor of philosophy
pk.	peck
pkg.	package(s)
P & L *or* P/L	profit and loss
p.m.	*post meridiem* (after noon)
PO	purchase order
P.O.	Post Office
p.o.e. *or* POE	port of entry
PP	parcel post
ppd.	prepaid
PR	public relations

pr.	pair(s)
pres.	president
prn	as needed (m)
prof.	professor
PROM	programmable read-only memory (IP)
pro tem	*pro tempore* (for the time being) (f)
P.S.	*postscriptum* (postscript) (f)
psi	pounds per square inch
PST	Pacific standard time
pstg.	postage
pt	pint(s)
pt.	part, point(s), port
PTA	Parent-Teacher Assn.
qh	every hour (m)
qid	four times a day (m)
qr	quire
qt	quart(s)
qtr.	quarter(ly)
qty.	quantity
q.v.	*quod vide* (which see) (f)
R & D	research and development
radar	radio detecting and ranging (ac)
RAM	random access memory (IP) (ac)
RBC	red blood cells; red blood cell count (m)
re *or* in re	regarding, in the matter of
recd.	received
reg.	registered
rep.	representative
req	requisition
retd.	returned
rev.	revised
RFD	rural free delivery
rm	ream(s)
R.N. *or* RN	Registered Nurse (m)
ROM	read-only memory (ac) (IP)
RPG	report program generator (IP)
rpm	revolutions per minute
R.s.v.p. *or* RSVP	*Répondez s'il vous plaît* (please reply) (f)
/S/	signed (before a copied signature)
SADD	Students Against Drunk Driving (ac)
SASE	self-addressed, stamped envelope
SAT	Scholastic Aptitude Test
SBA	Small Bus. Administration
scuba	self-contained underwater breathing apparatus (ac)
SEC	Securities and Exchange Comm.
sec	second
sec. *or* secy.	secretary

sect.	section
sen.	senator
shpt.	shipment
shtg.	shortage
SIDS	sudden infant death syndrome (m)
SO	Shipping Order
sonar	sound navigation ranging (ac)
SOP	standard operating procedure
SOS	Save our ship (distress call)
SPCA	Society for the Prevention of Cruelty to Animals
sq in	square inch
sq m	square meter
Sr.	senior
SRO	standing room only
SSA	Social Security Administration
St.	Saint, Street
stat	immediately (f) (m)
stat.	statistic
std.	standard
stge.	storage
stmt.	statement
TB	tuberculosis (m)
temp	temperature (m)
Th.D.	doctor of theology
TLC	tender, loving care
treas.	treasurer
TTL	transistor-transistor logic (IP)
TVA	Tennessee Valley Authority
UFO	unidentified flying object
ult.	in the last month (f)
UNESCO	United Nations Education, Scientific, and Cultural Org. (ac)
UNICEF	United Nations Children's Fund (ac)
UPI	United Press Intl.
UPC	universal product code
UPS	United Parcel Service (ac)
USIA	U.S. Information Agency
VA	Veterans Administration
VCR	videocassette recorder
VD	venereal disease (m)
VDT	video display terminal (IP)
via	by way of (f)—**not** an abbreviation
VIP	very important person
VISTA	Volunteers in Service to Amer. (ac)
viz.	namely (f)
vol.	volume
V.P.	vice president
vs. *or* v.	*versus* (as opposed to) (f)

WATS	Wide-Area Telecommunications Service (ac)
WBC	white blood cells; white blood cell count (m)
WCC	World Council of Churches
WDW	Walt Disney World
WHO	World Health Org. (ac)
whsle.	wholesale
wk.	week(s)
WP	word processing (IP)
wpm	words per minute (IP)
wt.	weight
yd	yard(s)
YMCA	Young Men's Christian Assn.
YMHA	Young Men's Hebrew Assn.
YWCA	Young Women's Christian Assn.
YWHA	Young Women's Hebrew Assn.
yr	year(s)
ZIP (Code)	zone improvement plan (ac)

Unit V  Word Division

Understand:
- When word division should not be used
- When word division may be used

Acquire:
- The ability to recognize words which may be divided
- The ability to divide words at the best point

Be Prepared To:
- Recognize incorrect or excessive word division
- Apply rules for word division to business writing

5

500 Avoiding Word Division

Word division should be avoided when possible. Divided words can be confusing to a reader and thus interrupt speedy comprehension of what is written. When words must be divided to maintain balanced margins, divide between syllables at the point which will hinder reader comprehension least.

With Word Division

The Pediatric Care Unit needs medical secretaries who recognize the importance of accurate medical records and careful treatment of patients. These areas were stressed in my medical transcription training.

Without Word Division

The Pediatric Care Unit needs medical secretaries who recognize the importance of accurate medical records and careful treatment of patients. These areas were stressed in my medical transcription training.

501 Word Division and Software

Most word processing software provides some assistance with word division by indicating (when reformulating a paragraph) a word falling beyond the right margin. This process allows the writer to determine an appropriate place for word division or to decide not to divide the word. If word division is not indicated, the program adds additional spacing to the current line to balance the right margin and carries the word not divided to the beginning of the next line. This automatic balancing of each line has resulted in less word division where word processing software is employed.

5

502   General Guidelines

One of the most common uses of the hyphen is to divide long words at the end of a line so that all lines of a typewritten document are balanced. Before reviewing how such words are divided, it is important to review some "do nots" of word division.

502.1   **Unnecessary division.** Do not divide words unless necessary. Avoid word division whenever possible.

502.2   **One-syllable and other short words.** Do not divide one-syllable or very short words (five or fewer letters) of more than one syllable. For example, do not divide the following words:

help	item	would	title	enter

502.3   **Confusing divisions.** Do not divide words if the divided word looks strange, or if the divided word would cause confusion or mislead the reader.

piz-	picto-	ide-
zazz	rial	alistic

502.4   **Division resulting in stranded letters.** Do not divide words if you leave only one (or two) letter(s) on the first line or if you carry only one (or two) letter(s) to the next line.

	enter		stranger
Not:	en-	**Not:**	strang-
	ter		er

502.5   **Words between pages.** Do not divide a word at the end of a page.

502.6   **Consecutive lines with divided words.** Do not divide words on consecutive lines or have many divided words on the same page. Remember that each divided word may cause a break in the reader's concentration and thus limit understanding.

502.7   **Contractions.** Do not divide contractions.

	wouldn't		haven't
Not:	would-	**Not:**	have-
	n't		n't

502.8   **Abbreviations.** Do not divide abbreviations.

	NAACP		UNICEF
Not:	NAA-	**Not:**	UNI-
	CP		CEF

502.9   **First and last lines of a paragraph.** Do not divide a word at the end of the last line of a paragraph. Avoid dividing a word ending the first line of a paragraph.

503   Words at the End of a Typewritten Line

With the aforementioned cautions in mind, use the following guidelines for word division at the end of a typewritten line:

503.1   **Only between syllables.** Divide words only between syllables. Refer to Unit 6 in this manual for syllable identification of commonly misspelled words, and consult your dictionary for syllables on all other words.

503.2   **Break in midword.** Divide at the syllable break that is as close as possible to the middle of the word. Since half the word will be on one line and half on the next line, the divided word will be easier to read. (/ = syllable break)

op/por/tu/ni/ties	oppor-tunities
com/pen/sa/tion	compen-sation
re/quire/ment(s)	require-ment(s)
in/ter/pret	inter-pret

503.3   **Divide for clear meaning.** Divide at natural syllable breaks which help clarify meaning.

ex/tra/cur/ric/u/lar	extra-curricular
en/vi/ron/men/tal	environ-mental
de/vel/op/ment	develop-ment
in/tro/duc/tion	intro-duction

Caution: When the same word can be used as both a noun and a verb, the pronunciation (and thus the syllabication) may also change.

	As a Noun	**As a Verb**
progress	prog-ress	pro-gress
founder	founder (do **not** divide)	foun-der
project	proj-ect	pro-ject

PRIMARY RULES OF WORD DIVISION

While words can be divided at most of the syllable breaks indicated in your dictionary, reader comprehension of the divided word will be assisted by using the following guidelines:

504   Compound Words

Divide hyphenated compound words immediately after the hyphen. With hyphenated expressions of more than two words, divide after the hyphen closest to the middle of the expression.

full-length	full-	length
self-educated	self-	educated
jack-in-the-box	jack-in-	the-box

Divide solid compound words between the word elements.

honeymoon	honey-	moon
checkbook	check-	book
firsthand	first-	hand

505   Double Consonants

When a root word ends in a double consonant, divide the word after the double consonant, prior to any added suffix.

falling	fall-	ing
recallable	recall-	able
businessperson	business-	person

However, sometimes the syllables change when the suffix is added and extra letters are eliminated (always consult your dictionary if you are unsure).

| impress + sion | impression | |
| im/pres/sion | impres- | sion |

When a root word . . .

- ends in a vowel plus consonant
- and the final consonant is doubled when adding a suffix
- and the suffix creates a new syllable, divide the word between the doubled consonant.

| omitted | omit- | ted |
| riddance | rid- | dance |

When a root word . . .
- contains a double consonant
- and has at least two syllables, divide between the double consonant.

| letters | let- | ters |
| accommodate | accom- | modate |

506   Family Relationships

Words containing the prefix *great-* should be divided immediately after the hyphen.

| great-grandfather | great- | grandfather |

Words containing the suffix *in-law* should be divided at the hyphen preceding the suffix.

| mother-in-law | mother- | in-law |

Solid compounds that describe family relationships should be divided between word elements.

| stepson | step- | son |
| grandmother | grand- | mother |

507   ## Hyphenated Words (See Compound Words, ¶504.)

508   ## Names

Every attempt should be made to keep full names together. However where space is limited in informal writing, names may be divided between the first name (including middle name or initial) and surname. (/ = break point)

Maria Elena/

Diaz de Villegas

Dr. William A./

McNae

When an extremely long title precedes a name, a break may occur immediately following the title. (/ = break point)

Administrative Assistant/

Winston Richter

Executive Vice President/

Sue Skidmore

509   ## Numbers

Avoid dividing numbers whenever possible. When word division **must** be used...

- divide **long numbers** after a comma, leaving at least four numbers on the first line and carrying at least six numbers to the following line.

  1,356,–   864,900

- divide **dates** following the comma, between the date and year, without a hyphen.

  February 18,/   1992

- divide **street addresses** between street name and descriptor, without a hyphen.

  2055 Belding/   Court

  or between words of a two-word street name.

  8625 North/   Bassett Way

- divide **numbered or lettered lists** immediately before the number or letter, without a hyphen.

  ... bringing the gift certificate,/

  (2) visit the store of your choice,   (3) ...

510   ## Places

Break names of places between the city and state, or between state and ZIP Code. Two-word city or state names may be broken between the two words.

FL 33313-0300

River, NJ 07458-0701

78705-0401

Fort Lauderdale,/

Upper Saddle/

Austin, Texas/

511   Prefixes and Suffixes

Divide words immediately following any prefix, or immediately before any suffix whenever possible or logical.

introduction	intro-	duction
photogenic	photo-	genic
activity	activ-	ity
extremism	extrem-	ism

Caution: Often when a prefix or suffix is added or changed, the syllabication of the root word changes.

| consist | con-sist | consistency | consis-tency |
| preventing | prevent-ing | prevention | preven-tion |

Sentence with a Dash. Divide sentences that contain a dash immediately following the dash.

When she arrives—and it will be late—/
the meeting will begin.

512   Vowels as Single-Letter Syllables

When a one-letter vowel syllable comes within a word, divide the word immediately after this vowel.

regulate	regu-	late
manipulate	manipu-	late
democratic	demo-	cratic

But when a single-vowel syllable immediately precedes an ending two-letter syllable, divide before the vowel.

| pacify | pac- | ify |
| humility | humil- | ity |

Or when a single-vowel syllable *a* is followed by an ending syllable *ble, bly,* or *cle,* divide before the vowel.

operable	oper-	able
probably	prob-	ably
miracle	mir-	acle

513   ## Two Vowels Together

Usually when two vowels come together within a word, with each vowel sounded separately, divide the word between the vowels.

	anxiety	anxi-	ety
	continuation	continu-	ation
	psychiatric	psychi-	atric
But:	psychiatry	psychia-	try

But, when the two vowels represent one combined sound, divide the word to keep the vowels together.

faithless	faith-	less
housewarming	house-	warming
millionaire	million-	aire

Unit VI   Spelling

Understand:
- The more common conventions for spelling
- The importance of precise pronunciation in spelling
- The value of the dictionary as the final "authority" on spelling

Acquire:
- The ability to recognize word roots
- The ability to recognize prefixes and suffixes

Be Prepared To:
- Spell words commonly used in business correspondence
- Spell the more troublesome words listed in ¶610
- Apply common conventions, precise pronunciation, and knowledge of word parts (roots, prefixes, and suffixes) to the spelling of more difficult words
- Use the dictionary when it is needed

601   Pronunciation

The most effective way to improve spelling is to improve pronunciation. Even though most spelling rules have numerous exceptions, correct pronunciation will provide at least the framework of letters that allows you to look the word up in the dictionary.

Correct pronunciation will reduce the number of errors caused by adding sounds (such as: atheletic instead of athletic; hinderance instead of hindrance). It will reduce the number of errors caused by dropping sounds (such as: reconize instead of recognize; liberry instead of library). It helps one avoid the transposition of letters (such as irrevelant instead of irrelevant). Finally, correct pronunciation helps eliminate simple phonetic errors (such as: bretzel instead of pretzel; zink instead of sink).

602   Dictionary Use

Another effective aid to correct spelling is the use of a good dictionary. Spelling in this manual is based on the 1987 printing of *Webster's Ninth New Collegiate Dictionary* published by Merriam-Webster, Springfield, Massachusetts.

On some computers, an automatic spelling checker (sometimes part of a word processing program; sometimes a separate single-purpose program) will scan completed text, identify misspelled words, offer the most likely correctly spelled substitutions, and substitute the correct form chosen by the computer operator.

603 Spelling Rules

Some spelling rules apply to only a few words and have numerous exceptions. The more useful rules apply to larger numbers of words and have fewer exceptions. Some of the more useful rules are discussed in ¶604–609.

604 Roots

Many English words are derived from Latin or Greek roots. The **root** is the *central part* of the word, the *core* of meaning. Familiarity with the structure of words (prefixes, roots, and suffixes) helps one remember and recognize spelling patterns.

Latin or Greek Root	English Root	Meaning	Words
corpus (L)	corp	body	corpse, corsage, corporation
credere (L)	cred	believe	credit, credible, credence
nomen (L)	nomin	name	nominate, nominal, nominee
novus (L)	nov	new	novel, innovate, novice

605 Prefixes

A **prefix** is a syllable (or syllables) placed before the root to qualify the meaning of the root.

Prefix	Meaning	Example
de	down, from	decry, debase, decline
dis	opposite, not	discredit, disable, disagree
re	again, back	repeat, rebuild, return

Adding prefixes: combine the prefix and the root without doubling or dropping letters.

in + tolerable = intolerable   im + mortal = immortal

606 Suffixes

A **suffix** is a syllable (or syllables) placed after the root to qualify the meaning of the root.

Suffix	Meaning	Examples
able, ible	capable of, fit for, worthy	workable, invisible, incurable
dom	condition of being, jurisdiction	wisdom, kingdom, freedom
ward	in the direction of	northward, seaward, inward

6

607

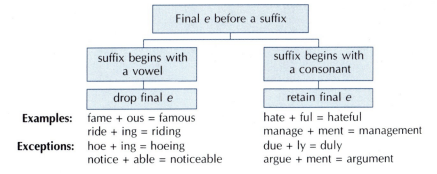

	Final *e* before a suffix
suffix begins with a vowel	**suffix begins with a consonant**
drop final *e*	retain final *e*

Examples: fame + ous = famous   hate + ful = hateful
                        ride + ing = riding   manage + ment = management
Exceptions: hoe + ing = hoeing   due + ly = duly
                        notice + able = noticeable   argue + ment = argument

608

Doubling the Final Consonant When Adding a Suffix

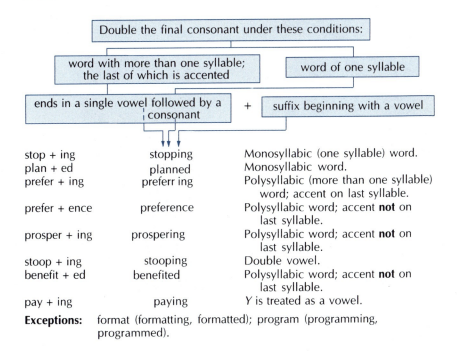

Double the final consonant under these conditions:

word with more than one syllable; the last of which is accented	word of one syllable

ends in a single vowel followed by a consonant   +   suffix beginning with a vowel

stop + ing	stopping	Monosyllabic (one syllable) word.
plan + ed	planned	Monosyllabic word.
prefer + ing	preferr ing	Polysyllabic (more than one syllable) word; accent on last syllable.
prefer + ence	preference	Polysyllabic word; accent **not** on last syllable.
prosper + ing	prospering	Polysyllabic word; accent **not** on last syllable.
stoop + ing	stooping	Double vowel.
benefit + ed	benefited	Polysyllabic word; accent **not** on last syllable.
pay + ing	paying	*Y* is treated as a vowel.

Exceptions: format (formatting, formatted); program (programming, programmed).

609

Ie or Ei

Use *i* before *e* except directly following *c*, if the combined vowels are sounded like long *e*.

Examples:	**Sounded Like Long e**		**Not Sounded Like Long e**	
	believe	field	deign	neighbor
	chief	niece	foreign	weight

Exceptions: neither*   seize   leisure   financier

*The exception for *neither* (and *either*) is because both words were originally pronounced with a long *i* sound — many people still prefer that pronunciation.

610 Word List

The following words are those most frequently misspelled. Some of the words **may** be spelled in more than one way; however, the most common spellings are provided here. The list is divided into groups of fifty words to facilitate study and quizzes.

absence	abundant	academic	academy	acceptable
accessible	accidentally	acclaim	accommodate	accompanied
accompanies	accompanying	accomplish	accurately	accuser
accusing	accustom	achieve	achievement	acquaintance
acquiesce	acquire	acre	across	actual
actuality	actually	address	adequate	admission
admit	adolescence	advantage	advantageous	adversity
advertisement	advice	advise	affect	against
aggravate	aggressive	aging	aisle	all right
alleged	alleviate	allot	allotment	allotted

allowed	amateur	amortize	analogous	analysis
analyze	annually	anticipated	anxiety	apologetically
apparatus	apparent	appearance	applying	appreciation
approaches	appropriate	approximate	arbitrary	architect
assistance	association	athlete	athletic	attack
attempts	attendance	attitude	attorney	audience
authoritative	autumn	auxiliary	bachelor	bankruptcy
bargain	basically	beautified	beggar	beginner
behavior	beneficial	benefit	benefited	biased
biscuit	breakfast	brilliance	Britain	Britannica

brochure	buoyant	buses	business	cafeteria
calorie	campaign	canceled	cancellation	capitalism
career	catalog	category	ceiling	cemetery
challenge	changeable	changing	characteristic	chauffeur
chronological	cite	coincidence	collateral	column
commission	commitment	committee	companies	comparatively
compelled	competition	competitive	compulsion	concede
conceivable	conceive	concentrate	conception	condemn
connoisseur	connotation	conqueror	conscience	conscientious
conscious	consensus	consider	considerably	consistency

continuously	controlling	controversial	convenience	coolly
correlate	council	counselor	courteous	courtesy
criticism	curiosity	curriculum	cylinder	debtor
deception	decided	deductible	defendant	defense
deferred	definitely	definition	dependent	describe
description	desirability	desperate	destruction	detrimental
devastating	development	dictionary	difference	dilemma
diligence	disappear	disappoint	disastrous	discipline
discrimination	discussion	disgusted	disillusioned	dissatisfied
dissimilar	doctrinaire	dominant	dormitories	dossier

drudgery
embarrass
entertainment
equipped
exaggerate
exercise
existent
explanation
fallacy
fictitious

ecstasy
emphasize
entrepreneur
equivalent
exceed
exhaustible
exonerate
extension
familiar
fiery

effective
encourage
enumerate
escapade
excellence
exhibition
exorbitant
extraordinary
families
finally

efficiency
enterprise
environment
especially
excellent
exhilaration
expense
extremely
fantasy
financially

eliminate
entertain
equipment
evidently
excitable
existence
experience
facsimile
fascinating
financier

fluorescent
friend
furniture
grammatically
guaranteed
happened
hesitancy
humorist
hypocrisy
imitation

forehead
friendliness
further
grandeur
guardian
happiness
heterogeneous
hundred
hypocrite
immediately

foreign
fulfill
gaiety
grievous
guidance
harass
hindrance
hunger
ignorance
immense

foreigners
fundamental
gauge
gruesome
handkerchief
height
hopeless
hurriedly
ignorant
imminent

forfeit
fundamentally
ghost
guarantee
handled
hemorrhage
hospitalization
hygiene
imagination
impasse

importance
indefinite
inevitable
innovation
intentionally
interpret
irresistible
laborer
lengthening
lien

incident
independence
influential
innuendo
intercede
interpretation
irritable
laboriously
liable
lieutenant

incidentally
indispensable
ingenious
inoculate
interest
interrupt
knowledge
ledger
liaison
liquefy

increase
individually
ingredient
insistence
interfering
involve
labeled
legitimate
library
literature

incredible
industrious
initiative
intelligent
interim
irrelevant
laboratory
leisurely
license
liveliest

livelihood
magnificence
material
memento
millennia
minutiae
misspell
negotiate
numerous
occurred

liveliness
maintain
mathematics
messenger
millionaire
misapprehension
moral
neither
obliged
occurrence

loneliness
maintenance
medicine
methods
miniature
miscellaneous
morale
notable
obsolescent
omission

luxury
manufacturers
medieval
mileage
minuscule
mischief
mortgage
noticeable
obstacle
omit

magazine
marriage
melancholy
milieu
minute
mischievous
necessary
nuclear
occasionally
omitted

opinion
optimistic
parallel
peculiar
perseverance
pertain
plausible
practically
preceding
prestige

opponent
organization
paralyzed
perceive
persistent
phenomenon
politician
practice
preferable
presumptuous

opportunity
original
parliament
performance
personal
philosophy
possess
prairie
prejudice
pretense

opposite
outrageous
partially
permanent
personnel
physically
possession
precede
prerogative
prevalent

optimism
pamphlet
particular
permissible
persuade
picnicking
possible
precedence
presence
primitive

principal	principle	privilege	procedure	proceed
profession	programmed	prohibition	prominent	promissory
pronunciation	propaganda	psychiatric	psychiatrist	psychoanalysis
psychological	psychology	psychopathic	psychosomatic	reference
referring	regrettable	reinforce	relative	relevant
reminisce	renaissance	rescind	reservoir	restaurant
revealed	rhapsody	rhetoric	rhetorical	rhyme
rhythm	ridiculous	sacrilegious	satellite	satirize
scent	schedule	science	scissors	secretary
separation	sergeant	siege	significance	simile
simple	simultaneous	sincerely	skillful	soliloquy
sophomore	souvenir	strength	stretch	subpoena
subtlety	subtly	success	succession	sufficient
suing	superintendent	supersede	suppose	suppress
surgeon	surreptitious	surrounding	surveillance	susceptible
syllable	symbol	symmetry	synonymous	tariff
taxing	technique	temperament	temperature	tendency
theater	theories	therefore	tragedy	transferred
traveler	tremendous	tyranny	unanimous	undoubtedly
unforgettable	unmanageable	unnecessary	unwieldy	usage

Unit VII

Numbers and Symbols

Understand:

- The various styles in which numbers are used: formal, ordinary text, scientific, and others

- The appropriate *form* (words or figures) for each *use* of numbers in each *style* (*figures* and *dimensions* in *ordinary text,* for example)

Acquire:

- The ability to write numbers in words or figures, using the correct *form* for each *use* in each *style*

Be Prepared To:

- Select the appropriate style(s) for writing the numbers in each document you process

- Apply the specific conventions for writing numbers explained in ¶711–732

7

GENERAL CONVENTIONS FOR WRITING NUMBERS

701   ## "Rules" for Writing Numbers

There is no single authoritative set of rules for writing numbers. There is, however, a set of reasonably clear conventions, developed and followed by those who write carefully and with attention to style. It is these conventions that are explained in the paragraphs that follow.

702

Table of Conventional Number Styles

NUMBERS	STYLE			
	FORMAL	**ORDINARY TEXT**	**INFORMAL**	**NUMERICAL**
	Proclamations Resolutions Invitations	Executive Correspondence Advertisements Slick-paper magazines Books	Business Correspondence Most Fiction Newspapers Some Textbooks	Instructions Scientific, Technical Material Statistics Tables
1–9	WORDS	WORDS	WORDS	FIGURES
11–99	WORDS	WORDS	FIGURES	FIGURES
100+	WORDS	FIGURES	FIGURES	FIGURES

NOTE: See ¶708.1, 708.2 on conventions for writing round numbers.

703

Formal Style

7

Formal style is employed in formal documents such as invitations to formal occasions (weddings, receptions, and the like), proclamations (of presidents, governors, and other rulers), and formal or ceremonial resolutions (of Congress, legislatures, boards, and the like). In formal style, all numbers are expressed in words.

at half past the hour
of
nine
in the evening

704

Ordinary Text

Ordinary text is employed by publications wishing to enhance their appeal to the educated and informed audience. The style is frequently used in top-level executive correspondence, advertisements for luxury items, books, and the like.

In ordinary text, numbers from one through ninety-nine are usually written in words. Numbers ranging upward from 100 are written in figures except for numbers one through ninety-nine followed by hundred, thousand, million, and so forth.

705

Informal Style

Informal style is widely used for speedy dissemination of knowledge. The numbers one through nine are written in words; 10 and above are written in figures. This style gives the text a pleasing appearance, avoiding the

awkwardness of expressing large numbers in words. Most business correspondence, newspapers, trade magazines, and the like, are written in the
informal style.

706   Numerical Style

Numerical style is employed in instructions, scientific writing, technical
writing, statistics, tables, and the like. In material of this kind, numbers
may be used so intensively that it would be impossible to express them
in words.

In numerical style, all numbers are written in figures.

707   Consistency

707.1   **Different styles within the same document.** It is not always
possible to maintain a consistent style throughout a document. However,
there should be a *reason* for *any* variation.

In an article written for a slick-paper magazine (ordinary text) it may
be necessary to lapse briefly into *numerical* style for a discussion of archi-
tectural specifications or the presentation of tabular material.

In informal style, a sentence, a paragraph, or even an entire section
consisting of statistics, tables, and the like, may require numerical style.

707.2   **Numbers in a set.** Use the same form (figures, words, or combined
figures and words) within each *set* of numbers. A set is a group of numbers related to one another for any one of several reasons.

   a. Numbers in the same category may be considered a set, even if
they are separated in the text.

> *Seven* beginners participated in the contest. *One* (the least experienced)
> scored *112*. Another scored *187*. The other five scored between *112*
> and *187*.

Some writers use words and figures to keep categories (sets) separate. In the paragraph above, the number of contestants is expressed in words; their scores are expressed in figures.

   b. Numbers in the same sentence or paragraph may be treated
as a set simply because they fall within the same sentence or
paragraph.

> All *7* beginners participated in the contest. The least experienced scored
> *112*. Another scored *187*. The other *5* scored above *112* but below *187*.

NOTE: Convert from words to figures to achieve consistency, unless that conversion causes a sentence to begin with a figure.
If the converted sentence would begin with a figure, it is preferable to spell out the number, even though figures are used later
in the sentence.

Not:	*3* surgeons used a total of *147* instruments.
But:	*Three* surgeons used a total of *147* instruments.
Or:	*The 3* surgeons used a total of *147* instruments.

708   Round Numbers

708.1 **Round numbers in informal writing.** Round numbers may be written in figures, words, or figure-word combinations—depending upon the intent of the writer.

  a. If the intent is formality, write round numbers in words.

  seven billion dollars   two hundred seventy-three million

  b. If the intent is smoothness, spell out round numbers that can be written in one or two words. (Those requiring three or more words are *usually* written in figures or figure-word combinations.)

  Three hundred   fifty-six* thousand   one thousand
  *NOTE: *Fifty-six* is a single compound word.

  c. If the intent is clarity—to emphasize the numbers—write round numbers in figures.

  500   7000 *or* 7,000   82,000,000

  d. Whether writing for smoothness or clarity, round numbers 1,000,000 or more may be written using figure-word combinations. (See ¶704 for use in ordinary text.)

  24 million   42.75 million   15-1/2 million

  See ¶719.4 on conventions for writing figure-word combinations.

708.2 **Round numbers in numerical style.** When writing in numerical style, express all numbers in figures or figure-word combinations.

  25,000   400   2.7 trillion   14 × 10   14 × 10[6]
  NOTE: Figure-word combinations may be used for numbers over 1,000,000. If the equipment you are using will not print exponents above the line, enclose them in brackets: 10[6]. See ¶719.4.

709   Adjacent Numbers

709.1 **Adjacent numbers stated similarly.** When adjacent numbers are both written in words or both written in figures, use a comma to separate them.

  On Flight *382, 12* passengers had carry-on luggage.
  If I make *six, seven* will be my next goal.

709.2 **Adjacent numbers and compound words.** When one of two adjacent numbers is part of a compound word used as a modifier, spell out the smaller number and write the larger in figures.

  48 four-pronged forks   three 4-pronged forks
  82 twenty-dollar bills   eight 20-dollar bills

710   Ranges

710.1 **Ranges expressed in words and figures.** The sizes of the numbers in the range and the context determine whether the range should be written in words or figures; see ¶702. Do not mix words and figures in the same range or set of ranges.

> The range of their ages is *3–11*.
> **Or:** The range of their ages is *3 – 11*.
> **Or:** The range of their ages is *three* through *eleven*.
> **Not:** The range of their ages is *three* through *11*.

710.2 **Selected numbers.** If selected numbers are listed rather than shown as a range, separate them with commas and spaces.

> Look for numbers *12, 39, 48,* and *137*.

710.3 **Abbreviating numbers in a range.** The higher number in a range may be abbreviated if both numbers have at least three digits *and* neither number ends in *00*. To abbreviate 101–109, retain the *changed* part of the higher number only. For 110–199, use two digits or more if needed.

> | 100–105 | → | 100–105 | 1005–1008 | → | 1005–8 |
> |---|---|---|---|---|---|
> | 105–108 | → | 105–8 | 125–145 | → | 125–45 |
> | 1000–1005 | → | 1000–1005 | 1522–1568 | → | 1522–68 |

NOTE: It is clearer to write both numbers in full than to change more than two numbers.

> 1245–1389
> **Not:** 1245–389

SPECIFIC CONVENTIONS FOR WRITING NUMBERS

711 ## Addresses

711.1 **House numbers.** House or building numbers under 100 are usually spelled out unless there is inadequate space.

> One Marina Avenue   Two Page Road   115 East Eighth Street

711.2 **Formal addresses.** Some persons write their addresses more formally than convention requires. It is considered courteous to address all persons and organizations as they prefer to be addressed.

> Three Hundred Wilton Terrace   Seven Thousand Gordon Drive

711.3 **Street numbers.** The numbers of streets (for those streets assigned numbers instead of names) are usually written in words if they are 100 or below, written in figures if they are 101 or above. In order to avoid confusion, use a hyphen preceded and followed by a space when figures are used for both the house number and the street name.

> 2447 Fifth Avenue South   122 - 143d street

711.4 **Highways.** State, interstate, and federal highways are identified with figures.

> S.R. 541   I-75   U.S. 41

711.5   **ZIP Codes.** Zoning *I*mprovement *P*lan codes are preceded by the standard two-letter abbreviation of the state name. Leave two blank spaces between the last letter of the abbreviated state name and the first figure of the ZIP Code.

> 10086* Sunset Boulevard   833 Georgetown Road
> Los Angeles, CA   90028-1015   Jacksonville, NC   28540-2086
> ***NOTE:** In street addresses *no* comma is used even in numbers of five or
> more digits.

712   ## Age

712.1   **Ages in ordinary text.** In ordinary text ages are expressed in words. See ¶702.

> Whereas Bessie Halper has reached the age of *ninety-seven* . . .
> He left home for good at the age of *twenty-one*.

712.2   **Ages in informal style text.** In daily business correspondence and other informal writing, ages ten and below are usually written in words. Ages 11 and above are written in figures. See ¶702.

> Their third son will soon be *nine* years old.
> Their children are eight, five, and three years old.
> They have *eight-, five-,* and *three*-year-old children.
> (See ¶211.34 on suspending hyphens.)
> They have a *23*-year-old daughter and a *9*-year-old grandson.
> (See ¶707 on consistency.)

712.3   **Ages in numerical style.** In technical or scientific material (statistics, tables, and the like) ages are expressed in figures.

> All of the subjects were between *2* and *8* years of age.
> Entries are made when the individual is *5, 7,* and *9* years old.

712.4   **Age with name.** When a name is followed by the person's age, the age is set off with commas.

> Wilma Byrnes, *twenty-three,* was observed at the scene of the accident.

713   ## Anniversaries

713.1   **Anniversaries in formal style.** Anniversaries are frequently written in formal style—all in words. When formal style is appropriate, spell out the number of the anniversary even if several words are required. See ¶702.

> This is their *twenty-fifth* wedding anniversary.
> They celebrated the *one hundred thirty-fifth* anniversary of the founding of
> the organization.

713.2   **Anniversaries in ordinary text.** In ordinary text, write anniversaries 1–99 in words, others in numbers.

> **NOTE:** The general conventions for writing numbers are applicable to anniversaries. See ¶702.

714   # Dates

The following conventions apply to dates appearing in text. See Unit 10 for conventions applicable to the dateline in business letters.

714.1   **Dates in normal order.** In most text, dates are written in month-day-year sequence. Use cardinal numbers (for example, 1, 23, 437).

January 1, 2000	July 4, 1776	January 24, 1925
Not: January 1st, 2000	**Not:** July 4th, 1776	

714.2   **Month out of normal order or not stated.** If the month follows the day or if the month is not stated, use ordinal numbers (1st, 2d, 3d, etc.) or ordinal words (first, second, third, etc.) to express the day of the month. (Also see ¶714.4.)

We plan to meet on the *twenty-first* or the *twenty-second*.
on the *21st* of May   on the *twenty-first* of May

NOTE: See ¶702 on expressing numbers (the day of the month) in words or figures.

714.3   **Dates in formal style.** In formal proclamations, resolutions, invitations, and the like, dates are written in words.

April eighteenth, seventeen hundred and seventy-five
the eighteenth of April in the year of our Lord seventeen hundred and seventy-five

714.4   **Military and foreign dates.** In the U.S. military services, dates are stated in day-month-year sequence. This style is also in *general* use in some foreign nations.

8 October 1955   27 May 2001

NOTE: In this format, the day is written in cardinal figures (for example, 1, 3, 15), not ordinals (for example, 1st, 3d, 15th).

714.5   **Decades and centuries.** Particular decades and centuries should be spelled out in all styles.

the twenty-first century   in the fifties
But: in the 1990s (identification of a decade by its century)

714.6   **B.C. and A.D.** The initials *B.C.* and *A.D.* are written after the number that identifies the year.

2225 A.D.   284 B.C.   14,500 B.C.

714.7   **Dates in contracted form.** Dates may be written as contractions ('44, '55) if:

a. They are of historical significance.

the armistice of '18

b. They are years of graduation.

the class of '50
the class of '03

c.   Several years of the same century are used in the same passage.

There was a severe flood in 1937 and lesser ones in '39, '41, and '47.

715   Decimals

715.1   Spacing with decimals. Do **not** space before or after a decimal.

3.58   .009 $245.67   327.1

715.2   Commas and decimals. Do **not** use a comma *to the right of* the decimal.

45,367.294739   .0095"

715.3   Zero before a decimal. Use a zero before a decimal only if the zero is necessary to call attention to the decimal.

0.87   .075 inches (The zero *after* the decimal is necessary to hold the "tenths" place in this example.)

715.4   Zero after a decimal. Use a zero at the end of a decimal only to right-justify a column of numbers, to indicate that a calculation has been carried to another decimal place, or for consistency among numbers in a set.

134.568   25.670 (correct to three decimal places)
36.500
37.510

716   Fractions

716.1   Fractions in ordinary text. In ordinary text, a fraction is written in words unless it is part of a mixed number, is awkward when written in words, or pertains to precise measurement or calculation.

At least *three-fifths* of those present agreed with the speaker.

Mixed number: Give the handle 2-1/2 turns clockwise.
Awkward if in words: divided into 7/8-acre tracts (*Seven-eighth-acre tracts* is awkward.)

Measurement: 1/2 cup   the 3/4-mile marker   1/4 pound   15/16 inch
Calculation: multiply by 1/8

716.2   Hyphenating fractions written in words. The numerator and denominator of a fraction written in words should be joined by a hyphen *unless* either numerator or denominator already contains a hyphen. See ¶211.9.

two-thirds   seven thirty-seconds   seven-eighths
three and two-thirds   forty-three hundredths

716.3   **Fractions and ordinals.**

a. Spell out ordinals from *first* through *ninety-ninth*. Hyphenate compound ordinals between *twenty-first* and *ninety-ninth* (do **not** confuse ordinals with fractions).

the fifty-ninth entry
(ordinal between *first* and *ninety-ninth*, spelled out, and hyphenated because it is compound)

the 1000th
(ordinal not between *twenty-first* and *ninety-ninth*, not spelled out)

one-thousandth of an inch   (fraction, hyphenated)

b. Do not use a word or suffix in the denominator of a fraction *written in figures*.

| **Not:** | 7/32ds | 9/64ths | 1/2 an inch | 5/8ths of an inch |
| **But:** | 7/32 | 9/64 | 1/2 inch | 5/8 inch |

c. An *of* phrase or similar construction may be used following a *spelled out* fraction.

| | one-quarter of an ounce | half an hour |
| **Not:** | 1/4 of an ounce | 1/2 an hour |

717   ## Measurement

717.1   **Units of weight, volume, count, and so forth.** In ordinary text, measurements are expressed in figures—except for occasional isolated measurements that are easily expressed in words.

The machines weigh *2375, 579,* and *1483* pounds respectively.
The drill press weighs *three hundred pounds.*

717.2   **Dimensions.** Dimensions are expressed in figures—except for isolated dimensions that are easily expressed in words.

a rug *8* feet *3* inches by *11* feet *7* inches
The room is *fifteen* feet long.

718   ## Metric Measurements

718.1   **Metric units.**

Basic Metric Units		
Quantity	**Unit**	**Symbol**
Length	meter	m
Mass	kilogram	kg
Time	second	s
Temperature*	kelvin	K

Basic Metric Units

Quantity	Unit	Symbol
Electric current	ampere	A
Luminous intensity	candela	cd
Amount of substance	mole	mol
*Common Unit	degree Celsius	°C

Supplementary Metric Units

Quantity	Unit	Symbol
Plane angle	radian	rad
Solid angle	steradian	sr

718.2   Derived metric units.

Quantity	Unit	Symbol	Formula
acceleration	meter per second squared	m/s^2	—
area	square meter	m^2	—
density	kilogram per cubic meter	kg/m^3	—
electric charge	coulomb	C	$A \cdot s$
electric field strength	volt per meter	V/m	—
electric resistance	ohm	Ω	V/A
energy	joule	J	$N \cdot m$
force	newton	N	$kg \cdot m/s^2$
frequency	hertz	Hz	s^{-1}
illumination	lux	lx	lm/m^2
power	watt	W	J/s
pressure	newton per square meter	N/m^2	—
quantity of heat	joule	J	$N \cdot m$
velocity	meter per second	m/s	—
voltage	volt	V	W/A
volume	cubic meter	m^3	—
work	joule	J	$N \cdot m$

718.3   Metric prefixes.

Value	Power of 10	Prefix		Symbol
1 000 000 000 000	10^{12}	tera	(ter'a)	T
1 000 000 000	10^9	giga	(jig'a)	G
1 000 000	10^6	mega	(meg'a)	M
1 000	10^3	kilo	(kil'o)	k
100	10^2	hecto	(hek'to)	h
10	10^1	deka	(dek'a)	da
0.1	10^{-1}	deci	(des'i)	d
0.01	10^{-2}	centi	(sen'ti)	c
0.001	10^{-3}	milli	(mil'i)	m

Value	Power of 10	Prefix		Symbol
0.000 001	10^{-6}	micro	(mi'kro)	μ
0.000 000 001	10^{-9}	nano	(nan'o)	n
0.000 000 000 001	10^{-12}	pico	(pe'ko)	p

718.4 Area, capacity, length, mass, weight, and volume.

Area

100 square millimeters	(mm^2)	1 square centimeter	(cm^2)
100 square centimeters	(cm^2)	1 square decimeter	(dm^2)
100 square decimeters	(dm^2)	1 square meter	(m^2)
100 square meters	(m^2)	1 square dekameter	(dam^2)
100 square dekameters	(dam^2)	1 square hectometer	(hm^2)
100 square hectometers	(hm^2)	1 square kilometer	(km^2)

Capacity

10 milliliters	(ml)	1 centiliter	(cl)
10 centiliters	(cl)	1 deciliter	(dl)
10 deciliters	(dl)	1 liter	(L)
10 liters	(L)	1 dekaliter	(dal)
10 dekaliters	(dal)	1 hectoliter	(hl)
10 hectoliters	(hl)	1 kiloliter	(kl)
1 cubic decimeter	(dm^3)	1 liter	(L)

Length

10 millimeters	(mm)	1 centimeter	(cm)
10 centimeters	(cm)	1 decimeter	(dm)
10 decimeters	(dm)	1 meter	(m)
10 meters	(m)	1 dekameter	(dam)
10 dekameters	(dam)	1 hectometer	(hm)
10 hectometers	(hm)	1 kilometer	(km)

Mass and Weight

10 milligrams	(mg)	1 centigram	(cg)
10 centigrams	(cg)	1 decigram	(dg)
10 decigrams	(dg)	1 gram	(g)
10 grams	(g)	1 dekagram	(dag)
10 dekagrams	(dag)	1 hectogram	(hg)
10 hectograms	(hg)	1 kilogram	(kg)
1 cubic decimeter	(dm^3)	1 liter(L) = 1 kilogram (kg)	

Volume

1000 cubic millimeters	(mm^3)	1 cubic centimeter	(cm^3)
1000 cubic centimeters	(cm^3)	1 cubic decimeter	(dm^3)
1000 cubic decimeters	(dm^3)	1 cubic meter	(m^3)

718.5 Conversion: metric → English; English → metric.

Metric-English Conversion	English-Metric Conversion
Approximate Values	**Approximate Values**
1 mm .... 0.04 inch	1 inch .... 25.4 mm
1 cm .... 0.4 inch	1 inch .... 2.54 cm
1 m .... 39.37 inches	1 foot .... 0.305 m
1 km .... 0.6 mile	1 yard .... 0.91 m
	1 mile .... 1.61 km
1 cm² .... 0.16 square inch	
1 m² .... 10.8 square feet	1 square inch .... 6.5 cm²
1 m² .... 1.2 square yards	1 square foot .... 0.09 m²
1 hectare .... 2.5 acres	1 square yard .... 0.8 m²
	1 acre .... 0.4 hectare
1 cm³ .... 0.06 cubic inch	
1 m³ .... 35.3 cubic feet	1 cubic inch .... 16.4 cm³
1 m³ .... 1.3 cubic yards	1 cubic foot .... 0.03 m³
	1 cubic yard .... 0.8 m³
1 ml .... 0.034 ounce	
1 cl .... 0.34 ounce	1 pint .... 0.47 L
1 L .... 2.1 pints	1 quart .... 0.95 L
1 L .... 1.06 quarts	1 gallon .... 3.79 L
1 L .... 0.26 gallon	1 ounce .... 28.35 g
1 g .... 0.035 ounce	1 pound .... 0.45 kg
1 kg .... 2.2 pounds	1 U.S. ton .... 0.9 metric ton
1 metric ton ...... 1.1 U.S. ton	

718.6 Temperature.

Celsius		Fahrenheit
0°C	freezing point of water	32°F
10°C	a spring day	50°F
20°C	recommended indoor temperature	68°F
30°C	a summer day	86°F
37°C	body temperature	98.6°F
100°C	boiling point of water	212°F

Converting from Fahrenheit to Celsius

$$C = \frac{5}{9}(F - 32)$$

Converting from Celsius to Fahrenheit

$$F = \frac{9}{5}C + 32$$

719   Money

719.1

General convention. Amounts of money are generally expressed in figures.

| $12.38 | $20 | nearly $50 | over $8000 |

719.2

Indefinite money amounts. An indefinite amount of money is written in words.

several hundred dollars   many thousands of dollars

719.3

Isolated money amounts. In ordinary text, an isolated money amount is spelled out if the result is not awkward or too lengthy. **Note:** All whole number money amounts under one hundred dollars should be spelled out.

twenty-five dollars   four hundred dollars   eight dollars

719.4

Large money amounts. Round number amounts of $1 million and more may be written in a combination of figures and words. In this format, the amount written in figures:
- must include a whole number
- may include a decimal of no more than three digits
- may include a fraction equivalent to a three-digit decimal instead of the decimal itself.

| $3 million | $5-1/2 million | $10.1 billion |
| $30 million | $7-3/4 million | $9.125 million |

Not: $7.3472 million   See ¶708.1
$7-15/49 million

719.5

Law documents; negotiable instruments. In law documents (wills, agreements, and the like) and negotiable instruments (checks, certain notes, bonds, and so forth), numbers (particularly amounts of money) are stated in words *and* figures for extra clarity and certainty.

seventy-three dollars ($73)
Three Hundred Seventy-Five and 43/100 Dollars ($375.43)

NOTE: Use the word *and* no more than once in a number. If the number consists of dollars and cents, the *and* should be used between dollars and cents.

Not: Two Hundred and Eight and 35/100 Dollars
But: Two Hundred Eight and 35/100 Dollars
Or: Two Hundred Eight Dollars
NOTE: Capitalization is optional; on checks and in some other applications, capitals as shown are preferred.

719.6

Decimal and zeros following money amounts. In running text when writing money amounts in figures, do not use zeros (or a decimal) after even amounts.

The initial rate is *$85* per month. After six months, it increases to *$105* per month.

But: Do keep the low-order (right) digits aligned in a column in lists and tables.

$352
  35
  18
$405

719.7 **Cents in general.** For amounts under one dollar in informal style, write the number in figures and spell out the word *cents*.

The price is *50 cents*.
There is a *50-cent* charge. (Compound modifier.)
The *five-cent* trolley ride is a thing of the past. (Isolated amounts of ten cents and less may be written in words.)

719.8 **Cents in formal style.** In formal style, cents are written in words.

The price is only *seventy-five cents*.
The purchase price is twenty-five dollars and *twenty-five cents*.

719.9 **Cents as part of a set.** If an amount is less than a dollar, but is part of a set in which some amounts are a dollar or more, use *$.44* as the form.

The prices were *$4.32, $.83,* and *$12.76.*

719.10 **Cents in functional writing.** In technical and statistical material, and catalog and other advertising copy, the cent sign (¢) may be used when all the amounts in a set are less than a dollar.

The price increased by *72¢* last year and *18¢* this year.

720 ## Ordinal Numbers

An ordinal number (written in figures or words) designates the place of an item in an ordered sequence.

1st, 9th, 100th   first, ninth, one hundredth

720.1 **Ordinal numbers in formal style.** In formal writing, ordinal numbers are written in words.

the *one hundred seventy-fifth* anniversary of the charter

720.2 **Ordinal numbers in ordinary text.** In general, write ordinal numbers below *100th* in words.

twenty-first   ninety-ninth   100th   121st   125th

720.3 **Ordinal numbers in functional writing.** In tables, bills, statistical or technical material, and other applications in which clear, concise communication is more important than formality, ordinal numbers may be written in figures.

the *3d, 5th,* and *9th* dials on the control panel
the *1st, 2d, 8th,* and *12th* columns in Table 14

720.4 **Ordinal numbers following surnames.** An ordinal number following a surname may be written in Arabic or Roman numerals. It is not preceded by a comma. However, the name should be written as the person prefers.

Jose Mendez 2d   Harry Hapstance III   Wilton Hargrave IV

721 Plural Forms of Numbers

721.1 **Plural forms of numbers written in figures.** To form the plural of a number written in figures, add *s*.

Some of the *2s* look like *3s*.
The *1990s* are, in some respects, similar to the *1930s*.

721.2 **Plural forms of numbers written in words.** To form the plurals of numbers written in words, follow the general conventions for creating plural forms as illustrated below:

four	thirty-five	thirty
fours	thirty-fives	thirties
fourths	thirty-fifths	thirtieths

722 Percent

722.1 **Percent in formal text.** In formal writing, spell out the number and the word *percent*.

Yes, *ninety-four percent* of the answers were correct.

722.2 **Percent in ordinary text.** In ordinary text, write the number in figures; spell out the word *percent*.

The report states that *78 percent* were correct, *20 percent* were incorrect, and *2 percent* were questionable.

722.3 **Percent in functional writing.** In tables, bills, statistical or technical material, and other applications in which clear, concise communication is more important than formality, use the % symbol instead of the word *percent*.

18%   58%   43%   122%

722.4 **Fraction of 1 percent.** A fraction of 1 percent is written as follows:

1/2 percent   .5%   0.5%   one-half of 1 percent

722.5 **Mixed number as percent.** A percentage may be expressed as a mixed number or as a decimal.

4-1/2 percent   4 1/2%   4.5 percent   4.5%

723 Proportions and Ratios

723.1 **Proportions and ratios generally written in figures.** Proportions and ratios are generally written in figures.

a 2 to 1 proportion   a 2:1 ratio   a 2-to-1 ratio

723.2   **Isolated proportions and ratios written in words.** Isolated proportions and ratios in ordinary text may be written in words.

> four parts water to one part pigment   a sixty-forty chance

724   ## Roman Numerals

724.1   **Uses of roman numerals.** Roman numerals are used most frequently to identify the main sections of an outline. They are also used in lowercase form (xiv, for example) to number pages in the front sections of many books. Roman numerals are used in the title and credits sections of motion pictures, on buildings, and in other applications in which the writer or designer wishes to convey an image of historical significance.

724.2   **Conversion table for roman numerals.** The following table shows the equivalent roman numerals for some arabic figures.

1	I	11	XI	30	XXX	400	CD
2	II	12	XII	40	XL	500	D
3	III	13	XIII	50	L	600	DC
4	IV	14	XIV	60	LX	700	DCC
5	V	15	XV	70	LXX	800	DCCC
6	VI	16	XVI	80	LXXX	900	CM
7	VII	17	XVII	90	XC	1,000	M
8	VIII	18	XVIII	100	C	2,000	MM
9	IX	19	XIX	200	CC	5,000	$\overline{V}$*
10	X	20	XX	300	CCC	10,000	$\overline{X}$*

*A line over a numeral multiplies the value by 1,000.

724.3   **Creating other roman numerals.** Other roman numerals may be created by prefixing and suffixing letters. Prefixing a letter is the equivalent of subtracting the value of the prefixed letter; suffixing a letter is the equivalent of adding the value of the suffixed letter.

> 49 (*L* minus *X*) plus (*IX*) *or* XLIX   64 is (*L* plus *X*) plus (*IV*) *or* LXIV

725   ## Scores

Scores of sporting events are written in figures.

> 102–94   15–6   9 to 5

726   ## Symbols and Abbreviations

726.1   **General convention.** Use figures with symbols and abbreviations. Normally, symbols and abbreviations are not used in formal style or in ordinary text.

> #5   14%   59¢ $58   144 sq ft   23″   23 in.

726.2   **Figures with #.** The number symbol may be used in functional writing (bills, tables, technical and statistical material, and the like). Since it is usually obvious that a number is a number, use of the symbol should be limited to those applications in which the symbol serves some purpose. Do not space between the symbol and the number.

> #AH2875   #SIG-824

726.3   **The word *number*.** The word *number,* if applicable, may be used at the beginning of a sentence to avoid beginning the sentence with a number written in figures.

> *Number 37789* has been assigned to your claim.

726.4   **The abbreviation *No*.** The abbreviation *No.* may be used before a number written in figures. This construction is particularly appropriate if there can be any doubt that the entire number is a number.

> License No. NKA 468 (*NKA* could be an abbreviation.)
> Invoice No. AV 2346
> **But:**   Invoice 2346

727   # Time of Day

727.1   **Times of day in formal writing.** In formal writing, all times of day are written in words.

> half past eight o'clock   half after seven o'clock

727.2   **Hyphenating time of day written in words.** Use a hyphen between the components of a two-word time-of-day expression; use a hyphen between the second and third words in a three-word time-of-day expression.

> seven-thirty   seven thirty-five   twelve forty-five

727.3   ***O'clock, a.m., p.m.*** Use the word *o'clock* with numbers written in words for the most formal statements of times of day. In less formal writing, use *a.m.* or *p.m.* with figures. See also ¶730.

> **Formal:**   quarter past seven o'clock in the evening
> **Less Formal:**   7:15 p.m.

727.4   **Time of day not on the *even, half, or quarter* hour.** In ordinary text, times of day **not** on the even, half, or quarter hour are written in figures. It is proper in any style to employ figures when the intent is to emphasize accuracy or punctuality.

> 8:35 a.m.   9:17 p.m.

727.5   **On-the-hour times of day.** In informal style, it is not necessary to add zeros to on-the-hour times of day.

> at *3* p.m.   before *8* a.m. and after *10* p.m.

727.6   **Approximate and even times of day.** In ordinary text, approximate times of day and even, half, or quarter hours are spelled out. See ¶727.4.

The advance party will arrive about *seven* o'clock.
The play will begin at half past *nine*.

727.7 **Colon separating hours and minutes.** When writing a time of day in figures, use a colon (without spacing before or after it) to separate hours and minutes. See examples in ¶727.4.

728 ## Usage of Numbers

Redundancy, inconsistency, lack of parallelism. Avoid constructions such as these:

Not:	**But:**
10:00 a.m. in the morning	10:00 a.m. *or* 10:00 a.m. tomorrow
tomorrow a.m.	tomorrow morning
7 p.m. o'clock	7 p.m., 7:00 p.m., *or* seven o'clock
11:30 p.m. until midnight	11:30 p.m. until 12 midnight
12 noon until midnight	12 noon until 12 midnight *or* noon until midnight

729 ## Voting Results

Voting results are written in figures.

7 to 5   49,385 to 18,483   8–3   23–17

730 ## Writing Numbers as Numbers

Numbers referred to as numbers rather than for their numeric value are written in figures.

Write a *5* in the blank.
The number is *48*.

NOTE: Since some instruments (including some automatic clock systems built into computers) do not indicate *noon* or *midnight,* it is sometimes necessary to substitute:

12:00 m.* for noon   12:00 p.m. for midnight
***NOTE:**   m. is used here because noon is the *meridian;* it is neither before (*a.m.*) nor after (*p.m.*).

731 ## Writing Numbers in Figures

731.1 **Comma used.** Whole numbers of four or more digits may be divided into thousands, millions, billions, trillions, and so forth, by using commas.

four thousand	4,000		
fifty thousand	50,000		
two hundred fifty thousand	250,000		
four million, two hundred fifty thousand	4,250,000	*or*	4.25 million
three billion	3,000,000,000	*or*	3 billion
sixteen trillion	16,000,000,000,000	*or*	16 trillion

731.2 **Comma omitted.** The comma is frequently omitted in writing four-digit numbers not included in a set containing numbers of five digits or more.

2836	9485	4937	2835

731.3 **Metric quantities.** Use spaces instead of commas in expressing metric quantities. In writing four-digit metric quantities, do **not** leave such a space unless the number appears in a column with at least one number of five digits or more.

2	384	874	485
	374	653	1973
	3	987	37
9	836	241	3876

732   Writing Numbers in Words

732.1 **Cardinal numbers.** Hyphenate all compound cardinal numbers (for example, twenty-three) between *twenty-one* and *ninety-nine* inclusive.

twenty-seven	thirty-eight	eighty-seven

NOTE: If a cardinal number in this range (twenty-one through ninety-nine) is part of a larger cardinal number, do not use additional hyphens.

one hundred twenty-seven   fifteen hundred thirty-eight
seven thousand three hundred eighty-seven

732.2 **Ordinal numbers.** Hyphenate all compound ordinal numbers (for example, twenty-third) between *twenty-first* and *ninety-ninth* inclusive.

twenty-seventh	thirty-eighth	eighty-seventh

NOTE: If an ordinal number in this range (twenty-first through ninety-ninth) is part of a larger cardinal number, do not use additional hyphens.

one hundred twenty-seventh   fifteen hundred thirty-eighth
seven thousand three hundred eighty-seventh

Unit VIII

Information Processing

Understand:

- The field of information processing and its components

- The field of *computer* information processing and its components

- The organization and functioning of word processing *systems*

- Computer processing of day-to-day transaction information

- Processing and subsequent use of management information

Acquire:

- The ability to prescribe effective techniques and efficient equipment for a variety of information processing tasks

- A working knowledge of how word processing, accounting, spreadsheet, and data base programs are used

- A vocabulary of word processing and computer terms

- The ability to identify common proofreader's marks

Be Prepared To:

- Compose effective business correspondence at the keyboard

- Proofread text at all levels of difficulty and correct using proofreader's marks

- Use common editing practices to improve the text of business documents

- Dictate effective business documents and edit them as necessary

801 Information Processing Explained

801.1 **Information processing described.** Most office work is information processing. To understand that concept, you will need to know how

173

the words *information* and *processing* are used in the world of computers and information processing.

Information is knowledge. It is usually expressed in characters: letters (AfDj), figures (3945), or special symbols (@#$%). Information looks like this:

(1) 2# @ $3/# = $6.

(2) two pounds at three dollars per pound equals six dollars.

(3) Melissa is 5' 8" tall; she weighs 121 pounds.

(4) Daryl is six feet one inch tall; he weighs 167 pounds.

Lines (1) and (2) contain the same information; they differ in form only.

Processing is refining data to make it more useful. Lines (3) and (4) can be made more useful (and more understandable, in this case) by expressing all the measurements of height and weight in figures—and arranging the information in tabular form.

Name	Height	Weight
Melissa	5' 8"	121
Daryl	6' 1"	167

Processing includes *compiling information* (gathering it from different sources), *categorizing information* (placing it in categories, such as accounts), *sorting information* (alphabetically, numerically, by weight, by date, and so forth), *ranking information* (by dollar value, size, ability, and the like), and other operations that refine information, making it more useful.

Processing may include calculations of all kinds. For example, if *quantity* and *price* are two items of information in the same application, having the computer multiply them together to determine the *amount* will probably be part of the processing to which the information (quantity and price) will be subjected.

Processing may also include formatting the information, which is what we did when we chose the tabular arrangement for the height and weight information.

Now suppose that Melissa and Daryl are members of the basketball team, and that we wish to compile height and weight information on all members of the team.

BASKETBALL TEAM		
Name	Height	Weight
Melissa	5' 8"	121
Daryl	6' 1"	167
Charlie	6' 6"	224
Gertie	6' 0"	159
Abner	6' 2"	219

Obviously, we could further process (refine) the information above by alphabetizing the name column, arranging the items by height or weight, and so forth.

We could add information such as age, grade, points scored, free throws made and missed, fouls committed, and other game statistics. We could *process* the *information* to produce all the statistics in which sports fans are so interested.

801.2

Information processing defined. **Information processing** is the recording and refinement of knowledge to make it more useful. Information processing systems receive, record, store, retrieve, alter, refine, transmit, or otherwise process information.

802

Information Processing Systems

It is convenient to analyze the field of information processing in terms of these major components:

a. Traditional information processing. (¶802.1–802.5)
- Hard-copy systems.
- Photographic and electronic storage and retrieval systems.

b. Computer information processing. (¶802.5–802.7)
- Word processing.
- Transaction processing.
- Management information systems.

802.1

Traditional information processing systems. Hard-copy systems and other traditional systems are discussed in other chapters in this manual (for example, Keyboarding, Business Correspondence, and Filing).

802.2

Hard-copy information systems. The most completely automated office still needs letters, memos, printed reports—all the traditional media for expressing, recording, and communicating information.

For easier access and retrieval, hard-copy information is filed in folders, bound in notebooks, and published in books and periodicals.

802.3

Photographic and electronic storage and retrieval systems. Microfilm, microfiche, and electronic recording systems of all kinds are designed to store and retrieve information **without altering it.**

Although these systems do not process information by changing it, the service of merely holding it available makes the information more useful. For that reason, library work and similar endeavors are called information services or information processing.

Some of these systems employ **some** computer technology. For example, microfilm and microfiche images can be produced directly as computer output. Storage and retrieval systems can be computerized.

802.4

Communication and transportation of information. Telephone systems, mail systems, courier systems, and the like, communicate and transport information within your office to an office across the street or to other offices across the nation and around the world. Although they are not normally thought of as information processing systems (probably because they communicate or transport information without changing it), telephone and mail systems do make information more useful simply because they get it to the people for whom it is intended.

Since telephone and mail systems carry information that is processed on all kinds of information processing systems, it is probably best to think of them as part of the system they are serving at the time: sometimes computer systems; sometimes noncomputer systems.

802.5   **Data processing.** Data processing and information processing are synonymous; data and information are synonymous.

802.6   **Computer information processing defined. Computer information processing** is the use of computers to record and refine knowledge in order to make it more useful. The major components of the field are word processing, transaction processing, and management information systems.

COMPUTER INFORMATION PROCESSING

Name of System:	Word Processing	Transaction Processing	Management Information Systems
Hardware:	Dictating Machines Word Processors Copiers Duplicators Computers	Computers	Computers
The Process:	From the unrecorded concept to the text of the finished document.	Processing the information necessary for day-to-day operation: accounts receivable, accounts payable, check processing, order entry, payroll, and so forth.	Deriving information useful to management from transaction information and other sources.

802.7   **Word processing defined. Word processing** is the sequence of operations used to record ideas, express them in text, and produce refined versions of that text in print. The writer may work alone at a word processor or may be assisted by one or more specialists who perform the highly specific tasks into which word processing can be organized. Those specialists may take shorthand (manually or on machines), operate dictating and word processing equipment, and employ other skills such as proofreading, formatting, and editing.

In its **broadest sense,** word processing encompasses all the operations from the initial recording of ideas to the final production of the document. It also includes **desktop publishing,** a process that produces entire publications with desktop equipment under the control of desktop computer software.

In its **narrowest sense,** word processing refers only to the operation of a word processor.

Word processing is used in this chapter to mean the work that begins with recording the writer's ideas and ends with the finished document. This is also the most common use of the expression *word processing*.

803 Input and Entry

803.1 **The author.** Each document begins with the ideas of an author. The author may be a professional writer—but is more likely to be a manager whose responsibilities are in sales, personnel, accounting, or a field other than writing.

Writing is a skill that is necessary in many management positions, and highly desirable in most others. It is difficult to imagine a management position in which writing is not at least a useful asset.

803.2 **Keyboard input.** As word processor hardware and software become cheaper and more useful, more authors keyboard their ideas directly into a word processor. The word processor screen is an ideal place for the author to manipulate words until they express ideas just as the author wants to express them. A thesaurus and spelling checker that remain resident in the computer while the word processing program is in use are among the most valuable tools an author can employ.

803.3 **Handwritten input.** Some authors prefer to write, draw, diagram, or outline their input directly on paper. In a few cases, the author is so effective at mental organization that the first draft on paper is usable—or requires a minimum of editing before it becomes usable.

Most authors work more effectively when they get a rough first draft on paper as soon as possible—a step that is usually the first in a series of rewrites by which the author gradually polishes the document until it is finished. For some authors, this series may consist of three or four drafts. For others, a document may go through a dozen or more drafts before the author is satisfied with it.

When there are several drafts, the word processor operator will be expected to follow the standards set by the author at each stage of production. In the early stages, the author may not require perfectly reproduced text—just a working copy. As the author refines the document, the standards will be raised, until the final version of the document is produced at the highest standards of which the author and the operator are capable.

804 Developing Dictating Skills

804.1 **The goal.** Begin each dictating session by reminding yourself that your goal is to produce documents that can withstand the most critical editing—documents that are accurate, brief, clear, direct, effective, and fluent. The same criteria that define good **editing** identify the characteristics of good **writing**, and therefore, good **dictating**.

804.2   **Dictating machines and word processors.** The dictating machine and word processor are ideal companions. Since the word processor displays text on the screen as it is written, corrections during transcription can be made by simply backspacing and keying strikeovers. (See ¶ 808.8.) Careful proofreading on the screen provides perfect text on the first printing.

Nevertheless, the text will look different on the page; corrections may be necessary even if the transcription is perfect. Those changes are easily made and subsequent drafts printed because of the ease with which text can be edited on the screen.

804.3   **Dictating and transcribing machines.** Most dictating systems employ units with which one can both dictate (record) and transcribe (play back and process). Some use single-function machines: separate units for recording and playing back.

804.4   **Indexing.** Each dictating system has one or more methods of **indexing**, locating reference points in the dictated material. Those reference points mark the locations of corrections and insertions and the beginning and end of each document.

One common indexing method employs electronic signals (beeps) placed on the recording medium when the dictator activates a control (button, lever, or the like) to indicate a reference point. Another method employs paper index strips on which reference points can be marked.

804.5   **Magnetic media.** Dictating systems employ a variety of magnetic media: disks, cards, belts, and tape in cassettes. The last, magnetic tape in cassettes, is the dominant medium.

804.6   **Organizing for dictation.** If you let the people around you, the telephone, and other distractions determine your priorities, you are not likely to find the quiet time you need to do the best job you can at dictating. Organize your *day* to give yourself the time you need for the task, then organize your *work* to use that time effectively.

    a.   Develop a system that brings the source documents you need for dictation to your desk when you are ready to dictate.

One system, called a tickler file, requires thirty-one file folders numbered from 1 through 31 and twelve file dividers—one for each month.

To use a tickler file, start by dividing the numbered folders into two stacks: 1 through today's date and tomorrow's date through 31. Put the second stack (tomorrow's number through 31) behind the guide for tomorrow's current month; put the first stack (1 through today's number) behind next month's guide.

As you receive documents that require responses, write yourself notes about future dictation, or collect information for future dictation, and file the information under the date on which you wish to bring it up for dictation.

Each morning, remove the folder for the day, remove its contents, and put the folder back in the file *behind yesterday's folder.*

b. Scan your stack of source documents quickly to see if there are top-priority matters that require your immediate attention. If necessary, make a quick telephone call, write and dispatch at once a brief note, dictate an urgent response—but do **not** be distracted from dictation by less important matters.

c. Review and place in order of priority the source documents. Begin a stack for urgent documents, one for routine but important documents, another for documents that are neither very urgent nor very important, and a fourth for documents for which you need additional source documents or additional information. Send for or get this information *before you begin to dictate.*

d. As you scan each document, make notes in the margins, brief outlines, and so forth. Use the backs of the source documents. You may wish to highlight important points, correct or update figures, and add or delete columns or categories. In documents to be revised or updated, you may wish to note reminders about the format, binding, or distribution of the document.

e. Go through all the stacks and decide on the exact order in which you will use the source documents for dictation. Number the source documents in that order.

804.7 **Dictating.** Dictating skills improve with practice. Use the following suggestions; do **not** give up and write your correspondence in longhand.

a. Think about the person or persons to whom your document is addressed. Tell your story as though they were present as you dictate. Not only will your writing sound natural and unstilted, but you will avoid almost without having to think about it the use of artificial phrases such as "will be forwarded under separate cover" (will be mailed) or "it is our wish to thank you for..." (thank you for...).

b. Dictate freely. Do not attempt to make the first draft your best formal text. Dictate naturally, then edit your work to your own satisfaction. As your dictating skills improve, you will learn to edit mentally; less rewriting will be required.

c. Dictate paragraph breaks and punctuation marks. When in doubt, create a paragraph break. Paragraphs that are a bit shorter than normal are more effective than paragraphs that are too long.

d. Use illustrations, tables, lists, and the like, freely. Give or send a copy to the person who will transcribe the dictation. Do **not** try to dictate tables, lists, and other technical data, unless doing so is absolutely necessary.

805 # Developing Transcribing Skills

805.1 **Organize for transcription.** As with most office tasks, transcription is easier and more rewarding if you are properly organized for the task.

a. Check for and transcribe first any document the author has identified as a priority document.

b. Before you begin to transcribe, do anything that done later would
interrupt your transcription.

c. Before transcribing, review references, notations on enclosures,
and so forth. Be sure you understand all special instructions. Locate any additional documents you need as enclosures or for reference; sort and correlate them to the documents by document
number.

d. Be sure you understand how each document is to be formatted.

e. Encourage each author to use a separate cassette, belt, or other
device. Keep a separate folder or bin for each author. You will
soon get to know the individual characteristics of each person
whose dictation you transcribe and how to deal with them: extra
fast or slow pace, unusual pronunciation patterns, and so forth.

f. Before transcribing, decide whether to keyboard a draft and then
a finished copy or to try for a finished copy the first time. Whether
or not you should type a draft depends on the difficulty of the
material, the recording skill employed by the author, and your
own transcribing skill. If you are in doubt, it is probably better to
format a draft. Some authors write best by editing a draft; some
may require several drafts before the finished text suits them.

g. Once you are familiar with the style of each author and with the
characteristics of your equipment, you will be able to estimate
the length of each dictated document by using the indexing
method built into your system.

805.2   **Transcribing.** Once you are organized for transcription, try to concentrate—and minimize interruptions. Controlling interruptions is not always possible, but it is an important goal to keep in mind as you plan
your daily routine.

a. If there is any doubt about an address, title, date, number, or
other data, confirm the correctness of the information before
transcribing that document.

b. If you are transcribing from shorthand notes, keep your eyes on
your notes. If you are using a dictation machine, keep your eyes
on the screen of your word processor or the paper in your typewriter.

c. Listen or read ahead to identify trouble spots before you reach
them. Develop a pace that allows you to work steadily and with
a minimum of errors. A pace that is just beyond your ability to
transcribe accurately is much less efficient than one that allows
you to work within your ability.

d. It is usually best for the author to dictate punctuation marks and paragraph breaks. However, not all do so. It is a good idea to remain alert for needed but undictated punctuation marks and paragraph breaks.

e. Unless you know that an author does not encourage the use of tables, take every opportunity to tabulate text. Tables are usually clearer and more effective than ordinary text.

Text can be itemized using bullets (●), numbers, or letters. Make bullets by keyboarding lowercase o's and then filling them in with a black pen.

● Bullets	1. Numbers	A. Capital Letters	a. Lowercase Letters
●	2.	B.	b.
●	3.	C.	c.

f. Keep a dictionary, reference manual, thesaurus, word division manual, and calculator within reach.

g. As each document is finished, recheck it for coherence and completeness. Be sure that all enclosures are in place and that copies have been prepared for those scheduled to receive them.

806 Correcting and Revising Text

806.1 **Proofreading defined.** **Proofreading** is the comparison of reproduced text with the original and the marking of errors on the former.

806.2 **Proofreading techniques.** The key to effective proofreading is concentration. The following are some techniques that will help you develop the ability to concentrate on finding *all* the errors the *first* time:

a. Establish a routine for proofreading. Many typists proofread each page before the sheet is removed from the typewriter. Word processor operators may proofread each screen before it is scrolled out of sight but wait until a section or chapter is finished to run the text through a spelling checker. (Some "realtime" spelling checkers check each word as it is keyed, beeping when the machine does not recognize the word.)

b. Match copy and proof. Check the text you have written against the original. Your text may be on the screen (not yet printed) or on paper. The original may be recorded on a dictating medium *or* printed or written on paper. If both the original and your text are on paper, you may wish to *match* them for proofreading each line by performing the following steps:

1. Lay the sheet containing the text you have written flat on the desk in front of you.

2. Grasp the original between the thumbs and fingers of both hands in normal reading position.

3. Place the original on top of the text that you have printed, rolling the bottom of the original back and under your fingertips so that only the first line of writing is visible.

4. Match this line with the first line of the text you have keyboarded.

5. Compare and check the text you have printed against the original. Roll the original up each time you finish a line, matching the two versions line for line until you reach the bottom of the page.

c. Read for content. After proofreading the document against the copy, read it again (without referring to the copy) for coherence and completeness. Does it make sense? Is there anything missing? It is easy to check all the areas in which you expect to find errors (difficult or obscure words misspelled, errors in punctuation, and the like) only to find entire words omitted, words written twice, or simple words misspelled — in headings or other obvious places.

d. Read aloud when proofreading. Ordinary text in typical documents is routinely proofread by the person who formats the reproduced text on a typewriter or word processor. Normally, the operator works alone, comparing the original and the reproduced text directly.

Some operators, faced with large or complex proofreading tasks, prefer to read the original into a dictating machine and then compare the reproduced text to the recorded text.

Some prefer to work with another person: one reads from the original while the other checks the reproduced text for correctness.

806.3   **Typical errors found in proofreading.** The following are some typical errors uncovered in the proofreading process:

a. Transposed letters.

This is the third time we   This is the third time we

b. Transposed words.

That is best the way to go   That is the best way to go

c. Omitted letter.

When the wilow tree was the   When the willow tree was the

d. Omitted word.

How were wearing our   How we were wearing our

e. Repeated letter.

There weere more than enough   There were more than enough

f. Repeated word.

When they ~~they~~ went to the   When they went to the

g. Errors or inconsistencies in paragraphing or indentation.

This was the first time that   This was the first time
the engine had failed to sta   the engine had failed to sta

806.4

Proofreader's marks. Proofreader's marks are used not only by those who read proof for publishers and printers, but by almost all who need to indicate corrections in text.

Proofreader's marks are sometimes applied at the location of the change:

Before Change	After Change
when i move	when I move
I ⌒when⌒ move	when I move

Proofreader's marks may appear in the margins instead of at the location of the change. When the former are used, *supplementary marks* are used *in the text* to indicate the exact location of the change.

Change	Mark in Margin	Supplementary Mark in Text	After Change
Align	‖	‖words on a list	words on a list
Capitalize	(Cap)	new york	New York
Close up space	⌒	win ter	winter
Delete	ℓ	leave out the	leave the
Delete and close up space	⌒ℓ	people	people
Insert	out	leave the	leave out the
Insert apostrophe	∨	Marie s dress	Marie's dress
Insert asterisk	✻	the end but	the end,* but
Insert brackets	[/]	run fast now	run [fast] now
Insert colon	⌃:	follow these steps	follow these steps:
Insert comma	⌃	ham, eggs and toast	ham, eggs, and toast
Insert diagonal	Ⓞ	and or the former	and/or the former
Insert hyphen	⊝	do it yourself project	do-it-yourself project
Insert parenthesis	(/)	run fast now	run (fast) now

Change	Mark in Margin	Supplementary Mark in Text	After Change
Insert period	⊙	the end͜	the end.
Insert quotation marks	ˇ/ˇ	the ˇend.ˇ	the "end."
Insert semicolon	⌃;	Row ͜row͜ row.	Row; row; row.
Insert space	#	the/space	the space
Let stand	stet	best well-wisher	best well-wisher
Lowercase	lc	the Summer season	the summer season
Move down	⌴	dowⁿ	down
Move left	⌐	move ⌐left	move left
Move right	⌐	move right⌐	move right
Move up	⌐	u⌐p	up
Spell out	sp	wouldn't run	would not run
Begin a paragraph	¶	⌃The first line and the second	The first line and the second
Straighten the line	═══	straighten the line	straighten the line
Transpose	tr	first to strike	to strike first

806.5 **Editing described.** Editing goes beyond the correction of mechanical errors in spelling, punctuation, format, and the like, to the improvement of the text itself—refining it in order to achieve higher levels of accuracy, brevity, clarity, directness, effectiveness, and fluency. Most writers edit their own text as an integral part of the writing process. They do their best work by producing several drafts, each somewhat more refined than its predecessor.

The first draft may be quite rough as long as the most important ideas are recorded. Careful and repeated editing through several additional drafts gradually shapes the rough first draft into the polished text that careful writers require of themselves.

Good writers and editors are always in demand—not necessarily to write best-selling novels or Hollywood screen plays, but to write the countless documents that are vital to the success of most business firms. Most people who do office work have a part in the *paperwork* that keeps the office going. One of the criteria by which they are evaluated, formally and informally, is the quality of their written work. In a very real sense, most office workers who hold positions of responsibility are *writers*, *proofreaders*, and *editors*.

806.6   **Editing the work of others.** If you edit the work of others, it is best to do so as diplomatically as possible. Offer suggestions, not sarcasm. Be sure of your facts. If you ridicule another person's writing, then turn out to be wrong, you can expect resentment on that person's part and embarrassment on your own.

Use notes written in the margins to explain any unusual changes. Question, explain, and suggest; do not dictate. Unless you have the authority to make unilateral changes, make it apparent in your manner that you are *suggesting* changes to improve the text. This is particularly important if you are editing the work of your boss.

Finally, try to avoid editing the work of anyone who rejects improvements. Some writers will continue to use words imprecisely, to write redundantly, and to litter their text with excess verbiage despite any advice they get. If your boss is one of these, it is probably best to avoid editing his or her work if you can. You are unlikely to improve either the text or your working relationship.

806.7   **Accuracy.** Question the accuracy of the text as you edit. Did the runner run the mile in 4.2 *seconds,* or should it be 4.2 *minutes?* How can net profit be greater than gross sales? Did the committee really *assume* their discussion after the break, or should it be *resume?*

Using the right word is very important. "No reading *aloud"* means that reading out loud is not permitted; "no reading *allowed"* means that all reading, including reading to oneself, is prohibited. The decedent who left her estate to be divided "equally *between* my niece and two nephews" intended that her estate be divided in *three* equal shares; however, the wording she used (*between* instead of *among* — see   143) indicates that the niece is to receive half the estate and the two nephews are to share the other half.

806.8   **Brevity.** Among reasonably literate writers, wordiness is probably the most common fault. The most direct way to improve your writing is to see how many words you can delete without changing the meaning or weakening the impact of your text.

a. Ordinary redundancy. Compare the following two sentences:

A word processing computer software program used in conjunction with a general-purpose digital computer can make possible greatly facilitated and easier editing of text on the screen of the monitor of the computer.

A general-purpose computer, programmed for word processing, makes the convenience of on-screen editing possible.

b. Redundancy of context. Once you have established the context (framework) within which you are writing, do not restate it unnecessarily.

Period instead of *period of time* in a document on punctuality, scheduling, and the like, where a *time* period will not be confused with the *punctuation mark.*

Tire instead of *automobile tire* in a document on automobiles or automobile tires.

806.9   Clarity. The best text is unambiguous and unmistakable.

> **Ambiguous:** She slammed the book down on the table and struck it with her fist.
> **Clear:**   She slammed the book down and struck the table with her fist.
>
> **Ambiguous:** He removed the boat from the trailer and painted it.
> **Clear:**   Having removed the boat, he painted the trailer.
>
> **Ambiguous:** Go to the second traffic light and turn left.
> **Clear:**   Go to the second traffic light (not counting the one overhead) and turn left.

806.10   Directness. Text can be written in a brief and clear style but still lack a compelling effect because it wanders indiscriminately toward its conclusions, distracting the reader with extraneous material. Get directly to the point through the orderly development of ideas. To do this, you need organization, a plan. Decide where to begin (how much background is necessary) and where to end (how much elaboration, if any, is needed once you have reached your conclusions). Careful outlining is the best way to eliminate unnecessary detours on your road to a conclusion.

If you are writing a piece on cleaning up Jackson's Pond in Titusville, there is probably no need to begin with a history of the environmental movement and conclude with the importance of Titusville to the nation's economy.

In some cases, it is desirable to put the central portion of a document into historic or geographic perspective, or to enrich the document by taking a few byways along the direct route. When the writer decides to digress, the digressions should be purposeful and well planned.

A composition may move logically from premise, through proof, to conclusion (Proper Maintenance Reduces Costs); it may explain how a process, machine, or principle works (The Roundabout Process of Production); it may appeal first to the intellect and then to the emotions (Why a Convertible Makes Sense for Me); it may be organized chronologically (My Trip), or proceed from bottom to top (The Oak Tree), or front to back (The Automobile).

Notice how the beginning of the following composition on the building of a house proceeds chronologically and from bottom to top. Notice also how it conveys growing solidity and strength as the house is constructed.

> The building gathered strength as it grew to fill the space between the thick layer of solid rock on which it was beginning to rest and the future location of its own ridgepole. One day, massive amounts of concrete were poured into the foundation forms, mating with the rock below and rising to support the upper members of the structure that were to come.
>
> Soon, wooden joists spanned the concrete walls of the foundation. Then, in rapid succession, came the subfloor, supports, rafters, and ridgepole. Each new member, carefully joined to its neighbors, added strength and solidity to the structure.

806.11   Effectiveness. Writing, to be effective, must have a purpose. The purpose may be to **inform, persuade, describe,** or **narrate.**

a. Exposition. **Expository** writing is undertaken
    to cause the reader to know or understand some
    subject. Although expository writing may persuade,
    clude a story (narrative), or rely partly on sensory perce
    (descriptive), its primary purpose is to explain: how a proce
    works, the importance of a historic event, a social problem, a
    political battle, and so forth.

b. Argument. **Argument** is written to persuade — to convince the
    reader. The appeal may be logical, using the informative tech-
    niques employed in exposition. The appeal may also be emo-
    tional, based on psychological factors such as the desire for
    affection, status, comfort, or security. Patrick Henry used infor-
    mation, logic, *and* emotion to craft his now famous argument.

c. Description. **Description** is the written sharing of the author's
    sensory perceptions: a beautiful sunset, a feeling of power, a nos-
    talgic experience.

d. Narration. **Narration** describes events, real or imaginary, within
    a framework of time (but not necessarily in chronological order).

e. Combining exposition, argument, description, and narration. Most
    compositions have more than one purpose and, therefore, em-
    ploy more than one writing style. While a novel may be primar-
    ily narrative, it is almost certain to contain a generous amount
    of description — and likely to contain lesser amounts of both ex-
    position and argument.

    An expository composition on a machine or process is likely
    to contain a discussion of the subject's effect on the writer, its so-
    cial or economic impact, and so forth.

    It would be difficult to advance most arguments without ex-
    plaining, describing, or using narrative examples.

806.12   **Fluency.** **Fluency** is the ability to use language with ease and grace —
to evoke explicit visual images and lucid abstractions that allow the
writer to communicate effectively with the reader.

a. Fluency and pretentious writing. Fluency should not be confused
    with pretentious writing, the unnecessary use of elaborate lan-
    guage. Fluent writing has the beauty and utility that can be
    achieved through simplicity; pretentious writing is ornate, but
    not necessarily beautiful or useful.

    Pretentious writing: Contemplating, the youth reclined in a supine po-
    sition and observed the visible nocturnal celestial
    bodies.

    Fluent writing: Deep in thought, the boy lay on his back and
    watched the moon and stars.

b. Fluent writing is evocative. Fluent writing evokes *explicit, se-
    quential, visual images,* as if the reader were leafing through a
    picture book.

.ten on the leg by a large red dog.

s:

∍n	Difficult to visualize when the reader does not know where or by what (whom?) the writer was bitten.
.e leg	Now the reader can visualize a leg, but the image of the bite remains indistinct. If this is a piece on dogs, the reader may visualize a dog bite — only to find that the sentence reads *I was bitten on the leg by a flea*.
by a large red dog.	Now the reader has the picture.

Fluent: A large red dog bit me on the leg.

Visual images:

A large red dog	The reader visualizes a large red dog.
bit me	Now the dog opens its mouth, bares its teeth, and prepares to bite.
on the leg.	Now the reader visualizes the dog biting the writer's leg.

806.13   Writing to obscure. The foregoing principles and examples presume the writer's intent to be effective and to communicate efficiently. If, however, the writer's intent is to shock, entertain, or mystify, then obscurity, ambiguity, and misleading visual imagery may be used to realize that intent.

> There, surrounded by barking, snapping dogs, I was bitten on the leg — by a flea.
> Henry said, "I heard Wanda say to the nurse that *she* killed the gardener." [Did Wanda say that *Wanda* killed the gardener, or did Wanda say that the *nurse* killed the gardener?]

807   Word Processing Systems

807.1   Components of a word processing system — hardware. The visible parts of a typical word processing system are the keyboard, system unit with disk drives, video monitor, and printer. Most of the electronic components (including memory) are out of sight inside the system unit.

807.2   Dedicated word processors. Dedicated word processors are specialized minicomputers that are built expressly for heavy-duty word processing. "Dedicated" means that these machines are not designed as or equipped for use as general-purpose computers.

Typically, a dedicated word processor is larger than a microcomputer, but small enough to fit on (*or* in) a special office-sized desk.

807.3   Microcomputers. A general-purpose microcomputer (desktop computer), loaded with a word processing program, is a capable, flexible word processor.

187

807.4

Dot matrix printers. **Dot matrix printers** form the image of each character by rearranging the pins that print the dots. If the dots are closely spaced, the quality of the printing may be near, but not equal to, that of a true letter quality printer (LQP).

Dot matrix printers (particularly those designed for graphics) can print graphs, charts, diagrams, and the like, but cannot compete with laser printers in producing quality text or graphics.

807.5

Letter quality printers. **Letter quality printers** (mostly **daisy wheel** printers—so called because of the shape of their printing elements) print text of the highest quality. They are, however, comparatively slow and have almost no graphics capability other than the ability to produce lines, charts, graphs, and the like, that require no drawing more complicated than straight horizontal and vertical rules.

807.6

Laser printers and desktop publishing. **Laser printers** can produce quality text and graphics of all kinds; they are widely used to produce camera-ready copy for offset reproduction. A microcomputer with a laser printer and an offset duplicating system constitute a complete desktop publishing system that is capable of printing line copy of all kinds economically and in quantity.

Laser printers are expensive, typically costing eight to ten times as much as a dot matrix or daisy wheel printer. Special, rather tedious programs or program routines are required for page makeup and printer control. Currently, this is an area of rapid technological change; both hardware and software are improving and prices are falling.

807.7   **Electronic typewriters. Electronic typewriters** have all the features of electric typewriters, plus limited text memory, correction memory, and text display. Typically, electronic typewriters can display a few words of text on a small display strip.

It is possible to equip some electronic typewriters with disk drives that provide additional storage — permanent storage. Some electronic typewriters can be used as computer printers.

As electronic typewriters become more sophisticated and as less expensive microcomputers are marketed, it seems apparent that we shall soon see an unbroken spectrum of systems ranging from the full-blown microcomputer-word processor at the top of the field down to the simplest electric typewriter.

807.8   **Word processing programs — software.** The software that enables a computer to function as a word processor is called a **word processing program.** The program is a set of instructions stored on a disk. After the program is *loaded* from the disk to memory (inside the system unit), the program will control all machine functions, responding to the commands issued by the operator through the keyboard.

808   # Keyboarding on the Word Processor

808.1   **The word processor as a typewriter.** The best way to understand the operation of a word processor is to begin by imagining the word processor as a typewriter. Information is keyboarded as it would be on a typewriter. If the word processor or computer is loaded with a simple program designed for typewriter emulation, the printer will print the character represented by each keystroke as you press the key, just as a typewriter does. You key in your name; the machine prints your name — just as a typewriter would.

808.2   **Word wrap.** When you come to the end of a line, however, you will encounter the first difference between the word processor and the typewriter: you do not have to press the carriage return key (on a word processor it is called the **enter key**).

As you approach the end of the line, each word keyed is **wrapped** around the end of the line, its beginning on the old line and its end on the new line. When the space following the word is keyed in, the entire word is *pulled* back to the old line *if it will fit there,* or *pushed* forward to the new line *if it will not fit on the old line.*

The cursor moves to the new line; keyboarding and entry continue there — without use of the carriage return or enter key.

808.3 **Displaying text on the monitor.** If a slight change is made in the typewriter emulation program, each character will appear on the *screen* as it is keyed (instead of being *printed* as it is keyed).

In normal operation, text is displayed on the screen as it is keyboarded; then it is edited (on the screen); then it is printed, or stored on a disk, or both. Be sure to "save" copy as you go along to avoid loss of data.

808.4 **Editing keys.** All word processing programs use function keys for editing. Each program assigns the keys differently; consequently, the Function-3 key may insert a blank line in one program and move a block of text in another. All the leading word processing programs have similar (but not identical) commands — despite the differences in key assignments.

808.5 **The cursor.** The **cursor** is a character, usually the underscore or a character-sized solid rectangle, that can be moved around the screen using the cursor keys. These keys, usually in a separate group, are identified with up, down, left, and right arrows indicating the direction in which each key moves the cursor.

The cursor always indicates the point at which the next character keyboarded will appear on the screen.

808.6 **Insert key.** The **insert** key is a toggle key: press it once and the system is in *insert* mode, press it again and the system is in *replace* mode. Press it again and the system is back in *insert* mode, and so forth.

808.7 **Replace mode.** The easiest way to correct a simple error is to backspace or use the cursor key(s) to get to the first character that is to be corrected and key the correct text directly over that which is incorrect. When the system is in **replace mode,** the new (correct) text replaces the old (incorrect) text on the screen, character by character as the new text is entered. In this case, there is no such thing as a strikeover — the new character *replaces* the old one.

808.8 **Insert mode.** If the system is in **insert mode,** newly keyed text will be inserted by pushing the old text forward. In the following example, the text should read *are not able to.*

Incorrect text:	are able to
Set cursor at the *a* in *able*:	are able to
Key *n*:	are nable to
Key *o*:	are noable to
Key *t*:	are notable to
Key *space*:	are not able to

808.9 **Deletion key.** The **deletion key** causes the character at the cursor to be deleted. All characters and spaces on the current line to the right of the point of the deletion move left one space.

Before deletion:	I tooke a look.
After deletion of e:	I took a look.

808.10   **Centering.** Centering is automatic. Simply key the line to be centered at the left margin (or any other place on the line) then press the function key(s) designated to control centering.

808.11   **Underlining and boldfacing for emphasis.** A special **control character** (the exact character varies with different word processing programs) is inserted in the text to begin automatic underlining or boldfacing; another such character is inserted at the point at which underlining or boldfacing is to end.

808.12   **Selecting a block of text.** A single character, a word, a sentence, a paragraph, or a number of paragraphs can be moved, copied, or deleted in a single operation *after* the block has been *selected*.
                To select a block of text:

    a. Move the cursor to the first character in the block.

    b. Enter the command your word processing program uses to designate a block, something like *Alternate B*.

> This will not be highlighted,
> but the following sentence will.
> This text is highlighted. It is
> the portion that will be moved,
> copied, or deleted. The text
> that is not highlighted will not
> be affected.
>
> *Text Before Highlighting*

    c. Move the cursor to the last character in the block; enter the block command again. This will cause the text you have selected to be highlighted.

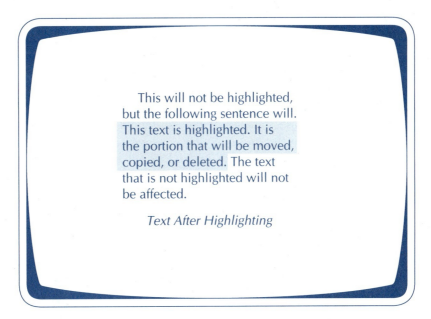

> This will not be highlighted, but the following sentence will. This text is highlighted. It is the portion that will be moved, copied, or deleted. The text that is not highlighted will not be affected.
>
> *Text After Highlighting*

808.13 **Moving a block of text.** To move a block you have selected, first move the cursor to the location to which you want the block moved. Then press the key your word processor uses to move a block, perhaps the letter *m*. The block will disappear from its original location and appear in the place you have designated.

808.14 **Deleting a block of text.** To delete a block you have selected, press the key(s) your word processing program uses to delete a block, perhaps the letter *d*. The selected block will disappear and the remaining text will close the gap.

808.15 **Copying a block of text.** To copy a block you have selected, move the cursor to the point at which you want the block copied. Press the key your word processing program uses to copy a block, perhaps the letter *c*. The block will be copied and inserted at the place you designated. The original of the block will remain in its initial location.

808.16 **Reformatting.** As a paragraph is edited, line fragments are forced past the end of the line to the beginning of the next. This process causes fragmentation of the next line, and the next, and the next, until the end of a paragraph is reached.

The leading word processors automatically reformat a paragraph that breaks up because of insertions. Normally, hyphens previously used for word division would be (improperly) placed within the line when the text is reformatted. To avoid unwanted hyphens after reformatting, each hyphen can be identified as a normal hyphen, optional hyphen, or non-breaking hyphen.

808.17 **Normal hyphens.** A **normal hyphen** (in a hyphenated word) is always visible. Even if you divide the word after the hyphen and the paragraph is reformatted, the hyphen will remain visible. For example, if you use a *normal* hyphen in *South-Western* and end the line after the hyphen, the word will appear as *South-Western* even if the text is reformatted and *South-* is no longer at the end of the line.

808.18   Optional hyphen. An **optional hyphen** is visible only when the word is divided at the end of a line. For example, if you use an *optional* hyphen in *South-western,* the word will be printed *South-western* if it is divided at the end of a line between *South-* and *western,* but it will be printed *Southwestern* (undivided) if it is printed on one line.

808.19   Nonbreaking hyphen. Use a **nonbreaking hyphen** if you do not want the word divided—even at the end of a line. For example, if you use a *nonbreaking* hyphen in *South-Western,* both words and the hyphen will be printed on the same line—the current line if there is room, the next line if there is not.

809   ## Special Word Processing Features

809.1   Spelling checkers. All leading word processing programs include routines for checking spelling. When a designated function key is pressed, the program begins scanning forward at the cursor, checking each word against a master spelling list. When a word is not known to the program, a window on the screen gives the operator these options:

  1. Ignore the word and continue the spelling check.

  2. Display a list of correctly spelled words, one of which will probably be the word desired.

  3. If the word is correctly spelled but is not on the word list (a proper noun such as your own name, a very obscure word, or the like) you can indicate that you want the word added to your **additional word list.** This list will be applied automatically whenever you spell check. You can add words to it and delete words from it.

If the second option is chosen, the list is displayed—along with instructions and a new list of options. Suppose the program has detected a word spelled *wirk,* and you have chosen option 2, asking for a display of correctly spelled words. A new window will open in the screen; it will look something like this:

<u>wiry</u>
wire
wink
work
wick
whir

Obviously, the correct spelling of your word is *work*. Press the cursor down key ↓ three times to highlight the word chosen; press the enter key. The word *work* will be substituted automatically for the incorrect *wirk*.

809.2 **Thesauri.** When you are composing at the keyboard, and you cannot think of the exact word you want, you can use a designated function key to enter the **thesaurus mode** (if your software offers this option). To see the synonyms for a word:

1. Enter the best word you can think of for your purpose. Move the cursor to any letter in that word.

2. Press the function key designated for synonyms. The program will highlight the word you have chosen and display a list of synonyms.

3. Choose the best word for your purpose; move the cursor to that word; press the enter key. The word of your choice will replace the original word with which you were not satisfied.

809.3 **Merge.** A **merge feature** in a word processing program permits the automatic insertion of variable information (a different name and address for each copy of a letter, for example) into form letters or other "boilerplate" (canned text).

The term **boilerplate** probably originated in journalism, with respect to which it refers to newspaper mastheads, syndicated columns, and the like, that fill up space with no effort on the part of the newspaper staff. It is also attributed to the law profession, wherein "canned" paragraphs supply the routine parts of contracts, wills, and other such documents; the attorney supplies the custom-written portion. Literally, boilerplate is the semifinished material from which boilers are made.

809.4 **Macro capabilities.** Macro routines are built into sophisticated programs of all kinds: word processors, spread sheets, and so forth.

A **macro routine** permits the operator to *record* a series of keystrokes, assigning the entire series to a single key (sometimes a pair of keys). An entire string of text can be assigned to a single key or key combination and subsequently be recalled with one or two keystrokes.

809.5 **Storing a document on a disk.** If you plan to save a document that has been entered and edited, you can store it on a disk by using a designated function key. You will be prompted for a filename. Usually, the filename must be no longer than eight characters.

When you key in the filename and then press the enter key, your document will be stored on a disk. You might choose a filename such as MYDOC for the name of your document.

809.6 **Retrieving a file.** At any time — now, next week, or next year — you can retrieve your document from the disk, call it back into memory, and display it on the screen. You would call for it by its filename: MYDOC.

809.7 **Using a retrieved file.** After a file has been retrieved, it can be edited or revised and printed as described in ¶810. The retrieved document can be stored under the same name (MYDOC), or given a new name such as MYNEWDOC.

If the same name is used (MYDOC), the revised version will replace the old version on the disk.

If a new name is used (MYNEWDOC) the new version will be filed separately under the new name; the old MYDOC will remain intact. Both versions (MYDOC and MYNEWDOC) will be present on the disk.

810   Formatting and Printing

810.1   **Formatting: screen and printer.** Formatting on the screen consists of setting margins and tab stops. Formatting on the printer consists of setting page length; type pitch; and double, single, or quadruple spacing. The left margin can be reset on the printer to move the text that is on the screen to the right, if that is desirable.

810.2   **Automatic formatting.** A word processor with **automatic page formatting** will store the format with the document on a disk. When the document is retrieved, the format is automatically retrieved and is instantly ready for use in editing or revising the document on the screen, or for printing it on the printer.

If a stored format is not to be applied, the new format must be set by the operator.

810.3   **Setting the screen format.** A designated function key calls to the screen the design used to set the screen format. Such a design may look something like this:

```
--------\----+---+----------------------------------------------------------/-------
```

This screen format shows margins set at 10 and 73, tab stops at 15 and 20.

810.4   **Setting printer format.** If no automatic format has been applied, the operator must enter the printer format by responding to the format menu:

CURRENT FORMAT

PRINTER TYPE 8
PAGINATION (Y/N) ....Y
LINES PER PAGE (2-255) 60
    FIRST TEXT LINE...............................3
    LAST TEXT LINE 54
LEFT MARGIN...1
EXTRA SPACING BETWEEN LINES 0
CONTINUOUS FORMS (Y/N) ....N
CHARACTERS PER INCH (10) (12) (15) 12

Format includes margins and tab stops.

810.5 **Printing.** Once a new format has been entered or an old format has been called from a disk file, one or two key strokes will cause the printer to print the document you have entered and edited.

811 ## Spreadsheets

811.1 **Spreadsheets and worksheets.** The accountant's multipurpose worksheet is the most useful single accounting form. Spreadsheets computerize the worksheet, making it easier to use, because all the calculations are automatic and immediate.

811.2 **The "what if" feature.** A single change on a spreadsheet may cause a number of other changes. On a computerized spreadsheet, all the changes will be shown automatically. Therefore, it is possible to try many combinations of factors to get the desired results. In trying to balance a budget, for example, one can try every conceivable way to increase income or decrease expenses—without having to recalculate each time a change is made.

The "what if" feature can answer such questions as the following:
- What if I get a 12% increase in salary?
- What if my income is decreased by 10%?
- What if I throw caution to the winds and take a Caribbean cruise this year?

811.3 **Capacity of spreadsheets.** Huge quantities of numeric information can be maintained on a single spreadsheet—and multiple sheets can be used to make the capacity even greater. Even modestly priced spreadsheet programs have 50 or more columns and 250 or more lines.

The "sheet" is actually an *imaginary* sheet stored in computer memory. Imagine a sheet of paper four feet wide and four feet high with 50 columns and 250 lines printed in regular pica type. Now imagine placing an empty 8" × 10" picture frame on the spreadsheet. The picture frame can be moved around to "see" every cell on the spreadsheet—but not all can be seen at the same time. (A **cell** is the rectangular intersection of a *column* and a *line*. The intersection of column *d* and line 12 is identified as *cell d12*).

811.4 **The capacity of the screen.** As with the picture frame, the screen can be moved around relative to the spreadsheet; it can see any section of the spreadsheet. Typically, the screen can see at one time 8 columns and 23 lines.

The entire spreadsheet (50 columns by 250 lines) contains 12,500 cells. The screen can see 184 cells, or less than 2 percent of the entire spreadsheet, at one time.

811.5 **Spreadsheet example.** In the following example, a spreadsheet program has been used to design a simple budget report. We have retrieved spreadsheet BUDGET from the disk on which it remains permanently and displayed it on the screen.

When we called the spreadsheet BUDGET file from the disk to the screen, the formulas were part of the sheet. They are not visible on the spreadsheet itself but are shown one at a time at the bottom (or top) of the screen as the cursor is moved from cell to cell. If the cursor is in a cell that does not contain a formula, no formula is shown at the bottom/top of the screen.

When the cursor is at cell h2, a notation near the cell reference on the screen will read *Formula: sum(b2...g2).* The three dots mean "everything between." The formula says that cell h2 will contain the sum of "everything between" cell b2 and cell g2, or b2 + c2 + d2 + e2 + f2 + g2. A designated row of cells, horizontal or vertical, is called a **range.**

SPREADSHEET BUDGET

1	a	b January	c February	d March	e April	f May	g June	h Total
2	INCOME							
3	**
4	Taxes							
5	Rent							
6	Food							
7	Misc Exp							
8	TOT EXP							
9	**
10	Savings							
11	Savings %							

Formula: sum(b2 . . . g2)

The cursor is at cell h2. The formula for that cell is shown at the lower left corner of the spreadsheet. As the cursor is moved from cell to cell, the formula for the cell in view will appear in this position—if the cell has a formula.

The formulas for *all cells* that have formulas are shown in the illustration below. The cells highlighted in blue are those in which information must be entered if the budget is to be complete.

SPREADSHEET BUDGET

1	a	b January	c February	d March	e April	f May	g June	h Total
2	INCOME		b2	b2	b2	b2	b2	sum (b2...g2)
3	**

4	Taxes	b2 × .17	c2 × .17	d2 × .17	e2 × .17	f2 × .17	g2 × .17	sum (b4 ... g4)
5	Rent		b5	b5	b5	b5	b5	sum (b5 ... g5)
6	Food							sum (b6 ... g6)
7	Misc Exp							sum (b7 ... g7)
8	TOT EXP	sum (b4 ... b7)	sum (c4 ... c7)	sum (d4 ... d7)	sum (e4 ... e7)	sum (f4 ... f7)	sum (g4 ... g7)	sum (b8 ... g8)
9	**							
10	Savings	b2 − b8	c2 − c8	d2 − d8	e2 − e8	f2 − f8	g2 − g8	sum (b10 ... g10)
11	Savings %	b10/b2	c10/c2	d10/d2	e10/e2	f10/f2	g10/g2	h10/h2

To complete the example, we shall first enter 2000.00 for January income in cell b2. The calculated amounts in the thirteen other cells shown will appear automatically.

	a	b January	c February	d March	e April	f May	g June	h Total
1								
2	INCOME	2000.00	2000.00	2000.00	2000.00	2000.00	2000.00	12000.00
3	**							
4	Taxes	340.00	340.00	340.00	340.00	340.00	340.00	2040.00

Monthly income is $2000.00, total income for the 6-month period is $12,000.00. Taxes are calculated at 17 percent of gross income.

Next we shall enter January rent of $520.00 in cell b5. The same amount ($520.00) will be recorded automatically for the five other months. Total rent will be calculated automatically and will appear in cell h5.

5	Rent	520.00	520.00	520.00	520.00	520.00	520.00	3120.00

Food expenses vary from month to month; consequently, we shall use actual expenditures from last year. Therefore, there is no automatic calculation other than that for the total appearing in cell h5.

6	Food	321.52	267.57	346.10	283.52	275.26	315.04	1809.01

Miscellaneous expenses also vary from month to month; hence, they are treated in the same manner.

7 Misc Exp	480.59	621.21	523.97	413.54	582.84	662.47	3284.62

The rest of the spreadsheet is calculated automatically.

	a	b	c	d	e	f	g	h
1		January	February	March	April	May	June	Total
2	INCOME	2000.00	2000.00	2000.00	2000.00	2000.00	2000.00	12000.00
3	***
4	Taxes	340.00	340.00	340.00	340.00	340.00	340.00	2040.00
5	Rent	520.00	520.00	520.00	520.00	520.00	520.00	3120.00
6	Food	321.52	267.57	346.10	283.52	275.26	315.04	1809.01
7	Misc Exp	480.59	621.21	523.97	413.54	582.84	662.47	3284.62
8	TOT EXP	1662.11	1748.78	1730.07	1557.06	1718.10	1837.51	10253.63
9	***
10	Savings	337.89	251.22	269.93	442.94	281.90	162.49	1746.37
11	Savings %	17	13	13	22	14	8	15

811.6 **General spreadsheet applications.** Spreadsheets are used in transaction processing to computerize many traditional accounting reports, including worksheets, income statements, and balance sheets.

They may be used as journals or ledgers by using only the traditional number of columns — typically debit, credit, and balance.

Spreadsheets are also used for *management information* reports, especially those that answer questions such as "What will happen to profits if we eliminate Product X?"

812 ## Data Base Systems

812.1 **Purposes of data base systems.** The purposes of **data base systems** are the consolidation of files and the coordination of applications.

Before a data base system is installed, some of the computer files of a firm might look like this:

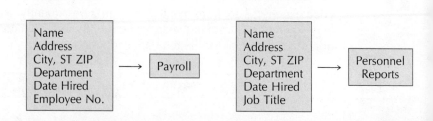

Payroll File		**Personnel File**	
Name Address City, ST ZIP Department Date Hired Employee No.	→ Payroll	Name Address City, ST ZIP Department Date Hired Job Title	→ Personnel Reports

After a data base system is installed, the data base might look like this:

Data Base

812.2   **Using a data base.** Whether it is the accounting department processing a payroll, the personnel department compiling a report, or some other department working on an entirely different project, any department (with access) in the firm can enter the employee number and thereby retrieve all the information currently on file for the employee. The information can be rearranged to suit the format and purposes of the user.

Access codes are used to limit each user to the information for which that user has a need. This device protects the confidentiality of the employee's file. Similarly, limitations are placed on the authority to *add* information to the file.

812.3   **Efficiency and economy.** Data base systems permit the use of a single data base by all users. With a single set of files to be updated, it is more likely that the information used will be accurate and current. The elimination of duplicate effort also reduces costs.

Properly administered, a centralized data base can provide greater accuracy, improved management information reporting, and reduced costs.

812.4   **Single-user applications.** A data base does not have to be shared among *users* to be useful. It may be shared among *applications* by a single user. For example, if you manage an apartment building, country club, lawn service, laundry, wholesale business, or any other organization in which you deal with the same people time after time, a data base system is likely to be useful if several applications require the same information in different formats.

812.5   **Data base systems and management information.** Management information systems are designed to provide the information upon which sound business decisions can be made by management.

A data base is usually the central structure in a management information system. One of the functions of such a system is to respond to queries such as "List and describe our customers who have switched from Brand A to Brand B in the last six months and summarize the reasons they give for switching" or "Tabulate the standard statistics on all the left-handed minor league pitchers over six feet tall who play west of the Mississippi."

The ability of a data base to store an item of information so that it can be retrieved in every possible combination with other items makes a data base a valuable management information tool.

812.6   **Client tracking.** Another useful data base application is a client tracking system that can be used to record all contacts for each client, record notes on the contact, and bill the client as applicable. This system is used by doctors, dentists, lawyers, and others who need to keep track of their clients but do not need sophisticated specialized systems.

812.7   **When data base systems are not useful.** Notice that all the applications described above have one thing in common: the information in the data base is stable and is used repeatedly.

A mail order business that does not specialize in repeat sales is probably well advised to key the information separately for each sale rather than to maintain a permanent customer file of any kind.

If a single user maintains a file for a single purpose (a directory, roster, or telephone list, for example) there is no advantage to using a data base program.

812.8   **General accounting software — useful application.** General accounting programs do the transaction accounting that keeps a business going on a day-to-day basis. Just as their pen-and-paper predecessors did, they process orders, journalize and post accounts receivable and payable, calculate payrolls, write checks, prepare routine reports, and so forth.

813   Integrated Applications

813.1   **The need for integration.** The user of a word processing program wants to incorporate a spreadsheet into a document. A spreadsheet user needs to write an explanation as part of a report. A data base user who wants to write a few pages of text for a newly compiled directory needs a built-in word processor.

The simplest, but least efficient, solution to these problems is to cut and paste the "finished" output of each program.

813.2   **Import-export routines.** Another solution is the import-export routines incorporated in many programs. **Import-export routines** make minor modifications in files that allow them to be stored on a disk (exported) by one program and retrieved (imported) by another program. In the first example of ¶813.1, the spreadsheet could export a spreadsheet file to a disk from which the word processing program could import it. Once the word processor has imported the file, it can be edited and otherwise treated as any other file by the word processing program.

The import-export routine is clumsy and time-consuming because of the manipulation of files that is required.

813.3   **Integrated software.** The problems outlined above have led to the development of **integrated programs:** word processing programs with built-in spreadsheets, spreadsheets with built-in word processors, and so forth.

813.4   **The ideal system.** The ideal software system would include a word processor with spell checker, thesaurus, grammar checker and writing coach, a full-size spreadsheet, and a data base system of adequate capacity and sophistication. Each of us could probably add something to that list!

While the ideal program does not yet exist, there are continuing and significant efforts to integrate and coordinate widely used programs. The three most significant approaches are as follows:

a. **The software family:** a group of several programs produced by the same software house and sharing similar commands. The purpose of this design is to permit sharing of information among the individual programs. For example, a spreadsheet analysis can be incorporated in a report prepared by a word processor — without re-keying either document.

   The greatest strength of this approach is that, since each program can stand alone, the individual programs can all be as powerful as single-application programs. The greatest weakness is the awkwardness of transferring information.

b. **Multiprogramming:** a system that brings together otherwise unrelated programs, keeping them on line (available almost instantly and ready to run) and permitting the user to switch from program to program without difficulty. For example, a spell checker and thesaurus can be used with a word processor, or one program can be printing files while the user works at the screen with another program.

c. **Integrated programs:** multiple-feature programs written in the image of the ideal program or at least incorporating many of the features of the ideal program.

814   Specialized Applications

814.1   Specialized programs. Word processors, spreadsheets, data base systems, and accounting programs are *generic* programs in the sense that they are designed to serve a variety of users who have a variety of needs. **Specialized programs** are designed to serve users with needs that are more narrowly defined: users in a single business, profession, or industry.

814.2   List of specialized programs. Some of the specialized programs available are as follows:

Architecture
Banking
Bill collection
Calendar, appointments, and note processing
Church systems
Condominium management
Construction management
Dental office systems
Engineering
Estate planning
Farming
Fund accounting for state and local government

Land surveying
Law office systems
Loan analysis for lending institutions
Maintenance
Management for vehicles, buildings, and machinery
Manufacturing inventory control
Medical office systems
Opinion surveys
Payroll management
Personnel management
Project management
Property management
Ranching
Shipbuilding
Statistics
Structural engineering
Trucking
Warehousing and inventory control
Will writing

814.3 **Computer graphics.** A word processing program permits the production of simple graphs, but the process is limited, slow, and tedious.

A **graphics program** facilitates the display of graphs, charts, and other line "art work" on the screen and the printing of graphics on paper. Computer plotters and laser printers produce high-quality graphs, charts, drawings, plans, and the like, from information stored in computers.

814.4 **Computer-aided design.** Graphics programs are used widely and intensively in computer-aided design (CAD). CAD programs draw alternative prototypes, simulate the testing of those prototypes, and tabulate the results of the tests.

814.5 **Computer networks.** A **computer network** consists of two or more computers connected by hard wires or telephone lines. In its simplest form, files and documents can be exchanged on the network.

More sophisticated networks, particularly hardwired systems within the same office or building, make it possible for several computers to share the same data base, printers, and so forth.

A widely used network configuration is a large mainframe supporting a comprehensive data base that is shared by several microcomputers.

814.6 **Communications.** Most computers are designed to accommodate a **modem**: a small hardware device, usually housed or added inside the computer, that enables the computer to transmit and receive information over telephone lines.

815 # Glossary

access: Occurs when the computer locates a record stored on disk, tape, or other storage medium.

access time: The time it takes the computer to locate a record stored on disk, tape, or other storage medium.

accounting: Collecting and storing data regarding transactions and other business activity; summarizing that data in periodic statements; preparing management information reports.

acronym: A word formed from the letters of other words, as COBOL from *common business-oriented language.*

address: A number, name, or symbol that identifies a specific location in memory.

ALGOL: *Algorithmic-oriented language.* An international programming language similar to FORTRAN.

alphabetic characters: The letters of the alphabet.

alphabetic data: Data consisting of alphabetic characters.

alphanumeric data: Data consisting of alphabetic and numeric characters.

analog computer: Uses electronic current to measure by analogy. Measures dimensions, temperature, illumination, humidity, and so forth. Used primarily for scientific and engineering applications.

ANSI: *American National Standards Institute.* Establishes commercial and governmental standards. Establishes standards for programming languages: ANSI COBOL, ANSI BASIC, and so on.

APL: *A programming language.* A programming language used in terminal-oriented systems.

application: A job performed by the computer. Typical applications are accounts receivable and payroll. See **applications software.**

applications software: Programs written to meet specific user needs rather than facilitate computer operation (for example, payroll, billing, or inventory control). Contrast with **systems software.**

architecture: The interaction of hardware and software to produce the type of facilities and performance desired.

archive: Storage of inactive files, usually on disks or tape.

artificial intelligence: An experimental field in which researchers are attempting to design computers that can solve problems seeming to require intelligence, intuition, and imagination.

ASCII: *American Standard Code for Information Interchange.* A standard code for representing data transmitted from device to device within the computer system, between systems via communication circuits, and between systems linked in hardwired networks. The system uses eight binary bits for character representation.

assembler: A program that translates assembly language programs into machine language programs.

assembly language: A midlevel, machine-oriented programming language. See **assembler**.

(wp) **author:** The person who creates the text of a document.

(wp) **automatic centering:** A feature that effects the horizontal centering of a line of text displayed on the screen.

(wp) **automatic record selection:** The data in a designated field determines what is to be printed for each record. In a billing application, for example, a large balance in the *amount overdue* field of a given record could cause a special collection message to be sent to the person to whom that record pertains.

(wp) **automatic file sort:** Sorts the records in a file into ascending or descending alphabetic or numeric order.

(wp) **automatic footnote follow:** The footnote is automatically printed on the page with the text to which it pertains. If the text is moved to another page, the footnote automatically follows.

(wp) **automatic hyphenation:** If necessary, the last word on the writing line is automatically divided and hyphenated. If the text is subsequently reformed, the hyphen is removed and the word is written solid. See **word wrap.**

(wp) **automatic line or paragraph numbering:** Automatically numbers lines or paragraphs sequentially in first draft text; removes the numbers in the finished document.

(wp) **automatic pagination and page numbering:** Automatically divides the document into pages and numbers them according to a format prescribed by the operator. If the document is revised or reformatted, it is automatically repaginated during its next printing.

(wp) **automatic printer control:** Printing instructions are stored as part of the document file or, in some programs, in a separate format file. The printer is adjusted during printing for single spacing, double spacing, ribbon color, underlining, boldface printing, pica type, elite type, condensed type, and so forth.

auxiliary storage: Storage in auxiliary devices such as disk drives and tape drives. Such devices store larger quantities of data than main memory does, but require longer access time. Also called **mass storage.**

background: On systems capable of multiprogramming, those applications that can run virtually unattended, with little attention from the processor, are said to run in the *background*.

background printing: A printer that can run for several seconds or even minutes on the contents of its buffer requires only occasional attention from the processor. The printer can run continuously in the background, leaving the rest of the system free to run other programs in the foreground.

back-up: The second copy of a program or data file stored on disk or tape for use in case of computer failure.

bar-code: A code in which patterns of printed lines or bars of varying width represent numbers. Each set of numbers identifies a product and its manufacturer. At retail check-out counters, bar-code scanners transmit the product code to a computer which records the current price of the item on the cash register. Also called **universal product code (UPC).**

bar-code scanner: An electronic device that reads bar-code (UPC). Widely used at supermarket check-out counters.

BASIC: *Beginner's All-purpose Symbolic Instruction Code.* A general-purpose high-level programming language. The most widely used programming language.

batch processing: A group of similar records are used as input under a program that subjects each record to the same process in the same computer run. Examples: A payroll application in which similar employee records are processed under the same program, or a billing application in which similar customer records are processed under the same program. See **batch file.**

batch file: An operating system file containing a group of instructions used in loading programs. Batch processing and running a batch program to load programs are different functions.

baud: A measure of the speed of transmission of digital data. Approximately equal to bits per second. Used to measure the speed of transmission over communication lines. See **modem.**

binary number: A number in a system using only two numerals: 0 and 1.

bit: A single binary digit. Always has a value of 0 or 1.

bits per second (bps): A measure of the rate of data transmission over telephone lines and other communication channels. Approximately equal to baud. See **modem.**

(wp)   **block:** One or more lines of text identified as a unit to be copied, deleted, or moved together.

(wp)   **block copy:** Reproducing a block of text in the edit field, leaving the original block undisturbed.

(wp)   **block delete:** Deleting a block of text in the edit field.

(wp)   **block move:** Reproducing a block of text in the edit field, deleting the original block.

(wp)   **boilerplate:** Stock sentences and paragraphs stored and kept ready for use in documents. Can be merged with each other and with custom-written text to create individualized documents. Also called **canned text.**

(wp)   **boldface printing:** Printing in characters made up of thick, heavy lines. Computer printers accomplish this effect by overprinting.

boot: To load the operating system, thus making the computer ready to accept an application program. Since the first few instructions get the computer ready to accept the remainder of the operating system, the process is called **bootstrapping**.

bootstrapping: See **boot**.

bubble memory: A memory device in which data is encoded onto a film of magnetic silicate in the form of a series of bubbles.

bubble sort: A method of sorting in which pairs of records are sorted until the entire file is in the proper order.

buffer: An area in memory assigned to an input/output device to compensate for the slowness of the device or for the fact that the CPU is not available when the input/output device is ready for it. See **background, background printing**.

byte: A group of adjacent bits (4, 6, or 8). Each byte represents one character in the character set of the computer.

canned program: An application program written broad enough to serve many users; marketed ready to use, complete with instructions and other documentation.

(wp)   **canned text:** See **boilerplate**.

card: Circuit board. Computer architecture employs slots into which basic circuits and enhancements are plugged. Cards can add the circuitry for graphics, hard disks, modems, and the like.

cathode-ray tube (CRT): Video display tube. The TV-like tube that is the display screen, or monitor, of the computer.

central processing unit (CPU): The processor for a mainframe.

chain printer: An impact printer in which the type characters are part of a rotating loop or chain. Impacts are provided by a row of print hammers, one for each print position. A full line is printed during each cycle of the printer.

character: A single letter, number, or other symbol that can be processed by a computer. See **alphabetic** and **numeric**.

character set: The set of characters that can be processed by a computer or a unit within the computer system.

chip: A silicon wafer on which the circuitry for a computer component is etched. See **microprocessor** and **memory**.

COBOL: Common *business*-oriented *language*. A programming language for business applications.

command: Instruction.

compatibility: The ability of programs to function with other programs, hardware components to function with other hardware components, and software and hardware to function together.

compile: To translate a high-level program into machine language.

compiler: A program that translates high-level programs into machine language.

component: A unit within the computer system: keyboard, printer, disk drive, and the like.

computer: A system, comprising electronic devices, that reads, performs high-speed calculations, stores, prints, and otherwise processes data while under the control of a program.

computer-aided design (CAD): The use of computers in design work. Permits the preliminary evaluation of many alternatives.

computer-assisted instruction (CAI): Instruction based on interaction between the student and the computer.

computer-aided manufacturing (CAM): Manufacturing in which the machines are under computer control.

computer language: A language consisting of words and symbols in which computer instructions are written following rigidly prescribed conventions. See **high-level language, machine language.**

conditional branch: The ability of the computer to vary its response depending upon the presence or absence of a specified condition. For example, one letter might be printed if a record contains an overdue balance, another if it does not.

configuration: Noun. The arrangement of the hardware in a computer system.

configuration: Verb. To fit a program to the hardware of a system by responding to the program's queries. Identifies hardware devices, enabling the program to adjust itself to the system.

console: The workstation from which a larger computer system is controlled. Usually consists of a display screen, keyboard, and one or more control panels.

constant: A numeric value that does not change, as a price that is applied to varying quantities. Contrast with **variable.**

CP/M: An operating system.

CPU: Central *processing unit.* The processor of a mainframe.

crash: A malfunction that makes it necessary to re-boot the system. All programs and data in memory are lost. Usually caused by software problems, operator error, or temporary power loss.

crossfooting: Totaling the columns of a spreadsheet; checking the totals for balance.

CRT: Cathode-ray tube.

cursor: The floating mark on the screen that indicates where the next character will appear. The cursor is usually a flashing underscore, but frequently a flashing block.

custom-written program: An application program written for the special needs of a specific user. Contrast with **canned program** and **packaged program.**

(wp) **cut-sheet feeder:** A paper-feed attachment for a printer that feeds individual sheets from a stack into the printer. Contrast with **tractor feed.**

daisy wheel printer: A printer based on a printing element that resembles the flower of a daisy. Each type character is at the end of a "petal." In printing, the element is rotated until the proper character is aligned with the printing position. The impact hammer then strikes the back of the type character, compressing the paper and ribbon between the platen and the type character.

data: Groups of numbers, letters, and other symbols representing facts.

data base: The files of a system in which data is commonly defined and consistently organized in integrated files that are shared by several applications. Contrast with the use of separate files for each application.

data base program: A packaged program that enables a user to design and use a data base tailored to the user's own applications.

data processing: The collection, input, and manipulation of data to make it more useful. Business data processing facilitates and records transactions and other day-to-day business activities, generates periodic and special summary reports, and produces management information.

debug: To correct errors (*bugs*) in a program.

(wp) **dedicated word processor:** A word processing machine that does not perform computer functions other than word processing.

(wp) **default:** Programs that permit the selection of variables such as format, hardware used, and so forth, usually specify commonly used default settings to which the program reverts if no variable setting is specified by the operator. For example, a word processing program might default to regular manuscript format if no format is specified by the operator.

(wp) **delete:** To strike out, cancel, erase. Characters on the screen may be deleted using the delete key; entire files may be deleted from the keyboard using operating system commands; selected records within a file may be deleted via the keyboard if the program is designed for that function.

desktop computer: A microcomputer.

desktop publishing: A microcomputer-based publishing system that produces professional quality graphics and text on a laser printer.

digital computer: A calculating computer that represents data electronically in discrete units. Compare with **analog computer.**

directory: A list of the files currently on the disk. Can be displayed on the screen to determine which files the disk contains, the current size of each file, and other directory information.

disk: A thin, flat, circular plate made of plastic or metal and coated with a material making it suitable for the magnetic recording of data. Metal disks are called hard disks. Plastic disks are called floppy disks, floppies, and (especially for 5¼-inch floppies) diskettes.

disk drive: A storage device that uses magnetic disks for the mass storage of data.

disk pack: A group of disks mounted coaxially in a removable canister. Permits the operator to load and unload large quantities of data without handling individual disks. Used in large systems, not with microcomputers.

diskette: See **disk.**

display: To cause data to appear on the screen.

(wp) **document:** Noun. Anything written or printed on paper.

document: Verb. To write running instructions and other explanatory material for a program. Usually done by the programmer. The finished material is called documentation.

DOS: *Disk operating system.* An operating system used on a disk-oriented system.

dot matrix printer: A printer that uses a pattern of dots to form characters. Each character in the printer's character set requires a different pattern of dots.

downtime: Time during which the computer is inoperable because of maintenance procedures or because of electronic or mechanical failure. Opposite of uptime.

drum printer: Employs a rotating metal drum embossed with a full band of type characters for each print position. As the character to be printed arrives at the print position, the print hammer for that position provides the impact to compress the ribbon and the paper between the type character and the hammer.

dumb terminal: A terminal that depends upon the mainframe to which it is connected for memory and processing circuitry.

(wp) **dual sheet feeder:** A feeder for a printer that feeds from two stacks. One stack is usually used for letterhead paper; the other feeds plain paper. Under program control, multipage letters are printed without operator attention to the printer.

duplexing: Computer transmission that is two-way, independent, and simultaneous.

EBCDIC: *E*xtended *B*inary *C*oded *D*ecimal *I*nterchange Code. A 256-character code widely used in computer systems.

(wp) **edit:** To enter new data or revise a displayed file using a word processing program or another program designed for editing.

(wp) **edit field:** That portion of memory that can be displayed by scrolling; the area in which screen editing can take place; the area in which a retrieved file exists.

electronic data processing (EDP): Processing data using computers and other electronic devices.

electronic funds transfer (EFT): The transfer of funds between financial institutions using computers and other electronic devices. Such funds may be those of the participating institutions or those of clients.

electronic mail (E-Mail): A system for the exchange of messages among subscribers using computers linked by communication lines, and to non-subscribers using the same devices, supplemented by other mail and courier services.

electrostatic printer: Uses dot matrix rods, electrostatic impulses, and heat to form and fix the printed image.

electrothermal printer: Uses hot dot matrix rods applied to heat-sensitive paper to create the printed image.

(wp) **elite:** Any typeface based on twelve characters per inch. See also **pica**.

encrypted data: Data translated into a secret code for security reasons.

enter: To put data into main memory via the keyboard.

enter key: Causes displayed data to be entered into main memory.

erasable programmable read-only memory (EPROM): A memory chip designed to be reprogrammed by a special programming device.

error code: A diagnostic code displayed when a malfunction occurs.

escape key: Permits the operator to leave one segment of the program and move to another—usually to the main menu.

execute: To run a program, causing it to perform the functions it was designed to perform.

feedback: Dimensions of the output of a computer-controlled process fed back to the controlling computer permitting the computer to make adjustments that keep the output within tolerances. Used in **computer-aided manufacturing (CAM).**

field: The location in a record in which a specific kind of data item is entered. For example, the names of customers are entered in the name field, which is part of the customer's record, which is stored in the customer file.

file: A group of related records stored on a disk or other mass storage medium under a common filename. For example, customer records could be stored together under the filename CUSTFILE.

filename: The name under which a file is saved and retrieved. One form is XXXXXXXX.EEE, in which X is an alphabetic or numeric character in the filename itself and E is an alphabetic or numeric character in an optional extension of the filename. The extension can be used to identify the *type* of file.

flexible disk: A floppy disk.

floppy disk: A data-storage disk made of thin, flexible plastic. Also called a **flexible disk.**

flowchart: A chart illustrating the organization of a program or process. A program flowchart is used to plan the logic of a program before the individual instructions are written. A *system flowchart* illustrates the flow of data through the data processing system, frequently illustrating the application of several related programs. Uses are similar to those of a hierarchy chart, logic chart, or tree chart.

(wp) **footer:** The text automatically entered at the bottom of each page in a document, usually a page number. Contrast with **header**.

(wp) **font:** A typeface employed on an element for a printer. Each font is given a distinctive name by the manufacturer (e.g., Courier, Prestige, Criterion, and so forth).

(wp) **format:** The arrangement, plan, or structure of a document.

FORTRAN (*formula trans*lation): A programming language used in mathematical and other scientific applications.

function keys: Special keys assigned to perform specific tasks by the program. For example, Fn-6 might control automatic centering under one program, set a margin under another, and delete a word under a third.

global: Applicable on the broadest scale possible. A global search searches an entire file; a global delete command deletes all the files on a disk.

graphic: Computer output in the form of a drawing, chart, or graph produced on the screen, a printer, or a plotter.

graphics program: A program that enhances the computer's ability to produce graphic output and expands the operator's ability to design the input from which it is produced.

hard copy: A printed copy, as opposed to a screen display.

hard disk: A rigid metal disk coated with magnetic material that makes it suitable for recording; used for storing data.

(wp) **hardwired:** Electronically joined by permanent connections. Used to refer to the connection of terminals and other units within a system or network, as opposed to those temporarily connected via modems and communication lines. Also used to refer to nonprogrammable ROM.

hardware: The physical devices making up the computer system: printer, monitor, disk drives, keyboard, system unit, and the like. Contrast with **software.**

(wp) **header:** The text automatically entered at the top of each page of a document: document name, chapter or section identification, page number, or the like. Contrast with **footer.**

hexadecimal: A base sixteen number system as opposed to a base two system in binary code.

hierarchy chart: A chart illustrating the organization of a program or process. Uses are similar to those of a flowchart, logic chart, or tree chart.

high-level language: Any English-like programming language oriented to the people using it and the applications for which it is used. Contrast with **machine language.**

impact printer: Any printer in which printed images are created by impacts that compress the ribbon and paper against raised type characters.

(wp) **indexing:** The capability of a word processing program to translate key words, identified by the operator during entry, into an index complete with page numbers.

information: 1. Data. 2. Data representing management abstractions, such as decision models, planning criteria, and performance standards.

information processing: 1. Data processing. 2. That portion of data processing dedicated to the production of management abstractions such as decision models, planning criteria, performance, standards, and the like. See **management information systems.**

ink jet printer: Uses an electronic field to form the character to be printed from droplets in an ink jet.

input: Data expressed in characters and entered into the computer.

input device: A device designed to receive input.

input/output (I/O) devices: Those devices in the computer system designed to receive input and produce output.

instruction: One line of a program. The smallest unit of a program the computer can execute.

integrated circuit (IC): A usually complex set of related subcircuits etched on a single silicon chip.

integrated software: Software in which functions ordinarily performed by two or more programs are combined in a single program.

interactive: Allowing or facilitating communication between the computer and the user. An interactive program will receive instructions from the user, ask questions, and react according to the answers.

interface: A device containing the physical connections and translating circuits that connect components within a system, or connect systems with other systems.

(wp) **justification:** Spacing text so that one or both margins are even. Text may be *left-justified* (left margin even) or *right-justified* (right margin even) or *fully justified* (all full lines the same length, both margins even).

k: Abbreviation for kilobyte, 1024 bytes. The standard method of stating the memory capacity of a computer, as 640k.

key-to-disk machine: A keyboard-driven machine that records data on disks for later entry into the computer.

key-to-tape machine: A keyboard-driven machine that records data on tape for later entry into the computer.

keyboard: A device containing an array of keys, similar to those on a typewriter, for entering data into the computer.

keyboarding: Using a keyboard to record data on an input medium (disk, tape, or cards) or to enter data directly.

kilobyte: 1024 bytes; 1k. See **k**.

language: A set of characters and conventions organized for the writing of instructions that make up programs. A low-level language is machine-oriented (machine language); a high-level language (for example, BASIC) is oriented to the user and the application.

laser disk: A disk used in a laser-based mass storage system.

laser printer: A nonimpact printer that uses a laser beam to produce graphics under computer control.

letter quality printer: A printer that produces high-quality printing like that of the best typewriters. Most commonly a daisy wheel printer.

light pen: A device with which the operator can identify screen locations. When the light pen is held against the screen, the computer can determine its location.

(wp) **list processing:** Processing files containing lists that are updated, sorted alphabetically or numerically on selected fields, and merged with other files to produce customized documents.

load: To place a program in memory preparatory to executing it.

local area network (LAN): A hardwired network of computers and terminals.

logic chart: A chart illustrating the logical organization of a program or process. Similar in use to a flowchart, hierarchy chart, or tree chart.

loop: A section of a program that repeats until a new condition causes the computer to leave the loop and continue with subsequent instructions.

For example, a program might calculate your future pension benefits by repeatedly adding a year to your age, applying your benefit at that age, and printing the result. The program could be written to break the loop and stop at any predetermined age.

machine language: The binary code into which all languages must be translated before a program can be run. Machine language is made up entirely of 1s and 0s, as 10010101.

magnetic ink character recognition (MICR): An input system employing a scanner that reads characters printed in a special magnetic ink. Widely used by banks to read the account numbers printed on checks in magnetic ink.

magnetic medium: A device on or in which data can be stored by means of magnetic impulses. Hard disks, floppy disks, tapes, drums, and core storage are all magnetic media.

magnetic scanner: An input device that reads the magnetic strips applied to credit cards and similar media.

magnetic tape: A long, narrow, reel-mounted band of thin plastic with a magnetizable surface layer that makes it suitable for the storage of data.

main memory: The RAM chips in the system unit of a small computer or the memory unit of a large computer.

mainframe: The central unit of a medium or large computer system. Does not include separate units such as terminals, mass storage units, or printers.

management information systems (MIS): That portion of a data processing system that is dedicated to the production of management abstractions such as decision models, planning criteria, performance standards, etc. Also called an information processing system.

mark sensing: An input system that employs carefully formatted and registered pencil marks on paper input sheets. Used to score answer sheets for objective tests and for similar applications.

(wp)   **mask:** A stored layout that pertains to a specific document. May consist of nothing more than marks that show where text is to be entered; may include text. An operator might store a form letter as a mask, then key an individual name and address into each document that is produced from it.

mass storage: Auxiliary storage units for storing large quantities of data off-line. Disk and tape units are the most common mass storage devices. Also called **auxiliary storage.**

matrix: A rectangular array. A spreadsheet is a matrix. One kind of dot matrix printer employs a matrix of seven dots by nine dots from which characters are formed.

media: Plural of **medium.** Means of storing data. Storage devices (disk drives and tape drives) use media (disks and tape) for the storage of data.

medium: Singular form of **media**.

memory: Temporary storage in the main memory unit. Usually silicon chip RAM. Memory stores data until the computer is turned off. Mass storage media (disks and tape) store data permanently.

menu: A displayed list of functions the computer is ready to perform and the key codes with which the user can cause each function to be performed. Most programs include a main menu listing the major sectors of the program and the key codes for entering each sector. Each sector has its own menu from which specific functions can be commanded.

merge: To integrate files, as to merge a name and address file with a file containing the text for a form letter, producing a series of individualized letters.

MICR: See **magnetic ink character recognition.**

microcomputer: A desktop computer system in which a central system unit contains the microprocessor and related circuitry, as well as main memory and one or more disk drives; a monitor, keyboard, and printer complete the system.

microprocessor: A processor etched on a single silicon chip.

minicomputer: A midsized computer falling somewhere between a large mainframe and a microcomputer. Usually capable of supporting time-sharing.

mode: Manner of operation; usually referring to operation in a specific sector of the program: input mode or print mode.

modem (*mo*dulator-*dem*odulator): A device that controls the transmission and receipt of binary data sent over telephone lines and through other communication circuits.

monitor: A video screen and the circuitry necessary to display data.

monochrome monitor: A monitor that displays data in one color as opposed to a color monitor that displays data in a variety of colors.

multiprogramming: A technique that permits two or more programs to reside in main memory together and, under control of the operating system, be executed simultaneously.

nonimpact printer: A printer that depends upon light, heat, xerography, electronics, or the like, rather than impact to transfer characters to the paper.

numeric address: A number identifying a specific location in memory.

numeric data: Data consisting of numbers. Compare with **alphabetic data, alphanumeric data,** and **text.**

object program: A machine-language program.

off-line operations: Operations that support the computer system, but do not require use of devices under the control of the CPU. Examples are the entry of data on key-to-disk machines or key-to-tape machines.

on-line operations: Operations that require the use of devices under the direct control of the CPU. Examples of on-line operations are the immediate processing of airline reservations or banking transactions.

operating system: A group of programs that coordinate and control the operation of the computer system. Frequently compared to an orchestra conductor, traffic officer, or short-order cook. See **disk operating system (DOS).**

optical character recognition (OCR): An input system capable of reading printed text.

optical mark sensing: See **mark sensing.**

(wp) **originator:** The author of a document.

(wp) **orphan adjust:** Preventing the first line of a paragraph from appearing alone at the bottom of a page.

(wp) **outlining:** Automatic formatting and insertion of numbers and letters to produce an outline from text.

output: The results of processing data, usually displayed on the screen, saved on disk or tape, or printed.

packaged program: An application program written broad enough to serve many users; marketed ready to use, complete with instructions and other documentation.

(wp) **page numbering:** After the user has specified the format for page numbering, each page is automatically numbered according to that format.

(wp) **pagination:** The automatic division of the text of a document into pages as it is printed.

parallel port: The interface between the system unit of a microcomputer and a parallel printer. Contrast with **serial port.**

parallel printer: A printer designed to receive data from the system unit over several parallel channels, thus increasing the speed of transmission.

parity bit: A bit added to those representing each character for the purpose of making sure the sum of all bits is always odd or always even.

password: A code word giving the user access to encrypted files.

personal computer (pc): A microcomputer or desktop computer.

(wp) **pica:** Printer or typewriter type printing ten characters per inch. Also called 10-pitch type. Compare with **elite.**

(wp) **pitch:** The width of type characters stated in characters per inch. The two most common sizes are pica (ten characters per inch) and elite (twelve characters per inch). Many printers can also print in condensed mode (fifteen characters per inch).

plotter: An output device that plots graphically one variable quantity against another.

printer: The computer unit that produces printed output.

processor: The computer unit that receives the step-by-step instructions of the program and executes them in the order in which they are received.

program: The step-by-step instructions that control the computer.

programming language: A set of codes and conventions that permit the programmer to write instructions that can be translated into machine language and run on the computer.

PROM (programmable read-only memory): A special read-only memory unit that can be programmed with special equipment at the factory or by a user who has the special equipment, but **cannot** be programmed in the normal course of computer operation. In normal operation, the user can cause PROM to be read, but cannot cause its contents to be changed. See **EPROM**.

prompt: A programmed query from the screen asking the user for input.

protocol: Electronic and procedural standards for the transmission of data from device to device within a system, between devices and systems in a network, and over communication lines.

random access memory (RAM): Memory that can be accessed directly without a sequential search for an address.

raw data: Data that has not been processed.

read in: To enter into memory via an input device such as disk or tape.

read out: To transfer from memory to an output device.

read-only memory (ROM): A memory unit, programmed at the factory, that can be read — but will not accept data for storage. See **PROM, EPROM**.

record: A group of related fields; a unit within a file.

(wp) **re-form:** An editing function that reconstructs paragraphs whose lines have been broken into segments by the deletion or insertion of characters.

rename: To change the filename of a file.

(wp) **replace:** To search text for a character or group of characters and replace them with different characters. See **search and replace.**

(wp) **retrieve:** To cause the computer to access a file and copy it in the edit field.

run: To execute an application program.

save: To store data as part of a file on a mass storage medium such as a disk or tape.

scanner: An input device that reads bar code, printed characters, magnetized characters, and so forth.

screen: The TV-like viewing surface of the monitor.

(wp) **screen editing:** Using the keyboard, under the control of an editing program, to edit text displayed on the screen.

(wp) **search:** The computer scans text for a character or a set of characters. Each time the object of the search is found, its location is indicated to the user.

(wp) **search and replace:** The computer scans text for a character or a set of characters. Each time the object of the search is found, it is automatically replaced with a substitute character or set of characters.

serial port: Interface for a serial printer (i.e., one to which data is transmitted over a single channel). Contrast with **parallel port.**

(wp) **shadow printing:** Printing with a double impression, the second slightly out of register with the first. Used for emphasis.

(wp) **sheet feeder:** A printer attachment that feeds individual sheets into the printer under program control. Also called a **cut-sheet feeder.**

silicon chip: A thin silicon wafer on which the circuitry and semiconductor components for an entire computer unit are etched. Also see **integrated circuit.**

smart terminal: A terminal equipped with memory and computing capacity of its own. Contrast with **dumb terminal.**

(wp) **soft hyphen:** A hyphen used to divide a word at the end of a line. If the document is later reformatted and the hyphenated word falls within the line, the hyphen will automatically disappear, joining the syllables of the word.

software: The operating systems, assemblers, compilers, and other programs that facilitate programming and running the computer.

sort: To arrange fields, records, or files in a predetermined sequence.

source document: A document containing input data.

(wp) **spelling checker:** A program or sequence within a program that scans text for misspelled words, displays correctly spelled alternatives, and gives the user an opportunity to select a replacement.

split screen: A technique used in programming that allows insertion of supplementary material by dividing the screen.

spreadsheet: A program modeled after an accounting worksheet. Uses a tabular arrangement of data consisting of columns and lines for calculation and the preparation of reports.

(wp) **stand-alone word processor:** A self-contained word processor that requires no support from a computer or any other device.

store: To save data in files on a storage medium such as disk or tape.

storage: The device or medium on which data is saved: disk storage or tape storage.

system: A group of elements organized to work together. The elements are usually people, devices, materials, or procedures.

system programmer: A programmer who writes systems software.

system unit: The central unit of a microcomputer. Usually contains the processor, memory, other system circuitry, and one or more disk drives.

systems software: Programs such as compilers, assemblers, and operating systems that facilitate operation of the system. Contrast with **applications software.**

tape: A long, narrow, reel-mounted band of thin plastic, coated with a magnetic surface enabling it to record data.

tape drive: An input/output storage device employing magnetic tape as the medium for data storage.

terminal: An auxiliary input/output device (usually consisting of a keyboard, a monitor, and a printer) connected to a mainframe. Usually located some distance from the mainframe; may be hardwired or connected via telephone line or other communication circuit.

(wp) **text:** The data making up a document.

tractor feed: A printer attachment employing two sprocket wheels that engage evenly spaced holes along the sides of continuous-form paper.

tree chart: Used to illustrate the logic of a program or process. Similar in use to a flowchart, hierarchy chart, or logic chart.

tutorial: Instructional text, usually included on the program disk, to instruct the user on the operation of the program. The user may display the program on the screen or print it.

(wp) **typeface:** A set of type characters of the same design contained on a single printer element.

universal product code (UPC): The code of variably spaced bars of varying width used to identify products sold in super markets. Also called a **bar-code**.

variable: A numeric value that may assume any one of a set of values, as a utility expense in a budget program. Contrast with **constant**.

video display terminal (VDT): A monitor.

(wp) **widow adjust:** A word processor adjustment that keeps the last line of a paragraph from standing alone at the top of a page.

window: A program feature that permits opening a rectangular panel anywhere on the screen to view additional applications without destroying the application already displayed.

(wp)   **word processing:** The creation, editing, and other processing of text to produce printed documents.

(wp)   **word wrap:** An adjustment that occurs at the end of every line entered. The word that falls at the end of the line is logically "wrapped" around the end of the line. If it is short enough to be placed on the current line, it is pulled back and placed there. If it is too long to be placed at the end of the current line, it is pushed to the beginning of the next line.

(wp)   **xerographic printer:** A computer printer that employs the principles developed for xerographic copying machines.

Unit IX

Keyboarding Basics

Understand:	■ Basic information to enable setup of the printed page
	■ Principles of centering, proofreader's marks, and making corrections
Acquire:	■ The ability to recognize correctly centered data
	■ The ability to identify common proofreader's marks (As recalled from Unit 8)
Be Prepared To:	■ Prepare attractively centered, tabulated reports
	■ Use proofreader's marks to correct rough drafts

900   This unit is a review of keyboarding. Though the information on centering and tabulation may be a review, the section on making corrections will probably be new to you.

901   ## Horizontal Centering Defined

Horizontal centering is the term used for centering a line in relation to the side edges of the paper. You probably use horizontal centering most often to center a line in typed material, such as a title.

Horizontal Centering

902   ## Steps for Horizontal Centering

1. Move margin stops to extreme ends of scale.

2. Clear tab stops; then set a tab stop at center of paper.

Formula for Finding Horizontal Center of Paper

	Example
Scale reading at left edge of paper	0
+ Scale reading at right edge of paper	102
Total/2 = Center Point	102/2 = 51

3. Tabulate to center of paper.

4. From center, backspace one time for every two letters, spaces, figures, or punctuation marks in the line.

5. Do not backspace for one leftover stroke at the end of a line.

9

223

6. Begin typing material to be horizontally centered where back-spacing ends.

NOTE: For centering on odd-size paper and cards, the same steps are used.

Automatic typewriters and word processing software programs generally center letters, words, and titles for you automatically when you key in a centering command.

903

Spread Headings

A spread heading looks like this:

A   S P R E A D   H E A D I N G

To type a spread heading:

1. Backspace from center once for each character or space (except the last letter or character) in the heading. Begin to type where backspacing ends.

2. When typing the spread heading, space once after each charac-ter and three times between words.

To type spread headings with automatic typewriters or word processing programs, type the heading as indicated in step two, and then key in the centering command.

904

Vertical Centering Defined

9

Vertical centering—also called top-to-bottom centering—is the term used for centering one or several lines between the top and bottom edges of the paper. You probably use this skill most often in typing tabulated material.

905

Steps for Vertical Centering

Vertical centering may be done using either of two methods:

mathematical
backspace-from-center

905.1

Mathematical method

1. Count lines and blank line spaces needed to type problem.

2. Subtract lines to be used from lines available (66 for a full sheet [11"] and 33 for half sheet [5.5"]).

3. Divide by 2 to get top and bottom margins. If a fraction results, disregard it.

4. If an even number results, space down that number of lines from the top of the sheet and begin typing the first line. If an odd num-ber results, use the next lower number.

Formula for Vertical Mathematical Placement

$$\frac{\text{lines available} - \text{lines used}}{2} = \text{top margin}$$

When using word processing programs, check the manual to determine the vertical default (the maximum number of vertical lines which will be typed on each individual or continuous paper sheet) for each sheet of paper. Use this number to substitute for the lines available in the above formula; then proceed with other steps as described.

905.2 Backspace-from-center method

1. Find total vertical lines available.

   full sheet: 11″ × 6 lines to an inch = 66 total lines available
   half sheet: 5.5″ × 6 lines to an inch = 33 total lines available
   Word Processing Programs: Refer to manual to determine vertical default, total lines available.

2. Find vertical center of paper to be used.

   total lines available/2 = vertical center

3. Space down from top edge of paper to vertical center.

   Word Processing Programs: Use the Return/Enter key to move to vertical center.

4. Roll platen (cylinder) back one time (one full line) for each two lines, two blank line spaces, or combination line and blank line spaces to be typed. Ignore odd or leftover lines.

   Word Processing Programs: Use the "up arrow" key to move back up the page once for every two typed and/or blank lines.

906 Tabulation

Tabulation is the term used to represent the typing of columns of information. Illustration 9-1 on page 226 shows a simple table with a main heading, secondary heading, and columnar headings. Tabulation is a way to present complex information in columns for easy reading and comparisons.

906.1 Typewriter/computer preparation

- Insert and align paper. If using computer, align top edge of continuous form paper.
- Clear margin stops by moving them to extreme ends of line-of-writing scale.
- Clear all tab stops.
- Move element carrier or cursor to center of paper or line-of-writing scale.
- Decide the number of spaces to be left between columns — preferably an even number (e.g., 4, 6, 8, 10).

ILLUSTRATION 9-1

Simple Tabulation with Main, Secondary Headings, and Columnar Headings

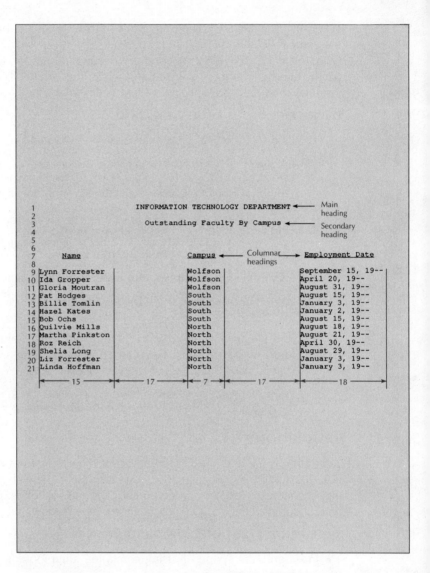

INFORMATION TECHNOLOGY DEPARTMENT ← Main heading

Outstanding Faculty By Campus ← Secondary heading

(Columnar headings)

Name	Campus	Employment Date
Lynn Forrester	Wolfson	September 15, 19--
Ida Gropper	Wolfson	April 20, 19--
Gloria Moutran	Wolfson	August 31, 19--
Pat Hodges	South	August 15, 19--
Billie Tomlin	South	January 3, 19--
Hazel Kates	South	January 2, 19--
Bob Ochs	South	August 15, 19--
Quilvie Mills	North	August 18, 19--
Martha Pinkston	North	August 21, 19--
Roz Reich	North	April 30, 19--
Shelia Long	North	August 29, 19--
Liz Forrester	North	January 3, 19--
Linda Hoffman	North	January 3, 19--

15 — 17 — 7 — 17 — 18

906.2 **Plan vertical placement.** Follow either of the procedures explained in ¶905.1 or ¶905.2 to determine vertical placement. Keep the following formatting requirements in mind:

- **Spacing of Headings.** Double-space (count 1 blank line space) between main and secondary headings when both are used. Double-space (count 1 blank line space) between the last table heading (main or secondary) and the first horizontal line of columnar headings or items. Double-space between columnar headings (when used) and the first line of the columnar entries.

- **Spacing Above Totals and Source Notes.** Double-space between the total rule (line) and the total figures. Double-space between the last line of the table and the 1-1/2" rule above the source note. Double-space between the 1-1/2" rule and the source note.

906.3 Plan horizontal placement. Follow the steps outlined in ¶902 to determine the horizontal center of the paper (or line-of-writing scale). Then, backspace from center one space for every two letters, figures, symbols, and spaces in the longest item of each column in the table. Then backspace once for every two spaces to be left between columns. Set left margin stop where backspacing ends.

If an odd or leftover space occurs at the end of the longest item of a column, carry it forward to the next column. Do not backspace for an odd or leftover character at the end of the last column.

Example:

William A. Stokes		February 2, 19--		Customer Services
17	4	16	4	17

William A. Stokes₁₂₃₄ February 2, 19--₁₂₃₄ Customer Services

906.4 Set tab stops. From the left margin, space forward one space for each letter, figure, symbol, and space in the longest item in the first column. Then space forward one space for each space to be left between Columns 1 and 2. Set a tab stop at this point for the second column. Continue this procedure for additional columns, setting tab stops for each.

NOTE: If a columnar heading is longer than the longest item in a column, it may be treated as the longest item in that column in determining placement. The longest columnar entry must then be centered under the heading and the tab stop set accordingly.

906.5 Center columnar headings

- **Backspace-from-column-center method.** From the point at which a column begins (tab or left margin), space forward one time for every two letters, figures, or spaces in the longest item in the column. This procedure provides you with the column center point. From it, backspace one time for every two letters and spaces in the columnar heading. Ignore an odd or leftover space. Type the heading at this point; it will be centered over the column.

- **Mathematical method.** To the number where each column begins add one half the letters and spaces in the longest line in the same column. This procedure provides you with the column center point. From it, backspace one time for every two letters and spaces in the columnar heading.

906.6   Horizontal rulings. Sometimes information provided in tabulated columns becomes very complicated. When this occurs, it often helps to arrange columnar information with ruled lines so that the reader can interpret the information more easily. An example of a table with complex ruled columns is presented in Illustration 9-2. To keyboard a ruled column, follow vertical and horizontal centering steps discussed previously. After the copy is completely keyboarded, insert the lines as described below.

To draw horizontal rulings (lines) in tables, depress the shift lock and strike the underline key. Single-space above and double-space below horizontal rulings.

With word processing software, it is possible to mark the beginning and end of a ruled line (mark a block) and copy the same line in other places within the same table.

906.7   Vertical rulings. On a typewriter, operate the automatic line finder. Place a pencil or pen point through the cardholder (typebar guide). Roll the paper up until you have a line of the desired length. Remove pen or pencil and reset the line finder.

With word processing software, it is often possible to draw vertical lines. With some sophisticated software programs, the vertical line can also be marked (blocked) and copied elsewhere in the table. If the word processing software used does not have this feature, vertical lines may be added by hand after the document has been printed.

907   ## Tabulation in Business Letters and Manuscripts

Detailed material in letters and reports may be easier to understand if it is tabulated. The tabulated material is keyboarded after double spacing below the preceding paragraph. Double spacing is also used after the tabulated material, before continuing the remainder of the letter or manuscript. See Illustration 9-3 for an example of a memo containing tabulated material.

908   ## Proofreading

Some of the time spent making corrections can be eliminated by careful proofreading of keyboarded material while it is still in the typewriter or computer.

908.1   ### Hints for accurate proofreading

- Take your time. Proofread slowly.
- Read aloud.
- Proofread each page line for line while it is still in the typewriter. With word processing software, proofread from the monitor before printing out the document.
- When proofreading for spelling, read the material backwards. Many word processing programs have a spelling checker as one of the features. Run the spelling check against your entire document, adding

ILLUSTRATION 9-3
Sample Memorandum with Table

TO: Horace Traylor
    Employee Relations

FROM: Marie Hydress
      Personnel

DATE: July 12, 19--

SUBJECT: Ten-Year Pins

Thank you for offering to order the ten-year pins for employees celebrating their tenth anniversary with Gonzalez & Co. The same style pins as those used last year will be fine, with the exception of the change in color to blue, as we discussed.

Following is a listing of employees' names for engraving on each pin:

Name	Date Employed	Department
Mary King	January 15, 19--	Personnel
William A. Stokes	February 2, 19--	Purchasing
Bennie Moore	April 27, 19--	Customer Services
Zelda Cecilia	June 10, 19--	Security
Gary Gosnell	July 21, 19--	Accounting
Arcie Ewell	October 18, 19--	Payroll

Please call me when the pins arrive, and I shall arrange to have them picked up and gift wrapped for each employee. Thanks again for your help.

mos

ILLUSTRATION 9-2
Sample Ruled Table

SCHOOL / Name, Address, and Contact	Type				How			From				Use					Students					Faculty					View Sample
	Video Tapes	Closed Circuit TV	Film	Slides	Comm. Prepared	Locally Prepared	Another School	Detailed Script	Brief L. Plan	Detailed L. Plan	Abbr. Script	Trad. Classroom	Open Lab	Combination	Article	Research	Ext/Enthusiastic	Enthusiastic	Satisfied	Unsatisfied	Ext/Unsatisfied	Ext/Enthusiastic	Enthusiastic	Satisfied	Unsatisfied	Ext/Unsatisfied	
Loop College, 64 E. Lake, Chicago IL 60601-7529, Mr. Guy Richards	X		X		X	X		X	X	X		X	X	X			X					X					
Heald Colleges, 1255 Post Street, San Francisco CA 94101-2137, Dr. Jim Deitz	X		X		X		X		X			X					X		X								
University of Tennessee, Business Education Department, Knoxville TN 37916-4419, Dr. E. Ray Smith & Dr. Dan Reese	X		X		X	X	X		X			X					X										

any often-used business terminology to the software dictionary. Correct all misspellings indicated. Remember, software spelling checkers will not catch a misuse of words such as *too* for *to*. Be aware of this kind of error.

■ Be on the lookout for these common errors:

> Errors in format
> Errors in content

908.2   **Proofreader's marks.** Proofreader's marks are used not only by those who proof copy for publishers and printers, but also by almost all persons who have occasion to indicate corrections in typewritten or printed material.

Proofreader's marks are sometimes applied directly to the location of the change. Proofreader's marks may appear in the margins instead of at the location of the change. When these marginal marks are used, supplementary marks in the text indicate the location of the change. To assist the typist in making subsequent corrections, try to use a bright colored pen to indicate proofreader's marks so all corrections will stand out. For more information and a table of proofreader's marks, see Unit 8, ¶806.1–806.4.

909   # Corrections

Even the best keyboard operators make errors. Therefore, each operator, together with the employer, must choose the best type of correction techniques to be used. Listed below are the important features of each method.

909.1   **Word processing software.** The fastest and most efficient method available for error correction is the use of word processing software. This software (used with stand-alone word processors or some automatic typewriters, and available for all computers) allows for rapid addition and deletion of letters, words, and even paragraphs. Paper costs are definitely reduced when such corrections/revisions are made before a copy is printed. Some software programs even allow you to "change your mind" and recover letters, words, or paragraphs which were just deleted.

The latest software packages have spelling checkers which check all words entered against 50,000+ words in electronic dictionaries. Many allow for the addition to the dictionary common business terms (or even names) specific to your organization. Medical, legal, and financial dictionaries are also available. An electronic thesaurus with 200,000+ synonyms provides assistance in finding just the word you need and in enlarging your vocabulary while writing. Companion software programs that check written documents against simple grammatical rules are now available and becoming more sophisticated each day.

Another method of electronic error correction is the use of software packages that provide math functions. When used correctly, such software will provide accurate answers to addition, subtraction, multiplication, and division problems within computer-generated documents.

All of this "electronic assistance" will serve to enhance and improve written correspondence. It is important that you keep current on new developments in this field.

909.2   **Automatic typewriters.** Many of the typewriters being sold today have some form of limited internal memory. Whether confined to a few key strokes, words, paragraphs, or even pages, these automatic (also called electronic) typewriters provide error correction by backspacing and retyping correct characters.

909.3   **Self-correcting typewriters.** Self-correcting typewriters are designed with a correction key and correction ribbon. Errors are lifted off the page or covered with a chalk-like substance. Self-correcting typewriters with a lift-off correction ribbon provide a fast, easy, and neat method of error correction on originals. A lift-off typewriter ribbon, including lift-off correction tabs, may be available for your make and model of typewriter— even if the machine was not designed to be self-correcting. Check with your local office supply store for information on your particular typewriter.

909.4   **Typewriters.** Traditional forms of error correction for typewriters still work efficiently.

Erasing—One of the oldest forms of correction. Pink or grey rubber typing erasers are available. The grey eraser contains more abrasive material than the pink eraser and should be used with high-quality bond paper. Use the pink eraser with thinner paper to avoid making a hole in the paper. Use an emery board to clean the carbon off of your erasers. Chalk or a white pencil can be used to put the "white" back in paper if an erasure noticeably damages the surrounding area.

Correction Paper—This is paper with a chalk-like substance on one side. It comes in rolls, small tabs, and tear-off sheets. It is available in white or in a variety of colors for use with colored paper. The correction paper is placed over the original, in front of the error; the error is retyped and thus covered by the chalk-like substance; the correction paper is removed; and the correction is retyped.

Correction Fluid—This fluid comes in small bottles and is available in white and in colors for use with colored paper. The opaque fluid is used to cover the error. Once the liquid dries, the correction can be typed. The fluid should be kept at a thin consistency and "dotted on" the error for best results.

Correction Tape—This is white pressure-sensitive paper (usually available in rolls) that can be used for covering a word, a line, or an entire paragraph. Errors corrected via this method are very obvious. Correction tape should not be used for copies to be distributed. It is excellent for copies prepared for reproduction.

Erasable Paper—This paper has been treated with chemicals to make errors easy to erase. It is seldom used in business, since it is more expensive than regular bond paper and because handling a letter may smear the freshly typed page. Typists do consider the use of this special paper for reports and other lengthy jobs.

Carbon Copy Corrections — Unfortunately, the new developments in error correction techniques listed in the foregoing text do not help when making carbon copies. Such errors must be corrected with erasing, correction paper, and/or correction fluid.

When erasing carbon copy errors, protect all following copies by using a stiff card or erasing shield in front of the following carbon, immediately *behind* the error being erased.

Correction paper must be used in front of *each* carbon copy error and removed before retyping the correction.

If correction fluid is used, "dot out" each carbon copy error. Let the fluid dry thoroughly before moving on to other corrections to avoid having the fluid adhere to the carbon paper rather than to the copy.

NCR and Other Carbonless Paper — NCR (*No Carbon Required*) and other carbonless paper is treated with chemicals causing typed letters to appear on the copy either from the back of the preceding sheet or from within the sheet itself. There is no way to correct errors made on this type of paper except with correction fluid and a pen, pencil, or strikeover.

909.5   **Material removed from the typewriter.** Errors discovered after pages have been removed from the typewriter or printed from the computer are more difficult and, therefore, more expensive to correct. They result in paper waste through reprinting or time-consuming realignment at the typewriter. Care should be taken to proofread carefully before the document is printed or released from the machine.

When using word processing software or automatic typewriters, errors are usually corrected and the document is reprinted. Both the reprinted document and original needing correction should be returned to the author. In this way, time can be saved through checking only the corrections, rather than rereading the entire document again before final signature.

When using a typewriter, such errors may be corrected through realignment. Use an *i* or *l* within the document to realign the page horizontally with the typewriter alignment scale.

909.6   **Squeezing and spreading letters.** When you need to add an additional letter to a word, or delete an extra letter from a word, proceed as follows to make the correction.

With word processing software, insert the additional letter or delete the extra letter, and reformat the sentence or paragraph. Reformatting will realign the revised material within the margins specified.

On a typewriter to insert an extra letter, begin the first letter of a word and all following letters a half-space to the left. In this way you may squeeze in an additional letter. When the correction contains one less letter than the original word, you must spread letters and spaces apart to make your correction undetectable. By beginning the first letter of the word and all following letters a half-space to the right (move the typewriter carriage by using the carriage release key; or push the element carrier), the extra space left from the omitted letter will be taken up at the beginning and end of the word.

910 Typing on Forms

Information on forms—such as applications, invoices, bills of lading, and the like—should be typed on the lines of the form so that only a slight space separates the letters from the underline (about the width of a hair). To give the forms you complete a professional look, align the beginnings of typed lines where possible. Fill in all requested information, inserting *N/A* (not applicable) or a dash for lines which do not apply.

911 Typing Index Cards and Labels

It is generally not possible to format index cards and small labels using word processing software, unless the cards and/or labels are available on continuous-form paper that aligns with your printer.

Index cards and labels tend to slip as you type them using a typewriter. To solve this problem, make a small pleat (1/4 inch wide) in a sheet of typing paper. Use cellophane tape to hold the ends of the pleat. Insert the index card or small label into the pleat and roll the sheet with card attached into the typewriter. Slippage will be eliminated.

Unit X

Letters, Memos, Envelopes

Understand:	■ How business correspondence represents an organization
	■ Formats used in today's business correspondence
Acquire:	■ The ability to identify essential parts of business letters, memos, and envelopes
Be Prepared To:	■ Attractively arrange and type error-free business correspondence
	■ Accurately type business envelopes with essential mailing notations

INCOMING MAIL

1000 See Unit 12, ¶1200–1210.

PREPARING BUSINESS CORRESPONDENCE

1001 ### Appearance

The appearance of the correspondence leaving your office is very important. How your letter looks to the recipient—the way it is centered on the page, how neatly the errors are corrected, the use of grammar and punctuation, and the skill with which your message is conveyed—will create an immediate mental impression of your office. From the initial preparation to the final review before mailing, your responsibility in preparing business correspondence is to make certain that you have created the best possible impression. Grammar and punctuation are discussed in other sections of this manual; this unit is a review of the basic guidelines for formatting and keyboarding business letters.

10

1002 ### Office Letterhead

Office letterhead is used for letters sent outside of your organization. This letterhead is printed on good quality bond paper and contains essential information such as the name, address, and telephone number(s) of the organization. Sometimes a listing of individuals within the office or department or both is included. Since both the printing and the quality of paper make letterhead expensive, you should use it carefully.

Several different letterheads may be used within the same office. For example, in a small legal partnership each attorney may employ an individual letterhead as well as the letterhead representing the legal practice. In a large organization, such as a manufacturing firm, the same basic letterhead may be used throughout the organization with a variety of listings added for specific departments or individuals. (See Illustration 10-1)

ILLUSTRATION 10-1
Sample Office Letterhead

DAWKINS BUILDERS
1560 Euclid Avenue
Berkley, CA 94708-0651
(415) 555-2922

Miller Dawkins, President

BOERSMA & IORINO ACADEMY
Specializing in Childern with Learning Difficulties

3256 Pebblebrook Lane
Cincinnati, OH 55239-5623
(513) 555-7990

Dr. Barbara Boersma
President

PALM CONTEMPORARIES
9943 Southwest 147 Court
Miami, FL 33176-9943
(305) 555-3446

"The best-built homes in Florida"

Elsa Agramonte, President
Nestor Agramonte, Vice President

10

1003   Letter Margins

Just as you would center a picture in a picture frame for attractive placement, you should center the text of your letter within the margins of the page. Once you have had practice judging margins, you will find you can quickly visualize where to place a letter. Until you have perfected this technique, however, a few guidelines will be helpful.

Most typewriters use one of two sizes of type—pica or elite. As shown in Illustration 10-2 pica type is larger and has ten letters to a horizontal inch; elite type is smaller and has twelve letters to a horizontal inch. With both styles, six lines are typed in one vertical inch.

ILLUSTRATION 10-2

Horizontal and Vertical Measures

Pica:	abcdefghij	**Ten characters per inch**
	�|←— 1 inch —→|	
Elite:	abcdefghijkl	**Twelve characters per inch**

```
This is an example          This is an example
of elite type to            of pica type to
show you that               show you that
there are six     1 inch    there are six
lines in a vertical         lines in a vertical
inch.                       inch.
```

One of the first steps in determining the most attractive margins to use for a business letter is to estimate what length your letter will be. Generally, letters fall into the following size categories:

ILLUSTRATION 10-3

Letter Placement Table

Letter Classification	5-Stroke Words in Letter Body	Side Margins	Margin Settings		Dateline Position (from Top Edge of Paper)
			Elite	Pica	
Short	Up to 100	2"	24-78*	20-65*	18
Average	101-200	1½"	18-84*	15-70*	16
Long	201-300	1"	12-90*	10-75*	14
Two-page	More than 300	1"	12-90*	10-75*	14
Standard 6" line for all letters**	As above for all letters	1¼"	15-87*	12-72*	As above for all letters

*Plus 5 spaces for the bell cue if you are using a typewriter.
**Often used with word processing equipment/software.

Although the bottom margin of the letter will vary depending upon letter length, always leave *at least* six blank lines (one inch).

If you use a word processor in your office, you will want to employ the same letter style and side margins in all correspondence. The standard six-inch line indicated in Illustration 10-3 (page 237) is most often used. Word processing software programs will automatically assist in pagination, leaving at least a one-inch bottom margin on each page.

If your automatic typewriter or word processing software program uses proportional spacing (that is, each character takes more or less space depending upon its width), refer to the machine or program manual to determine accurate margin alignment.

1004   Personal Business Letter

If you are typing a **personal business letter** (Illustration 10-4), use your home address in place of the company letterhead. All other guidelines for business letter preparation apply.

1005   Business Letter Styles

The most widely used business letter styles are the **block, modified block,** and **simplified.** Letters of various lengths appear in all styles. See Illustration 10-5 (page 240).

- **Block:** *All* lines begin at the left margin. See Illustration 10-6 (page 241).

- **Modified Block with Block Paragraphs:** All lines begin at the left margin except date, complimentary close, and signature lines, all of which begin at the center of the page. See Illustration 10-7 (page 241).

- **Modified Block with Indented Paragraphs:** Identical to the modified block, except that the first word of all paragraphs is indented five spaces. Also, the subject line may be centered or indented five spaces to match the paragraphs. See Illustration 10-8 (page 242).

- **Simplified:** All lines begin at the left margin. The date is placed on line twelve. To *simplify* the keyboarding of this letter: the inside address is keyed all in capital letters; the salutation is omitted and replaced by a subject line keyed all in caps; the complimentary close is omitted; the writer's name and title are keyed all in capital letters on one line. Since the salutation and complimentary close are omitted, the punctuation styles described in ¶1006 do not apply. See Illustration 10-9 (page 242).

1006   Business Letter Punctuation Styles

Two punctuation styles are used in office correspondence.

- **Mixed Punctuation:** This is the most widely used punctuation style. It requires a colon after the salutation and a comma after the complimentary close. See Illustrations 10-6 & 10-7 (page 241).

- **Open Punctuation:** No punctuation is used after the salutation or the complimentary close. See Illustration 10-8 (page 242).

ILLUSTRATION 10-4

Personal Business Letter

```
4408 Glen Rose Street
Fairfax, VA  22032-8044
January 15, 19--

Academic Advisement Department
Santa Fe Community College
111 Southeast First Avenue
Gainesville, FL  33333-1110

Ladies and Gentlemen:

I am interested in enrolling in the legal assistant
training program offered at Santa Fe Community College.

I should appreciate receiving information regarding
admission requirements and financial assistance
available at Santa Fe.  Also, please send me a copy of
your college catalog containing information on course
requirements and course descriptions for the legal
assistant and executive secretary programs.

Do you have dormitories on your campus?  If not, are
there student apartments near the campus?  Since I
shall be coming from Virginia to attend Santa Fe, I
shall need some help in finding a place to live.

Thank you for your assistance.

Sincerely,

Karen McMeekin

Karen McMeekin
```

PARTS OF A BUSINESS LETTER

All business letters have certain essential elements. Other elements may or may not be included, depending upon letter requirements.

Required Business Letter Parts

- Letterhead or Return Address
- Date

- Inside Address
- Salutation (**not** used in simplified style)
- Body
- Complimentary Close (**not** used in simplified style)
- Originator's Identification
- Reference Initials

1008   Optional Business Letter Parts

- Mailing/Special Notations
- Attention Line
- Subject Line
- Typed Company Name
- Title of Originator
- Enclosure Notation
- Copy Notation
- Postscript

ILLUSTRATION 10-5

Short, Average, and Long Letters

1009   Date

The date is a required part of business correspondence because it indicates to the reader when the letter was written. Use the Letter Placement Table (Illustration 10-3, page 237) to determine attractive vertical placement of the dateline (**Exception:** the simplified letter style; see Illustration 10-9, page 242). Horizontal placement depends upon the business letter style to be used (¶1005).

ILLUSTRATION 10-7

Modified Block Letter Style with Block Paragraphs
Mixed Punctuation

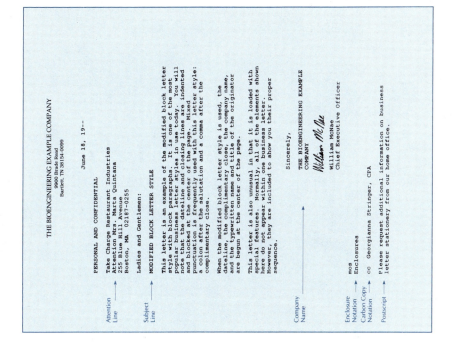

ILLUSTRATION 10-6

Block Letter Style
Mixed Punctuation

ILLUSTRATION 10-9

Simplified Letter Style

SEASIDE BUSINESS SCHOOL
100 Bay Boulevard
Miami, FL 33130-0101

February 1, 19—

ALMA GUERRA
CHANNEL 23—WLTV
2600 CORAL WAY
MIAMI FL 33135-0260

SIMPLIFIED BLOCK LETTER FORMAT

This letter illustrates the features that distinguish the
simplified block letter format from the standard block format.

1. The date is placed on line twelve so that the letter address
will show through the window of a window envelope when used.

2. The letter address is keyed in the style recommended by the
U. S. Postal Service for OCR processing: all-cap letters with no
punctuation. Cap-and-lowercase letters with punctuation may be
used if that is the format of addresses stored in an electronic
address file. Personal titles may be omitted.

3. A subject line replaces the traditional salutation which some
people find objectionable. The subject line may be keyed in all-
cap or cap-and-lowercase letters. A double space is left above
and below it.

4. The complimentary close, which some people view as a needless
appendage, is omitted.

5. The writer's name is placed on the fourth line space below
the body of the letter. The writer's title or department name
may appear on the line with the writer's name or on the next line
below it. The signature block may be keyed in all-cap or cap-
and-lowercase letters.

6. A standard-length line is used for all letters. A six-inch
line is a common length (60 pica or 10-pitch spaces; 72 elite or
12-pitch spaces).

The features listed and illustrated here are designed to bring
efficiency to the electronic processing of mail.

Kathie Sigler

KATHIE SIGLER, DEAN FOR ADMINISTRATION

mos

ILLUSTRATION 10-8

Modified Block Letter Style with Indented Paragraphs
Open Punctuation

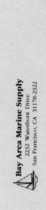

Bay Area Marine Supply
2232 Waterfront Drive
San Francisco, CA 31178-2322

April 10, 19—

REGISTERED MAIL

Nancy A. List, D.O.
1754 Maple Ridge Road
Haslett, MI 48840-4571

Dear Dr. List

It is a pleasure to confirm May twenty-
second as the delivery date for your new 32-
foot "Starlight" cruiser. The factory
representatives assure me that the special
options you ordered can be worked into the
production schedule without any difficulty.

Our original quotation of $198,600 is
now a firm price. It is payable at the time
the title is transferred. Please let me know
if you want any assistance with financing.

You have selected a fine boat; I hope
you will spend many enjoyable hours aboard.

Very truly yours

Eugene McDonald

Eugene McDonald, President

mq

As you know, a member of our staff will
be available to assist you on a shakedown
cruise at your convenience anytime within
sixty days of delivery.

1010   Mailing Notations and Other Special Notations

Special mailing notations (AIRMAIL, REGISTERED, SPECIAL DELIVERY, CERTIFIED) and other special notations (PERSONAL, CONFIDENTIAL) are keyed all in capital letters at the left margin a double space below the dateline.

1011   Inside Address/Salutation

The inside address provides all essential information for delivery of the business letter: addressee's name, title, company name, street number and name, city, two-letter state abbreviation, and ZIP Code. (For two-letter state abbreviations, see ¶1025 and 1026). The inside address also provides the information needed to determine the correct salutation to be used.

Following are several examples of inside addresses and appropriate salutations for each. Note that the city, state abbreviation, and ZIP Code are keyed on one line. Two spaces (but **no** comma) follow the state abbreviation before the ZIP Code.

1011.1   To an individual. (Colon after salutation indicates mixed punctuation)

Mr. Ted Livingston
Tulane University
Thirty-one McAlister Drive
New Orleans, LA 85555-3100
Dear Mr. Livingston:

Ms. Vicki Kissling
Two Linden Place
Elkhart, IN 46514-2222
Dear Ms. Kissling:

1011.2   To an individual at a business address. (Absence of punctuation after salutation indicates open punctuation)

Horace E. Traylor, M.D.
Instructional Resources
Los Angeles Pierce College
6201 Winnetka Avenue
Woodland, CA 91364-6200
Dear Dr. Traylor

Vice President
School of Architecture
University of Miami
1600 Northwest Tenth Avenue
Miami, FL 33136-0006
Dear Sir or Madam

1011.3   To a company/organization.

The Upjohn Company
Pharmaceutical Sales Office
1974 Lashly Court
Snellville, GA 30278-9741
Ladies and Gentlemen:

1011.4   Two-line address.

Mrs. Leota Schramm
Rogers City, MI 49779-3370
Dear Aunt Leota

1011.5 With apartment number.

Ms. Paula Epstein
7131 Wood Drive, Apt. 151
Austin, TX 78731-7131
Dear Paula

1011.6 Two people, different addresses.

Arthur Asher, M.D.   and   Ileana Gonzalez, D.O.
P.O. Box 2143   4408 Glen Rose Street
Riverview Road   Fairfax, VA 22032-8040
Riverton, WY 82501-2143
Dear Drs. Asher and Gonzalez:

1011.7 Two people, same address.

- Eliminate position titles, unless they are short and can fit on the same line with the name.

- Put names in alphabetical order.

- Eliminate department, unless both are from the same department.

- On individual envelopes, type full addresses.

Mr. Tom Petersen
Ms. Pam Stringer
Legal Services Association
1150 North Franklin
Dearborn, MI 48128-1105
Dear Tom and Pam:

1011.8 Titles. Change the position of titles to balance the inside address.

Dr. Pat Hodges, Director
Betancourt Health Center
15432 Kit Lane
Fort Worth, TX 75240-5324

Dr. Billie Marie Tomlin
Vice President
Betancourt Health Center
15432 Kit Lane
Fort Worth, TX 75240-5324

Roz Reich, M.D.
Vice President and
  General Manager
Betancourt Health Center
15432 Kit Lane
Fort Worth, TX 75240-5324

NOTE: When a house or building number is under 100, spell it out. Use figures for numbers 100 or greater. See Unit 7, ¶711.

Three Maple Lane
100 Woodward Avenue

1011.9 | ## Room, suite, building in address.

Ms. Renee Betancourt
Attorney at Law
429 Broad Street, Suite Thirteen
Richmond, VA 23219-4329
Dear Ms. Betancourt:

Columbus Employees Federal
   Credit Union*
Penobscot Building, Room 118
1800 King Avenue
Columbus, OH 48216-0011
Ladies and Gentlemen:

*NOTE: Long company names can be placed on two lines.

1011.10 | ## Husband and wife.

Dr. and Mrs. Doug Andrews
2050 Massachusetts Avenue
Washington, D.C. 20503-0500
Dear Dr. and Mrs. Andrews:

1011.11 | ## Foreign country.

Mr. Ryan Stringer
Trapp Interiors, Ltd.
Twenty-seven Monks Close
Leeds, York ALY-372
ENGLAND*
Dear Mr. Stringer:

*NOTE: Key the name of a foreign country all in caps.

1011.12 | ## In care of.

Alberta Goodman, D.O.
In care of John Roueche, D.O.   *or*   % John Roueche, D.O.
University of Texas at Austin
Austin, TX 78731-7001
Dear Dr. Goodman:

1012 | # Attention Line

Frequently an attention line is used to route a letter to a particular person when a letter is addressed to a company. The attention line indicates that the letter concerns company business and that the writer prefers that the letter be handled by the individual named in the attention line (or by another individual in a similar role if the individual named is no longer with the company). The attention line is keyed as the second line in the inside address. Note that the salutation agrees with the inside address, **not** the attention line.

Carolina Construction
Attention Ms. Sally Buxton
1005 Ala Lililoi Street
Honolulu, HI 96818-5000
Ladies and Gentlemen:

ExtraSuper Food Centers
ATTENTION Mr. Dan Derrico
2525 West Armitage Avenue
Melrose Park, IL 60164-2005
Ladies and Gentlemen:

1013 | # Subject Line

When a subject line is included, it serves as a title to the body of the letter and should be keyed a double space below the salutation. The subject line may be placed at the left margin. With the modified block letter, the subject line may be centered, begin at the left margin, or be indented five spaces (if the paragraphs are so indented). *SUBJECT* or *RE* is sometimes used with the subject line, but not required. The subject line can be keyed all in caps, in capitals and lowercase, or in capitals and lowercase underlined. A double space follows the subject line, before beginning the body of the letter.

Detroit, MI 48219-9106
Dear Mr. Gathercole:
            ANNUAL DATAFLEX CONFERENCE

Detroit, MI 48219-9106
Dear Mr. Gathercole:
SUBJECT: Annual Dataflex Conference

Detroit, MI 48219-9106
Dear Mr. Gathercole:
            RE: Annual Dataflex Conference

1014   Body

The message of your business letter is contained in the body. Each paragraph should be single-spaced with double spacing between paragraphs. Paragraphs begin at the left margin (except with the modified block, indented paragraph style).

Efforts should be made to balance paragraph size, with at least two paragraphs in a letter. A very short letter (six lines or less) may be double-spaced, or extra blank lines may be inserted between letter parts to achieve balance. See Illustration 10-10.

Quoted or tabular material within a letter is set off by a double space before and after the quotation, and by a five-space indention from the left margin.

1015   Complimentary Close, Company Name, and Signature Lines

A recent survey of businesses found that the majority used the **complimentary close** "Very truly yours" or "Sincerely." Two other popular ones were "Sincerely yours" and "Yours very truly."

- Key the complimentary close at the left margin in a block style letter (begin at the center in modified block style) a double space below the body of the letter.

- Capitalize only the first letter of the first word.

■ With mixed punctuation, place a comma after the complimentary close. With open punctuation, no punctuation is used.

ILLUSTRATION 10-10

Very Short Letter, Double-Spaced for Attractive Alignment
Mixed Punctuation

CARIBE MARKETPLACE
Loews Anatule Hotel
Dallas, TX 76135-1012

September 8, 19--

Ms. Rene McCullers
Tarrant County Junior College
5301 Campus Drive
Ft. Worth, TX 76119-5030

Dear Rene:

Congratulations on your appointment as Vice

President for Development of Tarrant County

Junior College. Please call on us if we can

be of assistance in your new role.

Sincerely,

Janet Seitlin
Conference Manager

mos

In some offices, the **company name** is keyed all in capital letters a double space after the complimentary close. The company name begins in the same place (left margin or center) as the complimentary close.

The **signature lines** are those lines which identify the writer of the letter and often the writer's title or department or both. They follow the complimentary close (or company name if one is used) by four line spaces. The signature line also begins in the same place (left margin or center) as the complimentary close.

Sincerely,	Very truly yours
PERSUTTI ASSOCIATES	PRIDE INTERNATIONAL
Delphine Persutti	Robert Ochs, Ph.D.
President	Dean of Students

- Titles may be on the same line as the writer's name, or on the following line.

- Titles of Miss, Ms., or Mrs. may be used with the typewritten name. Parentheses are optional. This allows the recipient of the letter to address his or her response correctly.

Sincerely yours,	Sincerely
(Ms.) Tomoko Sumida	Dr. Rene Garcia
Manager	Vice President

Hyphenated last names. Some hyphenated names are representative of two cultures. A hyphenated name such as Rivera-Wiggins is used by a Hispanic male or female. The two names represent the father's and mother's sides of the family. They are both used to indicate a pride in heritage. When a hyphenated Hispanic name is typed, the signature will always reflect the same hyphenation.

Sincerely yours,

Diana Rivera-Wiggins

Diana Rivera-Wiggins
Public Relations Director

Hyphenated last names are also a trend with many married people of other cultures who wish to use both the wife's family name and the husband's family name. Thus, Miss Bonnie Landsea who married Mr. Peter Diehl would become:

	And he would become:
Bonnie Landsea-Diehl	Peter Landsea-Diehl
Mrs. Bonnie Landsea-Diehl	Mr. Peter Landsea-Diehl
Mrs. Peter Landsea-Diehl	

Note that the wife's family name is first and the husband's second.

1016 Reference Initials

Reference initials identify the typist of the business correspondence. They are placed at the left margin, a double space below the final signature line. Reference initials are keyed in a variety of ways:

- Indicating the typist:

    kds   zz   map

■ Indicating the writer* (first initials) and the typist:

ALR:kss   TRD/POE   SR:cm

*The writer's initials are included in this way only if the writer's name is not typed.

1017 Enclosure Notation

When additional information is to be enclosed in the envelope with business correspondence, an enclosure notation should be used. This notation is placed at the left margin a double space below the reference initials. (See Illustration 10-11 on page 250 and its enclosure, Illustration 10-12 on page 251.) Enclosure notations are keyed in a variety of ways.

Enclosure	Enclosures (2)	Enclosures: Invoice
		Order Form
Enc.	Enc. 2	Check Enclosed

1018 Copy Notation

When copies of a business letter are to be sent to other individuals, a copy notation should be placed at the left margin, a double space below the enclosure notation or reference initials, whichever is last. (**NOTE:** pc = photocopy, cc = carbon copy)

cc   Dr. Hansen   pc   Research Department
     Dr. Kelly   Personnel

Also used:

Copy to: Ms. Meg Laughlin   Copy to Purchasing
         Dr. Joan Schaeffer

It is helpful to indicate when enclosures are (or are not) sent to those who are to receive copies of the letter:

pc   (w/enclosures)   Dr. Harriet Spivak
                         Dr. Charlotte Gallogly
cc   Dr. Harriet Spivak (w/enclosures)
     Dr. Charlotte Gallogly (w/o enclosures)

Sometimes the letter writer wants to send a copy of a business letter to someone without the addressee's knowledge. In this case, a **blind copy** notation should be used on the file copy **only**.

bcc: Mr. Oswaldo Lopez   or   bpc: Mr. Oswaldo Lopez
      Legal Department   Legal Department

1019 File Copies

Whether stored on paper or electronically (on a magnetic disk or other electronic medium), copies of all business correspondence should be available in the office.

Paper file copies, the most widely used storage device, may be made with carbon paper, made with NCR (no carbon required) paper, or made on the office photocopier. Some businesses have special sheets with simplified letterheads for copies sent outside the office. Paper copies are filed in a convenient cabinet for quick retrieval.

Electronic file copies are made automatically when letters produced on word processing equipment or computers are saved. While the original letter is made using the printer (and copies are usually made on a photocopier), the office file copy should be electronically stored. This practice will save much office storage space and allow for future electronic transmission of the document to other offices.

ILLUSTRATION 10-11

Letter of Application

NELSON A. BENEDICO

11621 Southwest 112th Street
Miami, Florida 33176-1621
April 6, 19--

Hank Meyer & Associates
2990 Biscayne Boulevard
Miami, FL 33131-9900

Dear Mr. Meyer:

What do the words PUBLIC RELATIONS mean without being followed with the words HANK MEYER? Regardless of whether I am in class, at a PRSSA meeting, or at work, your name enters the conversation. In the face of such omnipresence, one might be intimidated to write you. However, with the encouragement of Bill Stokes, I am taking that step. By way of my employment at Miami-Dade Community College/South Campus and through my mother, Zoila de Zayas, I have grown to know Dr. Stokes closely and value his opinion.

I am a student at the University of Miami and shall be graduated in approximately two months. I shall receive my Bachelor of Science in Communications degree in Public Relations and English.

I am interested in an entry level public relations position and should like the opportunity to discuss such a possibility with you. What makes me different? I love hard work. I love pressure. I love results.

I have completed internships with Beber Silverstein and Burson-Marsteller this semester and have grown accustomed to the environment that requires long hours, unexpected problems, but offers the satisfaction of results. Some may call it an "ulcer factory." I call it thrilling.

I can offer you the experience I have acquired from my internships. In addition, I can offer my bilingual skills, writing abilities, and zealous energy.

I should appreciate the opportunity to speak with you concerning any suggestions you may have about the notorious job search. I am enclosing a copy of my resume for your consideration and shall call you next week to schedule an appointment at your convenience.

In addition, Dr. Stokes asked me to offer him as a reference. He may be able to provide you with more information. I appreciate your time.

Sincerely,

Nelson A. Benedico

Nelson A. Benedico

Enclosure: Resume

ILLUSTRATION 10-12

Sample Resume

NELSON A. BENEDICO
11621 Southwest 112th Street
Miami, Fl 33176-1621
(305) 555-4107

EDUCATION
Bachelor of Science in Communication
University of Miami, School of Communication
Coral Gables, Florida
May 1990

MAJORS: Public Relations/English

Tulane University
New Orleans, Louisiana
September 1983 - December 1984

INTERNSHIPS
Beber Silverstein & Partners
Public Relations Division
Miami, Florida
December 1988 - May 1990

Responsible for: Reviewing publications for
client articles; Maintaining clipping files;
Establishing a computer system for generating
mass-mailing labels; Updating media contacts;
Producing a clipping file on Beber Silverstein; Preparing pasteup of articles into
camera-ready work for reproduction; Assisting
in the planning and execution of special
events; Assisting with technical aspects of
presentations; Writing, editing, and
preparing releases, proposals, and
correspondence for a variety of clients.

Burson-Marsteller
Chicago, Illinois
February 1987 - March 1987

One of six UM students to represent Burson-
Marsteller in a local project for Procter &
Gamble. Responsible for: Serving as Miami
representative for Chicago-based Burson-
Marsteller; Serving as liaison between the
company and local merchants; the media, and
the public; Executing events, including
advance preparation, and follow-up of event
at over 80 stores in three Florida counties;
Supervising work teams at each site;
Preparing paperwork, activity records, and
logs of expenses.

WORK EXPERIENCE
Miami-Dade Community College
Mitchell Wolfson New World Center Campus
Department of Public Affairs
Miami, Florida

Typesetter

Responsible for: Typesetting brochures, class
bulletins, and flyers for campus activities;
Providing specifications on unlabeled work;
Maintaining traffic schedule to insure
deadlines.

PERSONAL
LANGUAGES: Ability to read, write and
speak Spanish fluently.
Working knowledge of American
Sign Language.

OFFICE SKILLS: Typing, word processing,
computer operation.

AFFILIATIONS
Public Relations Student Society of America

REFERENCES
Eduardo Padron   William M. Stokes
Vice President   Vice President
Miami-Dade   Miami-Dade
Community College   Community College
(305) 555-3000   (305) 555-2000

1020   Additional Pages

When a letter extends to a second page, a plain piece of bond paper of the same quality as the original letterhead should be used. Following the same side margins, the second page of a two-page letter should begin on line seven with an identifying heading which indicates to whom the letter was written. See Illustrations 10-13, 14, & 15 (page 254).

Schaeffer Medical Research Group
Page 2
September 15, 19--

or

Schaeffer Medical Research Group   2   September 15, 19--

Following the second-page heading, double-space and resume keying the body of the letter.

- Do not divide a paragraph between pages unless two lines remain on the first page and at least two lines of the same paragraph begin the second page.

- Leave a uniform bottom margin of at least one inch at the bottom of all letter pages (except, perhaps, a larger margin on the last).

- Do not hyphenate the final word on a page.

- Do not use the second page to key only the complimentary close and following lines. At least two lines of the final paragraph should begin the second page.

To shorten a long letter that is not quite long enough to require two pages, the number of blank lines between the letterhead and date, between the date and inside address, or before the signature line may be reduced. In addition, single spacing may be used between reference initials, enclosure notations, and copy notations.

1021   Postscripts

A **postscript** is an additional word, line, or paragraph added after a letter has been completed. It is keyed as the **last** item in the letter, a double space below the reference initials, enclosure notation, or copy notation, whichever is last. The postscript should begin at the left margin, or be indented five spaces, depending upon the letter style chosen. See Illustration 10-8 on page 242.

CORRESPONDENCE WITHIN THE COMPANY

1022   Keyboarding an Interoffice Memorandum

Letters sent to individuals within the same company or organization are often keyboarded as interoffice memorandums. This practice allows for the use of less expensive stationery, as well as identifies immediately that the correspondence is from within the organization.

ILLUSTRATION 10-13

Two-Page Letter

NELSON A. BENEDICO

11521 Southwest 112 Street
Miami, FL 33176-1621
March 30, 19--

Ms. Elaine Silverstein
Beber Silverstein & Partners
3361 Southwest Third Avenue
Miami, FL 33145-6130

Dear Ms. Silverstein:

When my advisor first suggested the possibility of an
internship with Beber Silverstein, I was doubtful it would ever
come to fruition. I have now accomplished over 250 hours at
Beber and am walking away with more than my textbooks or
professors could have shown me in four years!

I want to take this opportunity to express my gratitude to
you for permitting me to enter the complex workings of an agency
of the magnitude of yours. For that, Ms. Silverstein, I shall
always be grateful.

Graduates today encounter that same horrible question, "What
experience do you have?" Unfortunately, few new graduates are
prepared to offer a positive answer. I am one of the lucky ones
that can respond to that question. Thank you.

I am sure you are aware that on April tenth my internship
will end, and I shall fall victim to exams, presentations, and
reports. I chose this date because it will permit me time to
prepare for the end of the semester. I realize the limitations
your new Public Relations Department is currently under and how
difficult personnel expansion may be at this time. I am,
however, enclosing a copy of my resume for you to consider for
any openings in the future. I can offer you my energy,
education, bilingual skills, and professionalism.

ILLUSTRATION 10-14

Second Page of Letter 10-10

Ms. Elaine Silverstein   2   March 30, 19--

I have enjoyed the time I spent within the walls of Beber
Silverstein and have prepared a report on my internship as part
of my requirements. If you are interested, I should be very
happy to present it to you. Please continue to offer your "real
life" expertise for students to add to their academic arsenal.
The experience is invaluable.

Sincerely,

Nelson A. Benedico
Nelson A. Benedico

mos

pc Ms. Lina Rodriquez

ILLUSTRATION 10-15

Second Page of Letter 10-10
Different Heading—Normally Used *Only* with Block Style*

```
Ms. Elaine Silverstein
Page 2
March 30, 19--

     I have enjoyed the time I spent within the walls of Beber
Silverstein and have prepared a report on my internship as part
of my requirements.  If you are interested, I should be very
happy to present it to you.  Please continue to offer your "real
life" expertise for students to add to their academic arsenal.
The experience is invaluable.

Sincerely,

Nelson A. Benedico

Nelson A. Benedico

mos

pc Ms. Lina Rodriguez
```

*Note, therefore, the change to block placement of the closing—on the first page, the inside address and date would also be flush left.

Interoffice memorandums are keyed on memorandum forms or on plain paper. The headings TO, FROM, DATE, and SUBJECT usually begin the memorandum. The subject line may or may not be capitalized. There are no complimentary close or signature lines in the interoffice memorandum. The writer signs (using name or initials) next to his or her name at the top. Reference initials, enclosure notations, and copy notations remain the same as in business letters. See Illustrations 10-16 & 10-17.

ILLUSTRATION 10-16

Interoffice Memorandum On Plain Paper

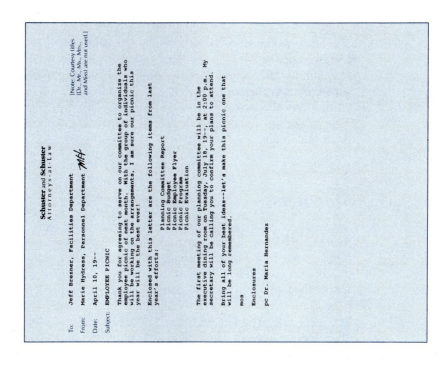

[Note: Courtesy titles
(Dr., Mr., Ms., Mrs.,
and Miss) are not used.]

TO: Jeff Brezner, Facilities Department

FROM: Marie Hydress, Personnel Department *MH*

DATE: April 10, 19--

SUBJECT: EMPLOYEE PICNIC

Thank you for agreeing to serve on our committee to
organize the employee picnic of next month. With the
group of individuals who will be working on the
arrangements, I am sure our picnic this year will be
the best ever!

Enclosed with this letter are the following items from
last year's efforts:

          Planning Committee Report
          Picnic Budget
          Picnic Employee Flyer
          Picnic Program
          Picnic Evaluation

The first meeting of our planning committee will be in
the executive dining room on Tuesday, July 18, 19--, at
2:00 p.m. My secretary will be calling you to confirm
your plans to attend.

Bring all of your best ideas--let's make this picnic
one that will be long remembered.

mos

Enclosures

pc Dr. Maria Hernandez

ILLUSTRATION 10-17

Interoffice Memorandum On a Company Form

Schuster and **Schuster**
Attorneys-at-Law

[Note: Courtesy titles
(Dr., Mr., Ms., Mrs.,
and Miss) are not used.]

To: Jeff Brezner, Facilities Department

From: Marie Hydress, Personnel Department *MH*

Date: April 10, 19--

Subject: EMPLOYEE PICNIC

Thank you for agreeing to serve on our committee to organize the
employee picnic of next month. With the group of individuals who
will be working on the arrangements, I am sure our picnic this
year will be the best ever!

Enclosed with this letter are the following items from last
year's efforts:

          Planning Committee Report
          Picnic Budget
          Picnic Employee Flyer
          Picnic Program
          Picnic Evaluation

The first meeting of our planning committee will be in the
executive dining room on Tuesday, July 18, 19--, at 2:00 p.m. My
secretary will be calling you to confirm your plans to attend.

Bring all of your best ideas--let's make this picnic one that
will be long remembered.

mos

Enclosures

pc Dr. Maria Hernandez

1023 Composing for the Employer's Signature

The office worker should become familiar with typical answers to routine correspondence, whether by letter or memorandum. In the electronic office, canned paragraphs can be stored for later rearrangement and use in subsequent correspondence. It will be helpful to the supervisor if the worker can draft routine correspondence. The supervisor will then review, make any necessary corrections or revisions, and sign the final, revised document.

OUTGOING MAIL

1024 Preparation of Envelopes

Envelopes should be prepared for outgoing mail before presentation of the letter to the writer for signature. Each envelope should include the return address of the writer (usually in preprinted form to match the letterhead), the complete address of the person or organization or both to whom the letter is to be sent, and any special mailing notations. Both addresses on the envelope should contain the two-letter state abbreviation and ZIP Code. The United States Postal Service prefers that all envelope addresses be keyed all in capital letters with no punctuation.

1025 Two-Letter State Abbreviations (See Unit 4, Table 4-1.)

1026 Two-Letter Canadian Province Abbreviations (See Unit 4, Table 4-2.)

1027 Return Address

Most of the time the business envelopes you use will be printed with the name and address of your office in the upper left corner of the envelope. It may, however, be necessary for you to type the name of the letter writer and/or department or account number (if you work for a large office). This information should be typed above the printed return address.

For personal business correspondence, or if your office does not use preprinted envelopes, the return address should be typed a double space from the top edge of the envelope and three spaces from the left edge.

1028 Mailing Address

The mailing address on the envelope should be typed four inches from the left edge and on line fifteen of a large envelope, two and one half inches from the left edge and on line twelve for a small envelope.

1029 Nine-digit Expanded ZIP Code

The U.S. Postal Service has added four more digits to the standard five-digit ZIP Code. Most companies are aware of their expanded ZIP Codes. This new code should allow faster processing and directing of all mail, which should also result in faster delivery. The increase in efficiency is important in view of the larger volumes of mail processed each year by the Postal Service. If you have any questions about your office's ZIP Code, call or write your local postal center.

1030 Envelope Notations

Notations that are intended for the office receiving the mail are called **addressee notations.** These notations are used by the person(s) delivering mail within the office and include information such as PERSONAL, CONFIDENTIAL, HOLD FOR ARRIVAL, or PLEASE FORWARD. Such addressee notations should be typed all in capital letters a triple space below the return address and three spaces from the left edge.

Mailing notations, those mailing directions intended for the U.S. Postal Service, include REGISTERED, RETURN RECEIPT REQUESTED, and SPECIAL DELIVERY. Such notations identify special mailing requirements for postal personnel and should be typed all in capital letters on line nine from the top edge, below the postage stamp (or postage meter mark).

Illustration 10-18 (page 258) shows the correct way to type both small and large business envelopes with a variety of mailing notations.

1031 Folding Business Letters

The correct procedure for folding business letters for insertion into envelopes varies according to the size of the envelope. Illustration 10-19 (page 259) shows how to fold a business letter for both a large and a small envelope. Also included are illustrations for folding business correspondence for insertion into a window envelope; make certain the complete address shows clearly through the window after insertion.

1032 Metered Mail

In most large offices, postage is applied to envelopes by a postage metering machine. This machine can add the various amounts of postage required depending upon the weight of the envelope or package being mailed. To facilitate rapid metering of mail, envelopes should be left open (the meter machine automatically seals all envelopes) with all envelope flaps up and addresses facing the same way. CONFIDENTIAL mail can be presealed before sending it to the mailroom, if desired. To avoid machine damage, letter envelopes containing bulky items, such as paperclips, should be sealed and marked "Hand Stamp" by the originating office. See Unit 12, ¶1234.

1033 Classes of Mail (See Unit 12, ¶1220–1227.)

1034 Special Mailing Services

Special mailing services and delivery schedules are available through the postal service and from private mail and parcel carriers. Consult your

ILLUSTRATION 10-18
Envelopes with Notations

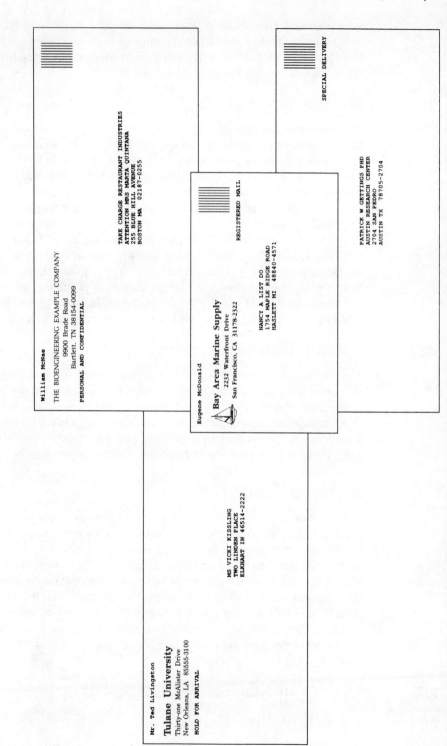

William McNae

THE BIOENGINEERING EXAMPLE COMPANY
9900 Brade Road
Bartlett, TN 38154-0099
PERSONAL AND CONFIDENTIAL

TAKE CHARGE RESTAURANT INDUSTRIES
ATTENTION MRS MARTA QUINTANA
255 BLUE HILL AVENUE
BOSTON MA 02187-0255

SPECIAL DELIVERY

PATRICK W GETTINGS PHD
AUSTIN RESEARCH CENTER
2704 SAN PEDRO
AUSTIN TX 78705-2704

Eugene McDonald

Bay Area Marine Supply
2232 Waterfront Drive
San Francisco, CA 31178-2322

REGISTERED MAIL

NANCY A LIST DO
1754 MAPLE RIDGE ROAD
HASLETT MI 48840-4571

Mr. Ted Livingston

Tulane University
Thirty-one McAlister Drive
New Orleans, LA 85555-3100
HOLD FOR ARRIVAL

MS VICKI KISSLING
TWO LINDEN PLACE
ELKHART IN 46514-2222

ILLUSTRATION 10-19

Choosing Envelopes and Folding Letters

Stationery	Envelope	Fold	Window Envelope Fold
Standard (8 1/2" x 11")	No. 10 (9 1/2" x 4 1/8") No. 6 3/4 (6 1/2" x 3 5/8")	3 2-3	W3 —
Monarch (7 1/4" x 10 1/2")	No. 7 (7 1/2" x 3 7/8")	3	W3
Baronial (5 1/2" x 8 1/2")	No. 5 3/8 (5 15/16" x 4 5/8")	2	W2

Fold 2

Fold into 2 parts.

Fold 2-3

Fold into 2 parts, then fold into 3 parts.

Fold 3

Fold W2
(Window
Envelope)

Fold into 2 parts.

Fold W3
(Window
Envelope)

Fold into 3 parts.

local telephone book for a complete list of providers. Special mailing services available include overnight delivery, special delivery, insurance for mail or packages, certificate of mailing (proves that you mailed something), certified mail/return receipt requested (proves that mail was delivered and provides you with the signature of the individual receiving the mail), registered mail (for items that cannot be replaced and/or are valued at $400+), COD (cash on delivery), money orders, and mail forwarding. Each of these services has special restrictions and requirements on time, size, weight, and so forth. Check with your local post office or private mail carrier for details. See Unit 12, ¶1228–1233.

Unit XI

Reports and Manuscripts

Understand:	■ The purposes for which reports and manuscripts are used
	■ How the various parts of reports and manuscripts work together
Acquire:	■ The ability to identify the required and optional parts of reports and manuscripts and to know how they are used
	■ The ability to identify correct formatting of reports and manuscripts
Be Prepared To:	■ Correctly keyboard the body of a report or manuscript in an attractive manner
	■ Keyboard the other parts of a report or manuscript with correct format matching that used in the body

1100   Business reports are written to convey information in a clear, concise manner. They may be formal or informal — but should always retain their clarity and conciseness. You quite likely know something about writing reports because you probably have written reports or manuscripts or both as part of your job or as a class assignment.

1101   ## Formal Reports

Formal reports may contain many parts. Some components are necessary; others are optional.

Business Report

Required	Optional
Title Page *or*	*Both* the Title Page *and*
Letter of Transmittal	Letter of Transmittal
Body of Report	Preface/Foreword
	Acknowledgments/Dedication
	Table of Contents
	Bibliography
	Appendix
	Footnotes

Each of the parts listed above is discussed in detail in the following pages. Examples are provided of several parts.

1102	## Report and Manuscript Spacing
1102.1	**Short and informal reports or manuscripts.** When reports or manuscripts are short and informal, they are usually bound by a staple inserted in the top left corner; such reports are said to be **unbound**. Margins for these and all reports are shown in Table 11-1.
1102.2	**Long reports — leftbound.** When reports are lengthy, they should be bound. When the report is bound (either with several staples, spiral, three-ring, plastic cover or other binding) at the left side, the report is **leftbound**. An extra half inch of space is left in the margin of the left side.
1102.3	**Topbound report.** If a similar binding is used at the top, it is a **topbound** report. An extra half inch of space is left in the margin at the top.
1103	## Title Page

The **title page** contains the report title, the writer's name (also title and department on a business report), and the date the report is submitted. Each item is centered horizontally; the title is keyed in capitals, with all capitals for the other lines optional. Vertical spacing is chosen for balance of the entire page. See Illustration 11-2 (page 264).

However, if the title page is to be bound in a leftbound report, one-half inch should be added to the left margin before horizontally centering each line. With a topbound report, an extra four to six blank lines should be left at the top of the title page.

1104	## Letter of Transmittal

The **letter of transmittal** introduces the report to the intended reader. It can be used to summarize important information, point out certain comparisons, and so on. Keyboarding instructions for the letter of transmittal are the same as those for any business letter (see Unit 10). However, if a letter of transmittal is to be a part of a leftbound report, one-half inch should be added to the left margin of the letter; in a topbound report, begin the dateline four to six lines lower on the page. See Illustration 11-3 (page 264).

1105	## Preface/Foreword; Acknowledgments/Dedication (Preceding Lengthy Reports)
1105.1	**Preface/foreword.** The **preface** (written by the author) or **foreword** (written by someone other than the author) is a set of introductory remarks to the reader, sometimes providing special information on methods used in gathering information for the report, and sometimes pointing out special parts of the report itself. See Illustration 11-4 (page 265).
1105.2	**Acknowledgments/dedication.** The **acknowledgments** or **dedication** page is a personal message from the author to individuals who have provided special assistance or to whom the volume is dedicated. See Illustration 11-5 (page 265).

11

TABLE 11-1

Business Report Margins

Type of Page	Unbound					Leftbound					Topbound				
	Top	Btm.†	Left†	Right†	Page‡	Top	Btm.†	Left†	Right†	Page‡	Top	Btm.†	Left†	Right†	Page‡
Title Page	*N/A				None	N/A				None	N/A				None
Letter of Transmittal	N/A				btm.	N/A				btm.	N/A				btm.
Preface/Foreword	Line 10 (Elite: 12)	1	1	1	btm.	Line 10 (Elite: 12)	1	1½	1	btm.	Line 12 (Elite: 14)	1	1	1	btm.
Acknowledgments/ Dedication	Line 10 (Elite: 12)	1	1	1	btm.	Line 10 (Elite: 12)	1	1½	1	btm.	Line 12 (Elite: 14)	1	1	1	btm.
Table of Contents	Line 10 (Elite: 12)	1	1	1	btm.	Line 10 (Elite: 12)	1	1½	1	btm.	Line 12 (Elite: 14)	1	1	1	btm.
List of Tables	Line 10 (Elite: 12)	1	1	1	btm.	Line 10 (Elite: 12)	1	1½	1	btm.	Line 12 (Elite: 14)	1	1	1	btm.
Body of Report															
First Page or Major Page Divisions	Line 10 (Elite: 12)	1	1	1	None	Line 10 (Elite: 12)	1	1½	1	None	Line 12 (Elite: 14)	1	1	1	None
All Other Pages	Line 8	1	1	1	top	Line 8	1	1½	1	top	Line 10	1	1	1	btm.
Bibliography/ Appendix															
First Page	Line 10 (Elite: 12)	1	1	1	None	Line 10 (Elite: 12)	1	1½	1	None	Line 12 (Elite: 14)	1	1	1	None
All Other Pages	Line 8	1	1	1	top	Line 8	1	1½	1	top	Line 10	1	1	1	btm.

*N/A = Not Applicable †Inches ‡Line 4: top, at right margin; bottom, at center.

ILLUSTRATION 11-2

Sample Title Page

THE CHANGING STUDENT PROFILE

by

JoAnn Falco
English Department

Bayside Community College
Central Campus

May 22, 19--

ILLUSTRATION 11-3

Sample Letter of Transmittal

Bayside Community College
Central Campus • 390 W. Tenth Street
Oakland, CA 94320-3990

July 12, 19--

Mr. John Neely, Editor
THE TEACHER'S AID
Central Publishing Co.
1653 Western Avenue
Montrose, CA 92174-7293

Dear Mr. Neely:

Enclosed is an article entitled "The Changing Student Profile" for your consideration for possible publication in THE TEACHER'S AID. This article is an examination of changes in the business education classrooms of the high school, community college, and university.

The topic is timely for today's educators as they attempt to meet the needs of classrooms of students with varied abilities. Reasons for increasing and decreasing enrollments, coupled with the effects of these changes on the classroom, are presented with a discussion of possible solutions.

Your publication committee's review of my article is most appreciated. I look forward to hearing from you.

Sincerely,

Dr. Carol Stevenson
Associate Dean

mos

Enclosure

ILLUSTRATION 11-5

Sample Dedication Page

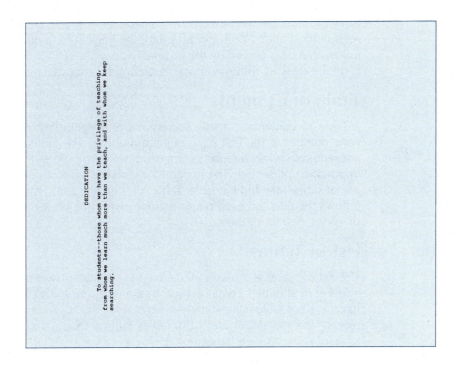

ILLUSTRATION 11-4

Sample Preface

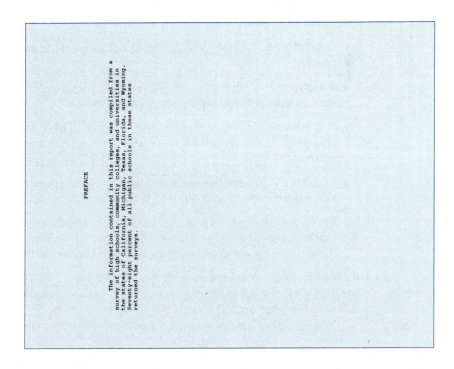

As Table 11-1 (page 263) indicates, the margins for both the preface/ foreword and the acknowledgments/dedication pages are identical. As seen in Illustrations 11-4 and 11-5 (both on page 265), a quadruple space follows the title, preceding the first paragraph. The remainder of the page is double-spaced with five-space paragraph indentions.

1106   Table of Contents

A **table of contents** is a list of every major division in a report and the page number of the first page of each division. The table of contents is not required; when a report is lengthy, however, it serves to organize the information presented. The margins for both the table of contents and the list of tables are indicated in Table 11-1 (page 263). A double space follows the title and each major division, with single-spacing within subdivisions. See Illustration 11-6.

1107   List of Tables

The **list of tables** is similar to the table of contents, except that it provides a listing of all tables contained within a report. Naturally, you would not have a list of tables unless there were *several* tables presented within the report. The spacing of the list of tables follows exactly that used for the table of contents. See Illustration 11-7.

1108   Outline

Just as the journey from one city to another is easier with a road map, the composition of a report is easier when you have an **outline** to guide you. Following the outline format in Illustration 11-8 (page 269), jot down ideas that will help you provide information on:

- **The Problem** — Upon what is the report to focus? State the problem briefly.

- **Background** — What situations have led to identification of this problem? Briefly, provide background information.

- **Procedures** — What procedures were used to gather the information presented in this report? What people were involved in the preparation?

- **Results** — What are the facts and figures of the situations analyzed? What have comparisons shown? What events have occurred?

- **Recommendations** — How can we use the results to make changes that will benefit the organization? What should we do differently with the knowledge we now have? What should we do in the same way?

If possible, share your outline with your colleagues. Discuss ideas to expand on your original outline. Compare your outline to reports previously submitted in your organization.

With your outline before you, write the first draft of your report.

ILLUSTRATION 11-7

Sample List of Tables

ILLUSTRATION 11-6

Sample Table of Contents

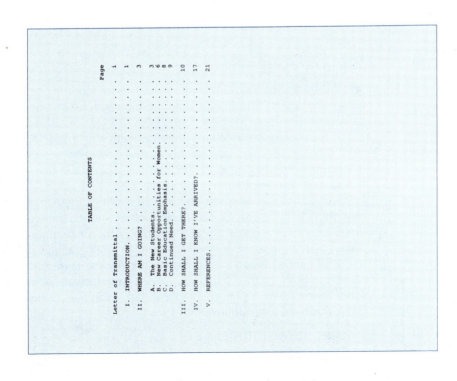

1109 Body of the Report

The **body of the report** is where the facts and figures of the report are found. The body is keyboarded in what is called **manuscript style** (double-spaced with five-space paragraph indentions) because it is easy to read. Margins for the first page and subsequent pages are indicated in Table 11-1 (page 263). Illustration 11-9 is the first page of the body of a sample report.

Double-space between the chapter reference and the title; a quadruple space is left between the report title and the first line of the body. First- and second-level subtitles are preceded and followed by a double space. Double-space the remainder of the body.

Each paragraph need not have a separate subtitle. Subtitles are used to provide the reader with additional information or to provoke interest in and clarification of the subject matter to be discussed in subsequent paragraphs.

1109.1 Quoted material. See Illustration 11-10 (page 270) for quoted material within a report. When **quoted material** is of more than two lines, it is indented five spaces from the left margin and single-spaced. A double space precedes and follows the quotation.

1109.2 Listed material. An example of **listed material** within a report is also shown in Illustration 11-10 (page 270). Listed material is also indented five spaces from the left margin and single-spaced.

Refer to Unit 8 for additional information on polishing your final report through the use of proofreading.

1110 Bibliography

The **bibliography** identifies all sources used, quoted, or paraphrased within the report. Spacing for both the bibliography and appendix pages is identified in Table 11-1 on page 263.

A quadruple space follows the title, with single spacing used within each bibliography item and double spacing between items. The first line of each notation begins at the left margin; subsequent lines are indented five spaces. See Illustration 11-11 (page 270).

Sometimes special forms are used when citing the name of the author or authors in bibliography entries. In footnotes when there are more than three authors of a single work, the name of the first author is given, followed by the phrase *et al* ("and others"); in bibliographies it is preferable to list all names. When two or more works by the same author are listed, repetition of the author's name is unnecessary. Instead, a line five spaces long, followed by a period, is substituted. Examples of these and other bibliographical forms follow:

1110.1 Book—One author

Bobbit, Franklin. *How to Make a Curriculum.* Boston: Houghton-Mifflin Company, 1924.

ILLUSTRATION 11-9

First Page and Sample Headings, Unbound Report

ILLUSTRATION 11-8

Sample Outline Organization

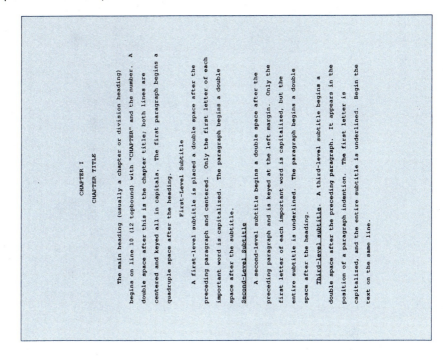

ILLUSTRATION 11-10

Sample Manuscript Page, Topbound Report

same time span will undoubtedly provide the greatest challenge to
date with classrooms of students with the maximum diversity of
skills and abilities.

Patricia Cross stresses the need for improvement in
education:

American higher education has worked hard for the past
quarter of a century to achieve educational opportunity for
all. It looks very much as though we shall spend the
remaining 25 years of this century working to achieve
education for each. The problems of attaining even minimal
educational opportunities for everyone have been so
consuming that we have not yet turned full attention to the
greater challenge of designing educational experiences that
will provide maximum learning for individuals. . . . we have
not demonstrated that we can deliver an education that
is attractive and useful to the majority of Americans.[6]

In his new book, Human Characteristics and School Learning,
Benjamin Bloom discusses a theory of school learning which can
account for most of the variation under a wide variety of
conditions. Simply stated, this theory consists of the
following:

1. Cognitive entry behaviors. The availability to the
learner of requisite entry behavior determines the extent to
which a specific task can be learned.
2. Affective entry characteristics. Affective entry
characteristics determine the conditioning under which the
learner will engage in a learning task.[7]

_____

[6]K. Patricia Cross, "Accent on Learning: Beyond Education
for All--Toward Education for Each" (Paper presented at the
meeting of the Symposium on Individualized Instruction,
Gainesville, April 8, 1976), pp. 21-23.

[7]Benjamin S. Bloom, Human Characteristics and School
Learning (New York: McGraw-Hill Book Co., 1976), p. 108.

8

ILLUSTRATION 11-11

Sample Bibliography Page

BIBLIOGRAPHY

Abdullah, Khalid Amin. "A General Survey of Shorthand Teaching
Devices." Masters thesis, Texas Technological College,
1966.

Anderson, Ruth I. "An Analysis and Classification of Research in
Shorthand and Transcription." Doctoral dissertation,
Indiana University, 1946.

_____. "Studying Shorthand--Reading vs. Writing." Business
Education World (September, 1948), p. 21.

_____. "Significant Implications of Research in Shorthand and
Transcription." Secretarial Education with a Future, 19th
Yearbook of the EBTA and NBTA. Somerville, N.J.: EBTA and
NBTA, 1962, p. 39.

_____. "Utilizing Shorthand Research in the Classroom."
National Business Education Quarterly (March, 1968): 48-49.

_____. "Methods of Instruction in First-Year Shorthand."
Effective Secretarial Education. Reston, Va.: NBEA, 1974,
pp. 31-45.

Arnold, Boyd Eugene. "The Effects of Combining Shorthand Plates
and Printed Materials as Out-of-Class Writing Assignments in
First-Semester College Gregg Shorthand." Doctoral
dissertation, Pennsylvania State University (University
Park), 1974.

Askew, Gloria H. "Structured Shorthand Sparks Student Interest
and Learning." Business Education Forum (October, 1974):
11-12.

Audiovisual Aids for Business. Economic and Distributive
Education. Monograph 92. Cincinnati: South-Western
Publishing Co., 1972.

Baggett, Harry W., Jr. "The Validity of a Measure of the
Difficulty of Gregg Shorthand Dictation Materials."
Doctoral dissertation, University of Minnesota, 1964.

Bobbit, Franklin. How to Make a Curriculum. Boston: Houghton-
Mifflin Company, 1924.

Hall, Laurence. New Colleges for New Students. San Francisco:
Jossey-Bass Inc., Publishers, 1974.

1110.2 ## Book—Repeating author

_____. *Curriculum and Instruction*. Boston: Houghton-Mifflin Company, 1926.

1110.3 ## Book—Two authors

Klausmeier, Herbert J., and William Goodwin. *Learning and Human Abilities*. New York: Harper & Row, 1966.

1110.4 ## Book—With editor

Skinner, Charles E., ed. *Educational Psychology*. New York: Prentice-Hall, 1951.

1110.5 ## Book—Chapter reference

Pullis, Joe M. "Variables Affecting Achievement in Shorthand and Transcription." In *Effective Secretarial Education*, 5–12. Reston, Va.: NBEA, 1974.

1110.6 ## Bulletins, pamphlets, or monographs

Pullis, Joe M. *Methods of Teaching Shorthand: A Research Analysis*. Monograph 126. Cincinnati: South-Western Publishing Co., 1973.

1110.7 ## Government publications

U.S. Superintendent of Documents, comp. *Checklist of United States Public Documents, 1789–1909*. Vol. I of *Lists of Congressional and Departmental Publications*, 3d ed., rev. and enl. Washington, D.C.: U.S. Government Printing Office, 1911.

1110.8 ## Magazine article—With author

Lambrecht, Judith J. "Aptitude Testing in Shorthand." *Business Education Forum*, October 1972, pp. 17–24.

1110.9 ## Magazine article—No author

"Air Thermometers." *Consumer Reports*, February 1966, pp. 74–75.

1110.10 ## Newspaper

New York Times, 15 January 1987, p. 3a.

1110.11 ## Paperback

Molloy, John T. *The Woman's Dress for Success Book*. New York: Warner Books, Inc., 1977.

1110.12 ## Unpublished dissertation

Stoddard, Ted Dee. "An Experimental Study in the Utilization of Staff and Equipment for the Teaching of Intermediate Collegiate Shorthand." Doctoral dissertation, Arizona State University, 1967.

1111 # Appendix

The **appendix** is a consolidation of examples, charts, graphs, memorandums, and the like, to further support and illustrate the information provided and recommendations made in the report. Each appendix item may be different in format, depending upon the type of information included. As much as possible, however, format should follow that recommended for the bibliography.

1112   Footnotes

Footnotes are references used to cite for the reader the source of any quoted or paraphrased material. An example of traditional footnotes is included in Illustration 11-10 on page 270. Traditionally, footnotes are keyed a double space below a divider line after the last line of text on the page. The secret to keyboarding footnotes is knowing how much space to leave so that the footnote(s) will appear between the manuscript material and the one-inch margin at the bottom of the page. At the left margin, an underline is keyed one and one-half inches long. A double space follows, and then the first footnote of the page is indented five spaces and single-spaced. Between two footnotes, there is a double space. Footnote numerical references are keyed as superscripts following the quoted material and in the reference at the bottom of the page.

1112.1   Examples of footnote formats

Book — One author

[1]Franklin Bobbit, *How to Make a Curriculum* (Boston: Houghton-Mifflin Company, 1924), p. 107.

Book — Repeating author

[2]Franklin Bobbit, *Curriculum and Instruction* (Boston: Houghton-Mifflin Company, 1926), p. 118.

Book — Two authors

[3]Herbert J. Klausmeier and William Goodwin, *Learning and Human Abilities* (New York: Harper & Row, 1966), p. 228.

Book — More than three authors

[4]Lawrence Hall et al., *New Colleges for New Students* (San Francisco: Jossey-Bass Inc., 1974), p. 97.

Book — With editor

[5]Charles E. Skinner, ed., *Educational Psychology* (New York: Prentice-Hall, 1951), p. 45.

1112.2   Repeated footnote references

When a footnote refers to exactly the same source as the previous footnote, the abbreviation *ibid.* ("in the same place") can be used.

[4]Ibid.

When a footnote refers to a work fully cited previously (*but not the one immediately preceding*), a shortened form for the footnote, including simply the author's surname and the reference page number, can be used.

[7]Douglas, p. 88.

At one time, scholarly references employed the abbreviations *loc. cit.* ("in the place cited") and *op. cit.* ("in the work cited") for subsequent references. However, this style is no longer recommended.

[16]Douglas, loc. cit.   (when reference is made to the same page in the work previously identified)

[11]Douglas, op. cit., p. 77.   (when reference is made to a different page in the work previously cited)

1112.3 Internal citations

A newer form of reference is called **internal citation.** In the internal citation form of reference, the quoted material is cited within the report using just the author's surname and the year of publication.

Sample Internal Citation

... important when we deal with children." (Myers, 1972)

The bibliographical reference for the internal citation is similar to what it would be in the traditional bibliography, with the addition of the exact page number of the quoted material.

Bibliography Entry for Internal Citation

Myers, Jerome L. *Fundamentals of Experimental Design.* Boston: Allyn and Bacon, Inc., 1972, p. 5.

In the internal citation form, works by the same author are identified by the difference in the year of publication. Should quoted material include sources by the same author written within the same year, one reference would read "(Smith, 1988A)" and the second "(Smith, 1988B)."

Understand:

- The services offered by the United States Postal Service (USPS)

- The services offered by private-sector firms that compete with or supplement USPS services

- The concept of electronic mail

- The services offered by wire service companies

- The telephone system and the services and devices available to business offices

Acquire:

- The ability to operate as many different communication devices as your school or office permits

- The ability to use the terminology of the communications industries

Be Prepared To:

- Devise or improve the system for handling mail in your office

- Choose the best postal service for outgoing mail items

- Select and recommend wire services that may benefit your firm

- Select and recommend telephone services that may be helpful to your firm

POSTAL SERVICE

Incoming Mail

1200   In a small firm, the mail carrier may simply give incoming mail to a designated secretary who will sort and distribute it. Larger firms, managing larger quantities of mail, usually have centralized departments and more formal procedures for processing their mail.

1201   ### Sorting and Delivering Incoming Mail

Usually, the mail for the entire office is delivered to a designated location—the mail department if there is one. There, it is sorted for internal delivery to the addressees—specific persons, departments, or offices.

275

1202 ## Opening the Mail

Some executives prefer to open their own mail; most have it opened by an assistant. Mail that is marked *personal* or *confidential* should be delivered unopened to the addressee.

1203 ## Mail not Addressed Specifically

Some mail is addressed to the company or office rather than to a specific department or individual. In each office, someone (frequently a person in the mail department or the chief executive's office) opens and routes all mail that cannot be routed by the address on the envelope.

1204 ## Date Stamping; Checking Enclosures

Many executives prefer to have their secretaries stamp their incoming mail with the date and time received, check it to be sure that listed enclosures are actually enclosed, and discard envelopes, wrapping, and other waste, after being sure that they do not contain addresses or other information that may be needed later.

1205 ## Scanning Incoming Correspondence

Some secretaries are responsible for scanning incoming correspondence, noting any information that may be useful, and retrieving from the files any documents that may be needed to answer the correspondence.

1206 ## Recording Incoming Mail

Whether or not mail is processed by a centralized mail department, management may choose to keep a **log** or **register** of important mail. Typical of the correspondence that would be recorded in such a log are:

- Mail between home office and branch office.
- Mail between parent firm and subsidiary.
- Correspondence with government agencies.
- Correspondence related to certain (or all) law cases.
- Insured mail.
- Special delivery mail.
- Registered and certified mail.

Mail Register

In	Out	Mo	Da	Yr	File Number	Document Name	Their Name	Our Person	Their Person	Response Mo	Da	Yr
x		9	1	90	234.572	Subsidiary Reports	Home Office	Werner	Algamond	9	15	90
	x	9	1	90	095.54	Sales Tax Return	State Revenue	Tadford	Billinks			

12

1207 Routing Slips

Any document that should be seen by several people can be controlled with a **routing slip** which contains the names of those to whom the document is to be routed. The slip is simply attached to the document, which is then passed from person to person. A routing slip is used for documents that are neither urgent nor of critical importance.

1208 High-priority Correspondence

One or a combination of the following methods may be used to fix the responsibility for answering high-priority correspondence and remind the person or persons responsible for meeting deadlines:

- Have a rubber stamp made to route and control high-priority documents.

Albert Martin, Director Public Relations Department		
Date **3/25/--**		
ROUTING SLIP		Date Forwarded
____ Everyone		____
____ Babb, B.		
✓ Gryder, H.		**3/25**
____ Igo, J.		
____ Mundt, K.		
✓ Primrose, N.		**3/25**
✓ Roehr, P.		**3/28**
____ Slaughter, G.		
✓ Tucker, C.		**3/28**
____ Wingfield, M.		
✓ *Brown, M*		**3/28**

Will you please:

____ Read and keep
____ Read and pass on
____ Read and return
✓ Read, pass on, and return

Date received	File
Document	
From	
Routed to	
Response required by	
The person to whom this document is routed is responsible for the response as indicated.	

Rubber Stamp for Routing
High-Priority Correspondence

- Circulate photocopies of the document (after it has been marked with the rubber stamp on which the blanks are filled in) to all who have an interest in or responsibility for response to the document.

- Register high-priority documents in a mail log. Include a check-off column to record in the log book the mailing of a response. Check the log book daily to be sure that deadlines are being met. Remind anyone who may be in danger of missing a deadline.

- Use a tickler file to prompt yourself to remind others of deadlines for reports, renewals, and the like, before each deadline.

1209   ## File-coding Incoming Correspondence

If a standard filing system is used throughout the office, department, or company, the logging procedure for incoming mail may include coding documents for filing purposes.

1210   ## Mail Expected Under Separate Cover

Whether or not other mail is logged, some firms keep a record of mail expected under separate cover. They do so to make sure that all the pieces of a mailing (letter and packages, several packages, and so forth) reach the addressee. This procedure should trigger a follow-up when an expected piece of mail does not arrive.

Outgoing Mail

1211   ## Proofreading

Regardless of the standards adopted by others, professional secretaries assume personal responsibility for the accuracy of their work. A final proofreading before each document is put into its envelope is the last opportunity to locate and correct errors. See ¶806.1–806.4 on proofreading.

1212   ## Signature

Develop a procedure for having the outgoing correspondence signed. Ideally, correspondence ready for signing should be taken in a batch to the executive. The secretary should stand by to answer questions and take last-minute instructions pertinent to the correspondence. A clipboard or folder may be used to organize the documents for signing. Stick-on notes may be used to indicate the proper location of signatures and to remind the executive of anything special about each document. If the secretary signs the executive's name to a document, the signature should be followed by the secretary's initials.

1213   ## Enclosures

Enclosure notations should indicate all the enclosures that will be included with a letter. If there is more than one enclosure, enclosures should be itemized in the notation. Double-check to be sure that enclosures are actually sent. The enclosure notation is placed flush with the left margin a double space below the reference initials, or a double space below the signature block if reference initials are not used. See Unit 10, ¶1017.

1214   ## Courtesy Copies

Whether *cc* (**carbon copy**) or *pc* (**photocopy**) is used, be sure that copies are sent to the proper persons. Use a check mark on the file copy or some other notation to record systematically the fact that such copies have actually been sent. Even though there is no notation on the original that blind copies have been sent, there should be a notation on the file copy. The notation used on the file copy is usually *bcc* or *bpc* for **blind carbon copy** or **blind photocopy.** The copy notation should be placed a double space below the signature block, reference initials, or enclosure notation—whichever is last. Be sure to save a file copy. When word processors are used, a standard procedure should be adopted for saving hard copies or saving the text on the magnetic medium or both. See Unit 10, ¶1018 and 1019. See Unit 13 regarding filing.

1215 Envelopes and Mailers

Stock a variety of envelopes—at least one of the large sizes and one of the small sizes. Mailers of several types are available; they are made with a variety of padding materials. If your firm does not have a department to prepare the outgoing mail, keep some kraft paper and string on hand to wrap packages that cannot be accommodated by standard mailers.

1216 Presorting Outgoing Mail

Small quantities of first-class mail are routinely *separated* into local and out-of-town categories by the postal service *customer.* Larger quantities (500 pieces or more in a single mailing) may be *presorted* by ZIP Code. Presorting, coupled with payment by postage meter, postage permit, or precanceled stamps, will save the customer about fifteen percent on first-class postage.

1217 Zip + 4

Five-digit Zip Codes sort mail down to the local zone. The four extra digits in the newer nine-digit codes permit sorting down to a specific firm, post office box, building, or carrier.

1218 Automatic Sorting

The use of two-letter state abbreviations, Zip Codes, and Zip + 4 make it possible for the Postal Service to use automatic sorting equipment. Usually, automatic sorting begins with an optical character reader (OCR). The OCR is a sophisticated, expensive machine that can read typewritten characters. The OCR imprints each piece of mail it scans with a bar-code. From then on, that piece of mail can be read by less expensive, faster bar-code readers as it passes through additional sorting points on its way to its destination.

Bar-Code

1219   ## Recording Outgoing Mail

Some firms have all pages of each outgoing mailing photocopied in order to have a complete record of everything sent. Others photocopy only the most representative pages of each mailing (the first and last pages of a multipage letter with enclosures, for example). Still other firms use a log or register to record outgoing documents. Any one of these methods provides a chronological record of the outgoing mail. See ¶1206 for an incoming/outgoing mail register.

1220   ## First-class Mail

First-class mail includes letters, bills, statements, invoices, checks, postal cards, business reply cards and envelopes, and greeting cards. First-class mail travels by the fastest means available to the Postal Service. Normally, such mail posted by 6:00 p.m. local time will be delivered to local addresses the following day, to destinations within 600 miles the second day, and to other destinations in the forty-eight contiguous states the third day. First-class mail cannot be opened for postal inspection.

1221   ## Priority Mail

Priority mail is first-class mail weighing at least twelve ounces, but no more than seventy pounds. Priority mail may not exceed 100 inches in combined length and girth.

1222   ## Minimum Size Limitations

Envelopes sent through the mail must be at least as thick as a postal card (.007") and at least 5" × 3-1/2". Articles not meeting these minimum size limitations are not mailable, since they cannot be processed by automatic sorting equipment and are difficult to process by hand.

1223   ## First-class Minimum Weight, Surcharges

A surcharge is levied on any envelope that weighs one ounce or less *and* exceeds six and one-eighth inches in height *or* eleven and one-half inches in length *or* one-fourth inch in thickness.

1224   ## Second-class Mail

Second-class mail consists of newspapers and magazines. It is a cheaper method of shipment. A special permit is required to send newspapers and magazines by second-class mail. Within the second-class category, there are separate classifications for single copies and bulk mailings (multiple copies of the same publication).

1225   ## Second-class Minimum Weight, Surcharges

A surcharge is levied on any article that weighs two ounces or less *and* exceeds six and one-eighth inches in height *or* eleven and one-half inches in length *or* one-fourth inch in thickness.

1226   Third-class Mail

Although **third-class mail** may be used for any merchandise or printed material, it is used primarily for the mass mailing of advertising material. It employs two rate structures: one for one-of-a-kind, one-at-a-time mailings — and another for batches of identical pieces. Sealed envelopes may be sent by third-class mail only if they are marked "Third-Class" on the address side. Third-class mail can be insured.

1227   Fourth-class Mail (Parcel Post)

Fourth-class mail accommodates parcels weighing one pound or more. There are maximums on size and weight. Charges are scheduled by weight and distance: higher rates for heavier parcels and more-distant zones. Parcels may be sealed or unsealed, but correspondence other than invoices or statements is prohibited. A common practice is to stamp or meter an envelope containing correspondence as though it were to be posted separately by first-class mail — then fasten the envelope to the outside of the fourth-class package. First-class rates apply to the correspondence; fourth-class rates apply to the package itself.

1228   Express Mail

Express mail is designed for rapid delivery. It is insured against loss at no extra charge. Several types of service are available:

	Picked-up at Sender's Office	Mailed at Sender's Airport	Delivered to Addressee's Airport	Delivered to Addressee's Office
Same day airport service		X	X	
Airport to addressee service		X		X
Office to airport service	X		X	
Pick-up and delivery service	X			X

Next-day service: Post the letter or parcel (or have it picked up at your office) by 5:00 p.m.; it will be delivered no later than 3:00 p.m. the next business day.

International Express Mail: Three-day service to major cities in foreign nations.

1229   Special Delivery

Special delivery service is available for first-, third-, and fourth-class mail. It provides delivery during regular business hours, during certain extended daily business hours, and during certain hours on Sundays and holidays.

    Special delivery mail moves with the regular mail in its class until it reaches the post office in the destination city. Normally, it is delivered to the addressee the day it reaches the destination post office.

1230   Certificate of Mailing

For a small fee, paid at the time an article is posted, the Postal Service will provide a certificate stating that the item was mailed. This certificate does not, however, insure the item against loss or damage.

1231   Return Receipt

For a small fee, the Postal Service will provide a receipt signed by the addressee or the addressee's agent at the time of delivery. A return receipt may be obtained as proof of delivery for insured mail valued at more than fifteen dollars, certified mail, registered mail, and COD mail.

1232   Insurance

First-, third-, and fourth-class mail can be insured up to a value of $400. First-class mail includes priority mail (all first-class mail weighing at least twelve ounces); fourth-class mail is also called parcel post.

1233   Registered Mail

Articles that cannot be replaced and those valued at more than $400 should be shipped by **registered mail.** Insurance of the actual value of the article up to $25,000 is included in the registration fee on all domestic deliveries (those inside the United States).

To ship an article by registered mail, the customer must declare the actual value of the article at the time it is posted. The article receives special care under controlled conditions all the time it is in the hands of the United States Postal Service (USPS). When the article is posted, the customer receives a receipt stating that it has been accepted for delivery by the USPS. For an extra fee, the USPS will provide a return receipt that indicates when, where, and to whom the article is delivered.

1234   Postage Meters

Postage meters can be purchased or leased from private manufacturers or leased from the USPS. The machine is taken to the post office periodically by the customer, who pays to have the meter reset (i.e., have it indicate more postage). Each time the user applies postage to an envelope or to a label for a parcel, the amount of postage necessary is set by the user. That amount is printed on the envelope or label and deducted from the postage indicated by the meter. The meter indicates the postage used since the machine was reset and the postage remaining for use. Misprints can be taken to the post office to obtain a refund.

For volume mailers, there are several advantages to the use of a postage meter. It is faster than stamping. It provides improved security (Postage is centralized; the imprint can be identified and traced.) Cancellation is not required as it is in the case of stamps. Postage meters can include a promotional message in their imprint.

1235   Postage Permits

Organizations can obtain a permit that allows the organization to have the postage printed on the envelope in the same impression used for printing the return address. One special kind of permit imprint is valid only for bulk mailing by the organization holding the permit; envelopes or other articles imprinted for bulk mailing cannot be mailed individually. Bulk mailing permits are available for first- through fourth-class mail. Postage permits make it unnecessary to affix stamps or run the pieces to be mailed through a postage meter.

1236   Collect on Delivery (COD) Service

The USPS will deliver an article to the addressee, collect at the time of delivery the amount specified by the sender (up to $300), and return the money to the sender. Charges may include all or part of the cost of the article, the postage, and the insurance. COD service is available for first-, third-, and fourth-class mail. COD service is also available from most of the private sector carriers that compete with the USPS.

1237   Money Orders

Postal money orders for payment in the United States are available at any post office. Most large post offices can arrange for money orders payable in foreign nations. The limit on an individual money order is $400, but more than one money order can be purchased if larger amounts are to be sent. Lost or stolen money orders will be replaced by the USPS if the user can establish ownership of the money order. Copies of money orders can be obtained for two years after the date of payment.

1238   Forwarding Mail

Individuals or organizations changing addresses should use the change of address kits provided by the USPS. Each kit contains forms with which to notify the USPS and those with whom the individuals or organizations correspond of the new address. First-class mail received at the old address is forwarded without charge for a period of one year; other classes are forwarded postage-collect.

1239   Business Reply Mail

Individuals or organizations can obtain permits to distribute self-addressed envelopes imprinted to indicate that the permit holder will pay the postage for the returned envelope. This allows business firms to distribute business reply envelopes freely with their advertising matter, hoping that a postage-free response will help persuade the potential customer to respond. Postage is collected from the permit holder when the envelope is returned. The permit holder may establish an account through which postage for individual items is deducted from a deposit for advance payments, thus eliminating payment in cash at the time of delivery.

1240 International Mail

Any post office will accept items for foreign delivery and answer individual questions about international mail. A USPS publication, *International Mail,* is a helpful guide, as are the other USPS publications on the subject.

1241 Postal Service Manual

Postal laws, regulations, services, and rates change from time to time. It is a good idea to have a copy of the *Postal Service Manual* in the office. It is available from or through your post office.

PRIVATE CARRIERS

1242 Private Delivery Services

Courier services, parcel services, airlines, bus companies, and taxicab companies offer a variety of delivery services. The yellow pages of the telephone book contain information on the services available.

1243 Private "Post Offices"

Small, private, storefront businesses offer many "post office" services in most communities. Typically, those services include postal boxes, USPS mailing services for all classes of mail, connections with private parcel carriers, connections with private courier services, package wrapping service, and photocopies.

1244 Airlines and Bus Companies

Most airlines and intercity bus companies accept packages at their baggage offices in one city for delivery at their offices in other cities.

1245 Courier Services

Courier services, such as Emery, Federal Express, and Purolator Courier, specialize in office-to-office delivery of envelopes and small parcels. They provide local and intercity service. Most items not delivered locally are moved by air.

1246 Taxicabs

Most taxicab companies offer local courier or messenger service.

1247 United Parcel Service

Parcels shipped via UPS can be dropped off at the local UPS office by the sender. They may also be picked up at the sender's place of business by a regularly scheduled UPS truck or during a special stop arranged by the sender the day before the pickup. Delivery is door to door. UPS competes with USPS and the private courier services.

ELECTRONIC MAIL AND WIRE SERVICE

1248 Cablegrams

Cablegrams are international telegrams that may travel by cable — or by microwave (satellite or relay-tower), radio, and the like. Cablegram service is available from Western Union and several other companies.

1249 Computer Networks

Almost any computer can be equipped inexpensively with a modem (modulator-demodulator) that permits the computer to send and receive data by regular telephone lines.

The computer user can "talk" to another user on the same network, check to see if there are any messages addressed to him or her, or "download" information. In **downloading**, the user simply copies over the telephone line data that is kept available in files maintained by the network.

1250 Electronic Mail

Several networks offer **electronic mail** (E-Mail) service. The service is given this name because electronic messages are held until the subscriber elects to "check the mailbox" for messages that are being held. The "mailbox" is actually a file in the central computer of the network. The subscriber calls in via computer and "checks the mailbox" by retrieving the messages in the file.

1251 Facsimile Devices

A **facsimile transmission (FAX) machine** is a scanning device that sends page-sized images by wire to similar machines throughout the world. Some operate over regular telephone lines; others are operated by various telephone companies and Western Union. A FAX machine operates like a photocopy machine that sends the image by wire. At the receiving end, a similar machine receives the electronic code for the image and translates it into the finished copy. The sending and receiving machines may be any distance apart so long as they are joined by a good connection.

Some FAX machines include a regular telephone handset so that the document can be transmitted and discussed in the same telephone call.

1252 Full-rate Telegrams

A **telegram** is a message sent by telex to someone who does not have a telex machine. It is sent to a Western Union office near the addressee by telex, then telephoned to the addressee. Delivery of the hard copy produced by the receiving telex machine is available for an extra fee.

1253 Inmarsat

Inmarsat is the marine sate lite system. It allows shore-to-ship, ship-to-shore, and ship-to-ship voice communication. Direct dialing is possible, using an area code for each ocean and a seven-digit number for each ship.

1254 Internetwork Service

If you have a computer equipped with a modem, you can reach anyone else equipped for telecommunication. If you know that the person you wish to reach has a computer that is part of a network, you may wish to go through that network. If not, you can dial a direct telephone line.

1255 Mailgrams

Mailgrams are made available through a cooperative effort of Western Union and the United States Postal Service. The sender sends a telex message (through the sender's own teletypewriter [or computer] or by calling Western Union) to the USPS telex installation nearest the recipient. At the receiving post office, the hard copy telex message is removed from the telex machine and delivered as mail. If the message is sent early in the day, it will be delivered the same day; if not, it will be delivered the following day.

1256 Overnight Telegrams

An **overnight telegram** is a telegram sent after regular business hours to arrive at the opening of business the next day. Since the charge is considerably less than that for a full-rate telegram, overnight telegrams are frequently used for longer messages.

1257 Telex

The **telex system** is a network of teletypewriters and computers connected through automatic exchanges making it possible for one user to communicate with another. Telex service is available in most of the major cities of the world. It is important to international trade because it helps overcome time and language differences and because it produces a hard-copy record. Western Union operates the largest telex network in the United States.

1258 Teletex

Teletex is an international system that permits properly programmed computers to serve as telex machines. It is operated by Western Union in the United States.

TELEPHONE SERVICES AND DEVICES

1259 Answering Machines

Answering machines provide most of the services of an answering service. They will answer your telephone with a prerecorded message, record a message, and give you your messages when you call in. Some include call screening: a speaker allows you to listen to messages and break in to answer if you choose to do so. The answering machine may be a separate unit or it may include a telephone.

1260

Automatic Dialing

Frequently called numbers are programmed into the individual's telephone. Each of those numbers can then be called by dialing only one to three digits (depending upon the capacity of the system).

1261

Basic Service

Basic telephone service consists of access to a local line. In most localities, the cost also includes placement and receipt of local calls. In some localities, there is a charge for local calls—either a flat rate per call or a charge based on the duration, distance, and time of day.

1262

Beepers (Pagers)

A **beeper** is a pocket-sized, battery-operated paging device that beeps to alert the user that a message has been received. Most beepers are used by physicians, security personnel, and the like, who are on standby status and by business people who are on call from their offices. Sophisticated units display brief messages (such as a telephone number) on a small liquid crystal screen. Usually, the user calls his or her office to get the message.

1263

Call Forwarding

If your telephone or system has a call forwarding feature, you enter a telephone number at which you can be reached, and the call forwarding feature automatically switches calls to that number. The number to which your calls are forwarded can be another conventional telephone, a pager, or a car telephone.

1264

Call Waiting

A call waiting feature sounds a soft beep when there is a call for a line that is in use. The beep tells the user that there is a call waiting and allows the user to switch to the second caller then switch back and forth between callers to complete both calls.

1265

Conference Calls

A conference call allows three or more telephones to be connected so that all callers can participate in a single conversation.

1266

Cordless Telephones

A cordless telephone consists of a base unit and a handset. The base unit serves as a relay station. It is stationary and is connected to a telephone line. It receives signals over that line and transmits them by radio wave to the handset. It also receives signals from the handset by radio wave and transmits them over the telephone line.

The handset is portable, not connected by wire to the base unit or the telephone line. The typical range between the base unit and the handset is about 700 feet.

1267   ## Credit Card Calls

The caller places a credit card call by dialing zero, the area code, and the number he or she wishes to call; an operator comes on line to obtain card information. The operator may record the caller's credit card number or route the call to a computer that asks the caller to dial his or her credit card number. In any case, the call is billed to the caller's credit card rather than to the telephone from which the call is made.

1268   ## Detail Recorders

Detail recorders are used to record data on telephone use. They vary in sophistication and in the kinds of data they can record. The most sophisticated units record all outgoing long-distance calls: the telephone number called, who made the call, the duration, cost, and other pertinent information.

1269   ## Dial Restrictions

Dial restrictions may be installed for a single telephone or an entire system, or for selected telephones in a system. Dial restricting devices block out certain exchanges, certain area codes, or all long-distance calls from the restricted telephones.

1270   ## Direct Distance Dialing

Long after most local telephone exchanges had been converted from manual switchboards to dial systems, long-distance calls were still placed manually by operators. Now, all domestic and many international calls can be made by direct dialing.

1271   ## Direct Inward Dial System

A direct inward dial system allows users within the system to be dialed directly from outside telephones. Outgoing calls are still routed through the user's PBX (see ¶1282) or key system. The user's switching circuitry may be part of the PBX system, a system installed to supplement the PBX system, or it may be at the telephone company's switching center. When the switching mechanism is furnished and maintained by the telephone company, it is sometimes called a Centrex system.

1272   ## Directory Assistance

Directory assistance (formerly "information") is reached by dialing the number listed in the front of your telephone book. The most widely employed system is to have the user dial 1-(the area code for the city in which the desired number is located—if different from the user's area code)-555-1212.

1273   ## Exchanges

Your telephone is connected by wire to the exchange which is identified by the first three digits in your telephone number. There, the automatic switching mechanism will connect you to another telephone in your exchange — or, if your call is destined for a telephone beyond your own exchange, route your call to the central office that serves your locality or service area.

1274   International Calls

For persons living near the boarders of Canada or Mexico, calls to those countries may be placed by dialing a number in the regular long-distance format — for example, 1-905-555-1234.

To reach other foreign stations, follow the instructions in the front of your telephone book. The usual procedure is to dial the international access code (011) first, then the code for the nation in which the station you are calling is located (two or three digits), then the city code (one to four digits; no code at all in some small nations), then the local telephone number.

If you are using a pushbutton telephone, depressing the # button after dialing is completed will speed up the switching process and get your call through more quickly.

1275   Key Systems

A **key (push-button) system** employs telephones that can be connected by depressing latching keys (buttons) that connect the telephone to any one of several lines and light up to indicate the line to which the telephone is connected. For example, you may be in an office in which eight people share two outside lines and two intercom lines. A simple key system can provide access to all four lines at any telephone in the system. Add a hold key, and it becomes possible to switch calls by alerting another user in the same office over an intercom line while the outside call is on hold.

1276   Last Number Redial

The last number redial feature makes it possible to redial the last number called automatically when a designated key is pressed (usually the # key). Last number redial is useful in trying to reach a busy number.

1277   Least-cost Routing

When the system is programmed for least-cost routing, it automatically tries to place outgoing calls through an 800 number or a reduced-rate line. If none is available, the call is dialed directly.

1278   Local Calls

Within your service area (city, county, and so forth) the automatic switching system routes our call to the proper exchange using the first three digits in the number you dial. Once your call has been routed to the proper exchange, it is further routed to the proper telephone using the last four digits in the number you dial.

1279 ## Long-distance Calls

To make a long-distance call, you first dial the long-distance prefix. The prefix depends upon the long-distance service you use, but it may be as simple as dialing the digit 1. Dialing the prefix connects you to your long-distance office or service which will route your call. From your own long-distance office or service, the next three digits in the number you dial (the area code) will route your call via cable, satellite, or microwave radio to the long-distance office in the destination city. In that office, the exchange number (the first three digits in the local telephone number) gets the local exchange; the last four digits route the call to the telephone you are calling.

1280 ## Long-distance Control System

When a long-distance control system is in operation, it places limitations on the calls that can be made from each telephone or by each individual. Individuals are identified by identification numbers. The long-distance control system may limit the telephone or individual to toll-free calls, local calls and 800 numbers only, certain area codes, domestic calls, or whatever.

1281 ## Message Waiting

The message waiting feature employs a special tone or light on the telephone to indicate that the receptionist or operator has a message for the user of that telephone.

1282 ## PBX Systems

A **PBX (private branch exchange) system** performs the same basic functions as does a key system: it permits the sharing of outside lines and provides intercom lines for internal calls. The original PBX systems were controlled from switchboards by operators who made plug-and-socket connections. Today's PBX system, or CBX (computerized branch exchange), or PABX (private automatic branch telephone exchange), employs a private dialing system for intercom calls and a dial code (usually the digit 9) for obtaining an outside line.

A PBX system can accommodate a larger number of telephones than can a key system. It also allows many embellishments to the basic line-sharing and intercom functions.

1283 ## Person-to-person Calls

When a person-to-person call is placed, the operator tries to reach a particular person for the caller. Charges do not begin until the caller is speaking with that person. Since the rate is high, it may be cheaper to make several attempts to reach the person with regular calls.

1284   Remote Station Answering

The remote station answering feature automatically switches incoming calls to a designated telephone. It is useful during times when a business is closed for switching calls to a single telephone—perhaps that of a night watchman or, in the case of a small business, the owner's home.

1285   Speakerphones

A speakerphone allows the caller to speak and hear through the telephone from anywhere in the room in which the telephone is located. It is useful when talking on the telephone and taking notes, or in bringing a telephone call into a meeting.

1286   Time and Charges

To receive a report of the time and charges pertinent to a call, the caller requests that information at the time the call is placed—and remains on the line after the call has been completed. The operator or a recording will then come on the line and report how long the call lasted and the charge for completing it.

1287   WATS Extender

A WATS extender may be incorporated into a PBX system. It enables users to call the PBX system from the outside and use the PBX's WATS lines.

1288   Third-number Calls

To make a third-number call, the caller asks the operator to charge the call to a number other than the one from which the call is placed. If the caller is traveling, he or she may wish to have the call charged to his or her home or business telephone.

1289   WATS

Wide-Area Telecommunications Service (WATS) is provided via a special telephone line over which outgoing long-distance calls may be placed. Generally, frequent users of long-distance services will pay less using WATS than they would using regular long-distance service.

Inward WATS permits the use of a number with an 800 area code to make incoming calls free to the caller. Long-distance charges are paid by the recipient of the call.

Unit XIII   Filing

FILING SYSTEMS IN GENERAL

1301   Filing Defined

Filing is the orderly arrangement of records for retention and retrieval. The records may be hard copies (written on paper), photographic images on film, or magnetic impulses stored on computer disks, tape, or other media.

1302   Purposes of Filing

Records are maintained for two general purposes. First, for transaction purposes: conducting the day-to-day affairs of the organization. Typical documents containing records of transactions are cash register tapes, sales slips, purchase orders, time cards, payrolls, and routine letters regarding the day-to-day operation of the organization.

The second purpose of maintaining records is the compilation and use of management information. Most management information is derived by refining the information stored in transaction records. Management information reflects past, present, and (projected) future sales, costs, profits, staffing, and the like; it provides a factual basis for management decisions.

13

1303 The Need for Rules

The orderly completion of transactions and effective use of management information are important functions in any organization. In a small organization, these functions may be relatively simple; they can probably be undertaken informally with some degree of success. In larger organizations, they are not simple — and *must* be undertaken methodically.

1304 Who Makes the Rules?

When only a few people use the files and those people can easily communicate with one another as the need arises, certain "common practices" will probably develop. Although those practices may or may not be the best way to maintain the records of the organization, they will work reasonably well — so long as they are used by everyone who has access to the files.

If some or all of those who use the files insist that their individuality be reflected in their work, the system will not work effectively. Worse still, a haphazard filing system makes periodic record-by-record searches for lost documents inevitable.

The records of larger, more complex organizations demand a more sophisticated approach — both because the problems of filing are more complex and because the results of misfiling or failure to retrieve are more difficult and costly to fix. The planning, organization, operation, and control of the more sophisticated filing systems is called **records management.**

In a large organization, many people may have access to the files. They *must* use the same rules for filing. Those rules are usually recorded in a manual; they are taught to each new employee who is given access to the files.

On a larger scale, many of those who work in records management belong to ARMA (the Association of Records Managers and Administrators). From time to time, ARMA publishes rules for alphabetic filing under the title *Guidelines to Alphabetic Filing.*

1305 Alphabetic-by-name Systems

Most organizations file alphabetically by the name of the person or organization the document concerns. A letter *to* or a letter *from* Suzanne Masters is filed in the *M* section under *Masters, Suzanne.* A bill from the Arvey Cable Company is filed in the *A* section under *Arvey Cable Company.*

1306 Subject Files

The military services, some other government agencies, and nongovernment organizations with special needs file by subject. Their systems are divided first into broad categories such as *Planning, Training, Intelligence,* or *Supply.* As with an outline, the system is divided into narrower and narrower categories until there is a file category for the subject of every document. The procurement of flour might be filed under:

Supply
     Procurement
          Food
               Flour

1307 Numeric Files

Although subject files can be arranged alphabetically, the various subjects are usually numbered. A few systems employ numbers separated by hyphens (12-2-23) or alphanumeric coding (A-23-G). Most numeric systems are decimal systems, similar to those used in libraries and in the military services.

When a subject filing system contains correspondence or other material pertaining to individuals or organizations, the filing order is *subject* first, then alphabetically by *name*.

A typical decimal filing system is organized something like the following:

100   Plans and Training

200   Personnel
     201   Applications
          201.1   Current Applications
                 Atwater, Ted B
                 Banters, Elma J
          201.2   Inactive Applications

Although those who work with the files soon get to know the numbers they use, an alphabetic card file is maintained as a key to the numbers. The alphabetic card file in a library is the key to the decimal subject system used for the books themselves.

1308 Subject Sections in Alphabetic Files

Organizations employing alphabetical-by-name systems frequently use a few *subjects* within the alphabetical system. Since the names of individual applicants are not long remembered, an *applications* section is frequently maintained. It is filed in alphabetic order under applications. Within the applications section, the names of applicants are filed alphabetically.

Similarly, a subject section within an alphabetic file may be set aside for sources of supply, a current construction project, a branch office, and so on.

1309 Geographic Files

Some organizations prefer to file some records geographically. This is particularly true in the home office of a decentralized organization that encourages those in each sales territory or branch office to manage their own correspondence. Geographic files are usually arranged alphabetically by state, then city, then name.

At first it might seem that such a system would operate very inefficiently when the home office receives a letter directly. In reality, a quick look at the address of the correspondent reveals the sales territory or branch office to which the letter should be assigned. Neither mass cross-referencing nor "shopping around" among branches is required.

FILING SEGMENTS AND INDEXING UNITS

1310   Filing Segments

A **filing segment** is the complete name, subject, or number used to file a record.

> Adeline R. Sweet (Personal name)
> Webster Word Company (Organizational name)
> Applications (Subject, filed alphabetically)
> 407.38 (Subject, filed by number [Decimal])

1311   Indexing Units

An **indexing unit** is a single character or group of characters (word, letter, number, or symbol) considered separately for indexing purposes. The name *Merrill T. Sinagra* has three indexing units: *Merrill*, *T*, and *Sinagra*.

ALPHABETIC FILING

Alphabetic Order

1312   Alphabetizing

In alphabetizing, the key unit is considered first, then the second unit, then the third unit, and so on. Within each unit, the letters are considered from left to right.

Name	Key Unit 1 2 3 4 5 6 7 8 9	Unit 2 1 2 3 4 5 6 7 8 9	Unit 3 1 2 3 4 5 6 7 8 9
Thackery T. Collins	C o l l i n s	T h a c k e r y	T
Madeline Jain Coyle	C o y l e	M a d e l i n e	J a i n

The order is determined at the third letter of the key unit by the first *l* in *Collins* and the *y* in *Coyle*.

1313   When Key Units are Identical

When key units contain the same letters in the same order, filing order is determined by comparing the letters in the second units (presuming that they are not identical also).

Name	Key Unit 1 2 3 4 5 6 7 8 9	Unit 2 1 2 3 4 5 6 7 8 9	Unit 3 1 2 3 4 5 6 7 8 9
William P. Caselton	C a s e l t o n	W i l _l_ i a m	P
Wilma E. Caselton	C a s e l t o n	W i l _m_ a	E

The order is determined at the fourth letter in Unit 2 by the second *l* in *William* and the *m* in *Wilma*.

1314 When First and Second Units are Identical

When the first and second units of a segment are identical, filing order is determined by comparing the letters in the third units (presuming that they are not identical also).

Name	Key Unit 1 2 3 4 5 6 7 8 9	Unit 2 1 2 3 4 5 6 7 8 9	Unit 3 1 2 3 4 5 6 7 8 9
Wilma E. Caselton	C a s e l t o n	W i l m a	E
Wilma P. Caselton	C a s e l t o n	W i l m a	P

1315 When all Units are Identical

When all units in a name are identical, the addresses determine the filing order. See ¶1328–1329 for identical personal names and ¶1344 for identical organizational names.

1316 Nothing Before Something

When all the letters of a unit are identical to the first letters in a longer unit, the shorter unit is filed first.

Name	Key Unit 1 2 3 4 5 6 7 8 9	Unit 2 1 2 3 4 5 6 7 8 9
Mari Sanchez	S a n c h e z	M a r i _
Marianne Sanchez	S a n c h e z	M a r i _a_ n n e

The *nothing* after *Mari* (the 5th letter position in Unit 2 of the first name) comes before the second *a* in *Marianne* (the 5th letter position in Unit 2 of the second name).

Personal Names

1317 Order of Indexing Units in Personal Names

The most important indexing unit in the segment is the *key indexing unit*. It is considered first for filing purposes and is written first when the segment is written in filing order. In the case of personal names, the key indexing unit is the surname (the last name). The given (first) name is the second indexing unit. The middle name or initial is the third indexing unit.

Name	Key Unit 1 2 3 4 5 6 7 8	Unit 2 1 2 3 4 5 6 7	Unit 3 1 2 3 4 5 6
George Siemer Glossman	G l o s s m a n	G e o r g e	S i e m e r
Merrill T. Sinagra	S i n a g r a	M e r r i l l	T

1318 Initials in Personal Names

Each initial in a personal name is considered a separate unit.

Name	Key Unit 1 2 3 4 5 6 7 8	Unit 2 1 2 3 4 5 6 7 8	Unit 3 1 2 3 4 5 6 7 8
B. B. Heller	H e l l e r	B	B
B. Bobbie Heller	H e l l e r	B	B o b b i e
Bobbie B. Heller	H e l l e r	B o b b i e	B

1319 Surname Prefixes

A prefix (particle) is combined with the word that follows it to form a single indexing unit. If a space separates the particle and the following word, the space is ignored for indexing purposes. Some common particles are a la, d', da, de, De, del, De la, della, Den, Des, di, Dos, du, El, Fitz, Il, l', la, Les, Lo, Los, Mac, Mc, O', St., Ste., Saint, San, Santa, Santo, van, Van der, von, Von der.

Name	Key Unit 1 2 3 4 5 6 7 8 9	Unit 2 1 2 3 4 5 6 7 8 9
Anthony DiSarro	D i S a r r o	A n t h o n y
Carla Disarro	D i s a r r o	C a r l a
Ilio Di Sarro*	D i S a r r o *	I l i o

*Indexed as one unit, **without** the space. Written **with** the space.

1320 Hyphenated Surnames

A hyphenated surname is considered as a single indexing unit.

Name	Key Unit 1 2 3 4 5 6 7 8 9	Unit 2 1 2 3 4
Hugh Ardmon-Watters*	A r d m o n W a t t e r s *	H u g h
Jani Diskin-Maran*	D i s k i n M a r a n *	J a n i

*Indexed as one unit, **without** hyphen or space. Written **with** the hyphen.

1321 Compound Personal Names

Each word in a compound personal name is treated as a separate indexing unit.

Name	Key Unit 1 2 3 4 5 6 7 8 9	Unit 2 1 2 3 4 5	Unit 3 1 2 3 4 5	Unit 4 1 2 3 4 5
Jani Ann Dill-Maran	D i l l M a r a n	J a n i	A n n	
Hugh John Armon Watts	W a t t s	H u g h	J o h n	A r m o n

NOTE 1: A compound name written open (Armon Watts) should be cross-referenced (under *Armon*).

NOTE 2: A hyphenated surname (Dill-Maran) is treated as a single unit. If the second element (Maran) may be used to identify the person, the name should be cross-referenced under the second element.

NOTE 3: If the first word in a compound surname is one of the standard surname prefixes (the *St.* in *St. John*, for example), the surname is indexed as a single unit. See ¶1319.

1322 Names of Married Women

The name of a married woman is indexed as she writes it. If more than one form of the name is known, it may be cross-referenced.

Name	Key Unit 1 2 3 4 5 6	Unit 2 1 2 3 4 5 6	Unit 3 1 2 3 4 5 6	Unit 4 1 2 3 4 5 6
Miss Doris B. Tate	T a t e	D o r i s	B	M i s s
Ms. Doris B. Tate	T a t e	D o r i s	B	M s
Mrs. Arthur F. Wood	W o o d	A r t h u r	F	M r s
Mrs. Doris T. Wood	W o o d	D o r i s	T	M r s
Mrs. Doris Tate Wood	W o o d	D o r i s	T a t e	M r s

1323 Royal or Religious Title Followed by a Single Name

A name consisting of a royal title (King, Princess, and the like) or a religious title (Father, Sister, and so on) and a single name (given name *or* surname, **not** both) is filed *as written* with the title as the first indexing unit and the name as the second.

Name	Key Unit 1 2 3 4 5 6 7 8 9	Unit 2 1 2 3 4 5 6 7 8 9	Unit 3 1 2 3 4 5 6 7 8 9
Princess Grace	P r i n c e s s	G r a c e	
Brother Clarence	B r o t h e r	C l a r e n c e	
Father Franklin	F a t h e r	F r a n k l i n	
But: Father John Franklin	F r a n k l i n	J o h n	F a t h e r

1324 Unusual Names

Some names are so unusual that it is impossible to distinguish between the given name and the surname. File unusual names in the order in which they are written. Cross-reference if doing so will be helpful.

Name	Key Unit 1 2 3 4 5 6 7 8 9	Unit 2 1 2 3 4 5 6 7 8 9
Sing Min	S i n g	M i n
Soong Ho	S o o n g	H o
Yeh Zabba	Y e h	Z a b b a

1325 Identical Names with Seniority Designations

When names are identical, seniority designations (if any) are used to determine filing order.

Name	Key Unit 1 2 3 4 5 6	Unit 2 1 2 3 4 5 6	Unit 3 1 2 3 4 5 6	Unit 4 1 2 3 4 5 6
T. Miles Aragon III	A r a g o n	T	M i l e s	I I I
T. Miles Aragon IV	A r a g o n	T	M i l e s	<u>I V</u>
Burton Ray Mayer, Jr.	M a y e r	B u r t o n	R a y	J r
Burton Ray Mayer, Sr.	M a y e r	B u r t o n	R a y	<u>S</u> r

NOTE: Seniority designations are indexed in their abbreviated forms (Jr., Sr., and so forth). The order is as follows:

First:	arabic numbers, in numerical order (2d, 3d) indexed as	2 3
Second:	roman numbers, in numerical order	II III
Third:	words, in alphabetical order, abbreviated forms	Jr Sr

See note at ¶1327.

1326   ## Identical Names Followed by Abbreviations

When names are otherwise identical, academic degree or professional designations (if any) are used to determine filing order. Abbreviations for academic degrees and professional designations are indexed alphabetically as written.

Name	Key Unit 1 2 3 4 5 6	Unit 2 1 2 3 4 5 6	Unit 3 1 2 3 4 5 6	Unit 4 1 2 3 4 5 6
Benja K. Hinton, A.B.	H i n t o n	B e n j a	K	A B
Benja K. Hinton, C.P.A.	H i n t o n	B e n j a	K	<u>C</u> P A
Benja K. Hinton, M.B.A.	H i n t o n	B e n j a	K	<u>M</u> B A
Benja K. Hinton, M.D.	H i n t o n	B e n j a	K	M <u>D</u>
Benja K. Hinton, Ph.D.	H i n t o n	B e n j a	K	<u>P</u> <u>h</u> D

See Note at ¶1327

1327   ## Identical Names Preceded by Titles

When names are otherwise identical, personal or professional titles (if any) are used to determine filing order.

Name	Key Unit 1 2 3 4 5 6 7	Unit 2 1 2 3 4 5 6 7	Unit 3 1 2 3 4 5 6 7	Unit 4 1 2 3 4 5 6 7
Dr. Jean B. Dwelley	D w e l l e y	J e a n	B	D r
Miss Jean B. Dwelley	D w e l l e y	J e a n	B	<u>M</u> i s s
Mr. Jean B. Dwelley	D w e l l e y	J e a n	B	M <u>r</u>
Mrs. Jean B. Dwelley	D w e l l e y	J e a n	B	M r <u>s</u>
Ms. Jean B. Dwelley	D w e l l e y	J e a n	B	M <u>s</u>

NOTE: In a rare case, one might find names that are identical including seniority designations, abbreviations, or personal titles. Consider the units in the following order:

	Unit 1	Unit 2	Unit 3	Unit 4	Unit 5	Unit 6
(Dr.) Avil R. Band III, P.E.	Band	Avil	R	III	PE	Dr
(Mr.) Avil R. Band III, P.E.	Band	Avil	R	III	PE	Mr

1328 Identical Names Without Titles, Degrees, or Other Identifying Units

When names are identical and there are no distinguishing titles, degrees, or other such units, indexing order is determined by the elements in the address in the following order:

Identical Units	City	State or Province	Street	House or Building Number
B K Hunt	Dallas	Texas	Longhorn Road	222
B K Hunt	Kansas City	Kansas	Walnut Avenue	313
B K Hunt	Kansas City	Missouri	Ellington Avenue	4309
B K Hunt	Kansas City	Missouri	Walnut Avenue	439
B K Hunt	Kansas City	Missouri	Walnut Avenue	4309

1329 Identical Names with Identical Titles, Degrees, and Other Identifying Units

When names are identical and titles, degrees, seniority designations and professional designations are also identical, indexing order is determined by the elements in the address in the following order:

Identical Units	City	State or Province	Street	House or Building Number
(Dr) R G Tate CPA	Atlanta	Georgia	Southern Ave	122
(Dr) R G Tate CPA	Columbus	Georgia	5th Avenue South	531
(Dr) R G Tate CPA	Columbus	Ohio	State Street	1022
(Dr) R G Tate CPA	Columbus	Ohio	Tucker Avenue	22
(Dr) R G Tate CPA	Columbus	Ohio	Tucker Avenue	237

1330 Names of Numbered Streets

The names of numbered streets are filed in ascending numerical order before street names expressed in words. Ordinal endings (*st, d,* or *th*) are disregarded. See ¶1331 for examples.

1331 Street Names with Compass Directions

A compass direction in a street name is indexed as it is written.

Name	Unit 1 in Street Name	Unit 2 in Street Name	Unit 3 in Street Name	Unit 4 in Street Name
3d Street	3	Street		
7th Street	7	Street		
7th Street SE	7	Street	SE	
7th Street Southeast	7	Street	Southeast	
South East 7th Street	South	East	7	Street
Southeast 7th Street	Southeast	7	Street	
Southeast Seventh Street	Southeast	Seventh	Street	

1332

House and Building Numbers

House and building numbers written in figures are filed in ascending order in a group. If an address contains both a street address and a building name, the building name is disregarded.

Building Designation	Unit 1 in Building Designation	Unit 2 in Building Designation
Allison Arms	Allison	Arms
Building 1	Building	1
Building 2	Building	2
Building C	Building	C
Meridian Club	Meridian	Club

Organizational Names

1333

Order of Units in Organizational Names

In the name of an organization, the words are indexed in the order in which they are written. The same rules apply to business firms, financial institutions, religious institutions, clubs, associations, and the like. The organizational name is filed as it appears in the letterhead, trademark, or the closing lines of letters.

Name	Key Unit 1 2 3 4 5 6 7 8 9	Unit 2 1 2 3 4 5 6 7 8 9	Unit 3 1 2 3 4 5 6 7 8 9
American Historical Association	American	Historical	Association
Collier County Bank	Collier	County	Bank
Community General Hospital	Community	General	Hospital
East Seattle Nursery	East	Seattle	Nursery
East Side Carpet	East	Side	Carpet
First Methodist Church	First	Methodist	Church
First National Bank	First	National	Bank
Long Island Lumber	Long	Island	Lumber
The Ritz-Carlton Hotel	RitzCarlton	Hotel	The
Truxton Department Store	Truxton	Department	Store
University of Florida	University	of	Florida

NOTE: *The* at the beginning of an organizational name is counted as the *last* indexing unit in that name.

1334   Personal Name Within an Organizational Name

Organizational names containing personal names are indexed as written; personal names are not transposed. See ¶1349.

Name	Key Unit 1 2 3 4 5 6 7	Unit 2 1 2 3 4 5 6 7	Unit 3 1 2 3 4 5 6 7 8 9	Unit 4 1 2 3 4 5 6 7
Juan Estero Insurance Agency	J u a n	E s t e r o	I n s u r a n c e	A g e n c y
Mario Deconda Pizza Parlor	M a r i o	D e c o n d a	P i z z a	P a r l o r

1335   Compound Words in Organizational Names

Compound words in organizational names are indexed as written. Hyphenated words are treated as though written solid.

Name	Key Unit 1 2 3 4 5 6 7 8 9	Unit 2 1 2 3 4 5 6 7 8	Unit 3 1 2 3 4 5 6 7 8 9	Unit 4 1 2
New York Deli	N e w	Y o r k	D e l i	
Pan American Travel Co.	P a n	A m e r i c a n	T r a v e l	C o
South West Properties	S o u t h	W e s t	P r o p e r t i e s	
Southwest Property Management	S o u t h w e s t	P r o p e r t y	M a n a g e m e n t	
South-West Property Management Co.	S o u t h W e s t	P r o p e r t y	M a n a g e m e n t	C o

1336   Married Woman's Name in Organizational Name

A married woman's name in an organizational name is filed as it is written.

Name	Key Unit 1 2 3 4 5 6 7	Unit 2 1 2 3 4 5 6 7 8 9	Unit 3 1 2 3 4 5 6 7	Unit 4 1 2 3 4 5 6 7
Mrs. Abbie Dabney's Place	M r s	A b b i e	D a b n e y s	P l a c e
Mrs. Henderson's Candies	M r s	H e n d e r s o n s	C a n d i e s	

1337   Minor Words in Organizational Names

All words in an organizational name—including minor words such as articles, conjunctions, and prepositions—are indexed in the order in which the organizational name is normally written, except for an initial *the*. Each word—including minor words—is indexed as a separate unit.

Name	Key Unit 1 2 3 4 5 6 7	Unit 2 1 2 3 4 5 6 7	Unit 3 1 2 3 4 5 6 7	Unit 4 1 2 3 4 5 6 7
At the Village Green	A t	t h e	V i l l a g e	G r e e n
The Green Banana	G r e e n	B a n a n a	T h e	

1338 Numbers in Organizational Names

Numbers spelled out in organizational names are indexed as written and filed alphabetically. Numbers written in figures are filed before numbers written in words. Arabic numbers are filed before roman numbers. Numbers written in figures with ordinal endings (1st, 2d, and so on) are indexed without the endings (1, 2, and so on). Inclusive numbers (24–47) are indexed by the lower number only (24).

Name	Key Unit 1 2 3 4 5 6 7 8 9	Unit 2 1 2 3 4 5 6 7 8 9	Unit 3 1 2 3 4 5 6 7 8 9
1st Texas Grill	1	T e x a s	G r i l l
6–9 Shop	6	S h o p	
Chapter 13	C h a p t e r	1 3	
Chapter XIII	C h a p t e r	X I I I	
Fifty-Four Forty Club	F i f t y F o u r	F o r t y	C l u b
First Texas Grill	F i r s t	T e x a s	G r i l l
One Twenty-Three Restaurant	O n e	T w e n t y T h r e e	R e s t a u r a n t
Patton's Marker 3	P a t t o n s	M a r k e r	3
Patton's Marker 27	P a t t o n s	M a r k e r	2 7
Patton's Marker South	P a t t o n s	M a r k e r	S o u t h
Size 6–9 Shop	S i z e	6	S h o p

1339 Symbols in Organizational Names

Each symbol in an organizational name is indexed as a unit and treated as though it were spelled out (¢ = cents, + = plus, and so forth).

Name	Key Unit 1 2 3 4 5 6 7 8 9	Unit 2 1 2 3 4 5 6	Unit 3 1 2 3 4	Unit 4 1 2 3 4 5	Unit 5 1 2
2 @ 1 Price Co.	2	a t	1	P r i c e	C o
The $ Wise Shop	D o l l a r	W i s e	S h o p	T h e	
!s Shop	E x c l a m a t i o n s	S h o p			
Take #s Off	T a k e	P o u n d s	O f f		

1340 Hyphenated and Coined Organizational Names

Each hyphenated or coined word in an organizational name is a single indexing unit.

Name	Key Unit 1 2 3 4 5 6 7 8 9	Unit 2 1 2 3 4 5 6 7 8 9	Unit 3 1 2 3 4 5	Unit 4 1 2 3 4 5 6
E Z Way Stores	E	Z	W a y	S t o r e s
E-Z On Brace Co.	E Z	O n	B r a c e	C o
EZ Ride Cab Co.	E Z	R i d e	C a b	C o
Ezzard Charles Gym	E z z a r d	C h a r l e s	G y m	
Southwestern Properties	S o u t h w e s t e r n	P r o p e r t i e s		
South-Western Publishing Co.	S o u t h W e s t e r n	P u b l i s h i n g C o		
Two-for-the-Show Theater	T w o f o r t h e S h o w T h e a t e r			

1341 Punctuation in Organizational Names

All punctuation is disregarded when indexing organizational names.

Name	Key Unit 1 2 3 4 5 6 7 8 9	Unit 2 1 2 3	Unit 3 1 2 3 4 5	Unit 4 1 2 3 4 5
H. W. Baker Co.	H	W	B a k e r	C o
Hughes, Win, and Baker	H u g h e s	W i n	a n d	B a k e r
Hughes-Win Co.	H u g h e s W i n	C o		
Hughes-Win, Inc.	H u g h e s W i n	I n c		

1342 Titles in Organizational Names

Titles in organizational names are indexed as written.

Name	Key Unit 1 2 3 4 5 6 7 8 9	Unit 2 1 2 3 4 5 6 7 8 9	Unit 3 1 2 3 4 5 6 7 8 9
Doctors' Hospital	D o c t o r s	H o s p i t a l	
Dr. Well	D r	W e l l	
Miss Bangles Fashions	M i s s	B a n g l e s	F a s h i o n s
Mr. Bob	M r	B o b	

1343 Abbreviations and Single Letters in Organizational Names

Abbreviations and single letters in organizational names are indexed as written. Each abbreviation is indexed as a separate unit (*Ave, Inc*).

Single letters separated by spaces are indexed as separate units. An **acronym**, a pronounceable word formed from the first letters or first few letters of several words (*radar, laser, BASIC*), is indexed as a single unit regardless of how it is written: closed, with spaces, with or without periods. The call letters of a radio or television station are indexed as a single unit.

Cross-reference the spelled-out form to the abbreviated form if that will be helpful (*Alcoholics Anonymous* to *AA*, *American Automobile Association* to *AAA*, and so on).

Name	Key Unit 1 2 3 4 5 6 7	Unit 2 1 2 3 4 5 6	Unit 3 1 2 3 4 5 6 7 8 9	Unit 4 1 2 3 4
A. A. Able's TV	A	A	A b l e s	T V
A Able Inc.	A	A b l e	I n c	
A. Able Incorporated	A	A b l e	I n c o r p o r a t e d	
Mad Harry's Used Cars	M a d	H a r r y s	U s e d	C a r s
MADD	M A D D			
Madison Ave. Theater	M a d i s o n	A v e	T h e a t e r	
Madison Avenue Bowling	M a d i s o n	A v e n u e	B o w l i n g	
WBBH	W B B H			
WBBH-TV	W B B H T V			
WNOG	W N O G			

1344 Identical Organizational Names

Identical organizational names are indexed by address. The elements of the address are employed as follows.

Identical Units	City	State or Province	Street	House or Building Number
Hamburger Hideaway	Covington	Georgia	Hamilton Ave	8436
Hamburger Hideaway	Covington	Kentucky	Garrard St	343
Hamburger Hideaway	Covington	Kentucky	Greenup St	822
Hamburger Hideaway	Covington	Kentucky	Greenup St	1833
Hamburger Hideaway	Denver	Colorado	Walton Ave	245

Governmental Names

1345 Federal Government

All federal government agencies are indexed under *United States Government*. Each agency is then indexed under the most distinctive word at each governmental level listed in the agency's name, starting with the level (subdivision) of highest rank and working down to the name of the agency itself. If the words *Department of, Bureau of,* and so on, appear at any level, they are indexed as separate units *if they are needed.*

Written As	Indexed As

Bureau of the Census
Department of Commerce
	United States Government
	    Commerce Department of
	    Census Bureau of the

Federal Aviation Administration
Department of Transportation
	United States Government
	    Transportation Department of
	    Aviation Federal Administration

1346 State and Local Governments

The name of the state, province, county, parish, city, town, township, or village is indexed first. If such words as *State of, City of,* and *County of* are included in the official name of the agency and those words are needed for filing purposes, they are considered as separate indexing units.

Written As	Indexed As

Division of Meat Inspection
Department of Agriculture
State of Ohio
Columbus, Ohio
	Ohio State of
	    Agriculture Department of
	    Meat Inspection Division of
	    Columbus Ohio

Division of Meat Inspection
Department of Agriculture
State of Ohio
Cincinnati, Ohio
	Ohio State of
	    Agriculture Department of
	    Meat Inspection Division of
	    Cincinnati Ohio

Bureau of Plant Inspection
Division of Plant Industry
Agriculture & Consumer Services
    Department
State of Florida
Tallahassee, Florida

Florida State of
    Agriculture and Consumer
        Services Department
    Plant Industry Division of
    Plant Inspection Bureau of
    Tallahassee Florida

Detective Division
Police Department
City of Rochester
Rochester, Minnesota

Rochester City of
    Police Department
    Detective Division
    Rochester Minnesota

1347 Foreign Governments

The first indexing unit of the name of a foreign government agency is the English name of the nation itself (Canada, Mexico, and so forth). If the official name of the nation includes words such as *Republic of* or *Dominion of*, each of these words is included as an indexing unit *if needed.*

Agencies and political subdivisions of foreign governments are indexed in descending hierarchical (rank) order. The most important word is the first indexing unit at each level; other words at that level are used if necessary. The city in which the agency is located (if needed for filing purposes) is the last element to be indexed. However, if all other elements are identical and the same agency has more than one location in the same city, the street address is indexed also.

Written As	Indexed As
Department of Transportation	Canada Dominion of
Dominion of Canada	Transportation Department of

Cross-Referencing

1348 The Need for Cross-referencing

No set of rules for filing could possibly designate a single place for filing every name and subject so clearly that everyone would understand and agree upon it. Not every document is confined to a single subject or even to a single name.

Suppose you are neatly set up to file customer names and job applicants by subject; however, a customer writes to place an order **and** apply for a job. Or suppose you work for a theatrical agency and Thelma Bledsoe writes to say that from now on her professional name will be Rita LaTour. Each of these documents requires cross-referencing.

1349 Organizational Name Including Personal Names

There are circumstances under which personal names included in organizational names should be cross-referenced. If your firm employs as an attorney the *Zwick* of the firm *Alton, Zwick,* and *Milton,* the correspondence should be filed under *Alton* and cross-referenced under *Zwick.*

The firm of A. B. Kensington Inc., usually called "Kensington's," should be filed under *A* and cross-referenced under *Kensington* or *Kensingtons* or both. See ¶1334.

<h2>1350   Compound Names</h2>

A compound name that is hyphenated is indexed as a single unit (¶1320, 1340). If there is a possibility that the person may also be known by the second element in the compound name, it should be cross-referenced under the second element. The name *Sandi Frazer-Hilton* would be filed under *FrazerHilton* and cross-indexed under *Hilton*.

The elements of a nonhyphenated compound name are filed as separate indexing units, last name (element) first. A married woman may take the surname of her husband and retain her maiden name as a middle name. If she chooses to continue use of her maiden name for professional purposes, her name should be cross-referenced. If Susan Spencer marries Tom Wilson, she may choose the name *Mrs. Susan Spencer Wilson*. For professional purposes, she may wish to be known as Ms. Susan Spencer. Her name would be filed as *Wilson Susan Spencer;* it would be cross-referenced under *Spencer Susan.* See ¶1321, 1322, 1336.

Unit XIV

Getting the Job— Getting Ahead

Understand:
- Where to find employment opportunities
- What to consider before applying for a job

Acquire:
- The ability to prepare a letter of application
- The ability to prepare an effective resume

Be Prepared To:
- Successfully prepare for a job interview
- Advance on the job

1400   The modern office may vary in size and specialty; however, the kind of office work will be similar in each. Office workers may handle many and various duties including appointment scheduling, routine correspondence, general accounting, telephone, and reception. Although each office may employ a limited number of workers, the great number of offices requiring assistance will provide many employment opportunities.

THE EMPLOYMENT SEARCH

1401 Employment Opportunities Exist in Many Situations Which Require Various Abilities

1401.1 **Traditional one- or two-employer offices.** Single doctor, lawyer, and CPA practices are still numerous today. Such small offices may have one to three individuals practicing the same, or different, specialties. Employees may handle a variety of duties each day.

1401.2 **Medium-sized offices where many employers work together.** These offices employ more workers who may share responsibilities, or specific tasks may be assigned to each office worker.

1401.3 **Large corporate offices.** In such office settings, office workers are generally assigned to specific departments or divisions with very specialized tasks. One employee might assist with the complex duty of organizing the delivery schedule, while another might work solely in the accounting department.

1402 Types of Work to Choose From

The choice of fields is unlimited. Careful thought should be given to the kinds of things you like to do and the areas in which you have an interest. For example, if you enjoy working with people and are interested in

14

sales, you might like working in an automobile dealership, employment office, art gallery, or retail shopping mall.

1403 Employment Skills Needed

To be successful in finding employment as an office worker, one of the first things you need to know is *what employers are looking for*. The following skills are the ones most requested by employers today:

- Basic academic skills—These are the ability to read, write, compute, and reason. Today the lack of these skills is a problem for many office workers. Correct grammar usage and spelling are a must for the production of excellent office correspondence.

- Secretarial skills—These are the ability to keyboard quickly and precisely, to transcribe accurately from machine dictation, to arrange attractively material on a typed page, to file and retrieve materials, and to use professional telephone techniques.

- Human relations—These skills involve the ability to deal with people (whether a boss, fellow worker, or customer) in a pleasant, friendly manner. It is important that all interactions be smooth and agreeable. Employers are looking for office workers who keep a positive and cheerful attitude, even in times of stress.

- Specific knowledge, experience, and skills. You may be surprised to find that specific abilities, while desirable, are ranked as the least important for today's office employee to possess. If you have basic academic, secretarial, and human relations skills, most employers are willing to train you. Nevertheless, additional business knowledge (knowledge of business terminology and actual work experience in the specific field) will make you the strongest possible candidate for a job opening.

1404 Where to Look for Employment Possibilities

Remember that job opportunities should be open to all persons—regardless of sex, race, ethnic heritage, religion, creed, age, or physical disability.

1404.1 Look through job openings currently advertised or posted.
There are many places where you can find such notices of office positions.

- The classified section of a newspaper

- Public or private employment agencies (WARNING: If you use an employment agency, make sure you know who pays the agency fee, if there is one. Many times the employer pays the agency to locate qualified individuals.)

- School bulletin boards or placement offices

- Magazines, professional journals, and periodicals

- Bulletin boards in personnel offices

14

1404.2

Find out about job vacancies not yet advertised. There are several ways you can do this:

- **Talk with family or friends.** They may know of upcoming employment opportunities in a particular field.

- **Visit personnel offices of employers.** Since personnel offices are responsible for posting and advertising all employment openings, a visit will often provide valuable advance information on upcoming openings.

- **Look for new or expanding office facilities.** The local newspaper often contains information regarding the opening of new offices, businesses, or departments within a university. The opening or expansion of any of these would require additional personnel. Once you know of such possibilities, a visit or job inquiry/application letter (see Illustration 14-1, page 312) is your next step. You may wish to send such a letter on cream-colored, gray, or beige paper. Using colored paper for your cover letter, envelope, and resume can make your application stand out from the rest; however, keep the overall look professional, not garish. The final package sent to the employer should contain no strikeovers; all corrections should be neatly made and not obvious to the reader.

- **Review the yellow pages of the telephone directory to find potential employers.** Once you have a list of possibilities, send a job inquiry/application letter (see Illustration 14-1, page 312) along with your resume to each company on your list.

APPLYING FOR THE JOB

1405

Application Form

When you write, call, or visit an employer, you will usually be asked to fill out an **application form.** The application form requests similar information to that given in your resume (an item that will be discussed later in this section). You should have your resume available when completing your application so that all dates and other information are accurate.

Since your application form, application letter, and resume will be the three written items considered before an interview is granted, it is important that all three represent you well. If you have the opportunity, ask to complete the application form at home, and then type the information requested (see Illustration 14-2, page 313). If you are requested to complete the form in the employer's office, do so neatly and in ink (see Illustration 14-3, page 314).

Some other important points you should remember when completing application forms are as follows:

1405.1

Read through the entire form. Before you begin to write, read through the entire form and note all of the questions asked. You will avoid putting answers in the wrong blanks by reviewing the form first. Follow directions carefully. Watch for special instructions such as last name first.

Fill the form out completely. Answer all questions fully and accurately. Complete all lines. If any question cannot be answered (for example, information requested on military service if you have not been in the military), put N/A on the blank line to show the question is "not applicable" to you and to show that you did not miss answering the question. All information provided on the application form and resume should agree exactly.

ILLUSTRATION 14-1

Job Inquiry/Application Letter

9090 Southwest Eighty-fifth Avenue
Miami, FL 33156-1900
June 1, 19--

Ms. Annie Betancourt
Personnel Manager
Jackson Memorial Hospital
1611 Northwest Twelfth Avenue
Miami, FL 33136-1106

Dear Ms. Betancourt:

The May 20, 19-- issue of The Miami Herald contained an article of interest to me about the upcoming expansion of the Pediatric Care Unit at Jackson Memorial Hospital. I am happy to hear of this expansion, as it will provide an opportunity to extend the excellent treatment now available to our sick and injured children.

Since such growth will require additional personnel, could the Pediatric Care Unit use a secretary who...

o can work with little supervision, taking initiative in completing complex tasks?

o will be dependable in attendance and be punctual?

o can deal with the public in a positive manner?

If so, I am the medical secretary for you!

The Pediatric Care Unit needs concerned medical secretaries who recognize the importance of accurate records and who are concerned with the treatment of patients. These areas were stressed in my medical transcription training at Miami-Dade Community College.

Jackson Memorial Hospital would be assured of a dedicated medical transcriptionist who sincerely cares for children, if you should decide to add me to your medical team.

In your hiring of the expanded Pediatric Care Unit, please give serious consideration to the enclosed resume. An immediate interview can be arranged by calling 555-5123. I look forward to hearing from you soon.

Sincerely,

Scott McMeekin

Scott McMeekin

Enclosure

ILLUSTRATION 14-2
Typed Sample Application Form

Jackson Memorial Hospital
the health team that cares.
Application for Employment

INSTRUCTIONS: This application must be filled out personally. Use black or blue ink. False or misleading statements are cause for rejection. All statements are subject to investigation. Answer all questions accurately and completely. PLEASE PRINT CLEARLY.

Position(s) applied for: Medical Secretary   Medical Treasurer

LAST NAME (Print in full): McMahin   First Name: Scott   Middle/Maiden Name: Social Security Number: 205-74-3859

Present Address: 6890 Southwest Rugby nfra Street   City: Miami   State: Florida   Zip Code: 33136-1900
Residence Telephone: (305) 866-6122
Other phone numbers where you may be contacted: Mother: 555-7492

Are you a citizen of the U.S.? Yes ☒ No ☐   If no, do you have a legal right to remain and work in the United States? Yes ☐ No ☐

EDUCATION – TRAINING

Place "X" in column indicating highest grade completed: 5 6 7 8 9 10 11 12   GED   College: A.B. X

Foreign Language Proficiency - Print the word "Good", "Fair", or "Poor" in the boxes titled Read, Write, Speak which best describes your ability to use this language.

Language	Read	Write	Speak
Spanish	Good	Good	Good

	Name and Location	Dates From	To	Grad-uate?	Major & Minor Subjects	Degree	Activities or Honors
High School	Coral Gables High School, Coral Gables, Florida	19–	19–	yes	Business Education	diploma	National Honor Society; Student Council Vice President
College	Mitchell Wolfson New World Center Campus, Miami/Dade Community College, Miami, Fl 33132-2800	19–	19–	yes	Medical Transcription Major	A.B.	Asst. Editor, METROPOLIS; President, Pi Theta Kappa
College	N/A						
Other	N/A						

Occupational or professional license(s)
If you have one: Type: Certificate from MDCC   Number: none
Date obtained: March, 19–   Renewal Date: N/A
If one is pending: Type: N/A   Date to be received:

OTHER SKILLS: Typing 60 wpm   Shorthand/Speedwriting 100 wpm
Other: Word Processing Equipment, Knowledge of Medical Terminology, Medical Transcription

Have you ever been a member of the Armed Services? Yes ☐ No ☒
Dates: From N/A   To
Type of discharge: Honorable ☐ Other (Explain) ☐   N/A
Date of Discharge: Month / Day / Year   N/A

V. Health Record
Do you have any reason that precludes you from performing any part of the job for which you are being considered?
None, excellent health

Since your 16th birthday, have you ever been convicted of a felonious offense? Yes ☐ No ☒
If "Yes", state the court, nature of offense, disposition of case and date. N/A

Prior to employment, your fingerprints will be taken for routine check by the F.B.I. and other agencies.

Employment Record
Have you been previously employed by Jackson Memorial Hospital? Yes ☐ No ☒
If "Yes", state department and dates N/A

List in order, starting with present or last employer.

Month/Dates Year	Company	Street	City	State	Zip	Telephone
From: April 19– To: Present	BAPTIST HOSPITAL	8900 S.W. 89 Street	Miami	FL	33156-8900	555-8076

Job Title: Volunteer   Department: Volunteer Services   Supervisor: Dr. Castell Bryant
Major Duties: typing, filing, delivery, candy/magazine carts, word processing equipment
Starting Salary $ N/A Per   Final Salary $ N/A Per   Reason for leaving: Still a volunteer   Telephone: 555-1191

| From: August 19– To: Present | CHICKEN SHACK | 11905 S.W. 88 Street | Miami | FL | | 555-1109 |
Job Title: Cook   Department: Kitchen   Supervisor: Mr. Louis Monzon
Major Duties: Food Preparation
Starting Salary $ 3.35 Per Hour   Final Salary $ 3.70 Per Hour   Reason for leaving: Still working   Telephone:

| From: To: | N/A | | | | | |
Job Title: Department: Supervisor:
Major Duties:
Starting Salary $ Per   Final Salary $ Per   Reason for leaving:

| From: To: | N/A | | | | | |
Job Title: Department: Supervisor:
Major Duties:
Starting Salary $ Per   Final Salary $ Per   Reason for leaving:

| From: To: | N/A | | | | | |
Job Title: Department: Supervisor:
Major Duties:
Starting Salary $ Per   Final Salary $ Per   Reason for leaving:

CERTIFICATION: I hereby certify that all statements made on this form are true to the best of my knowledge. I fully realize that should an investigation disclose any misrepresentation, I will be subject to immediate dismissal.
Date: 6/28/--   Signature: Scott McMahin

We are an Equal Opportunity Employer and participate in Affirmative Action Programs. Our application forms are designed to obtain an applicant's skills, knowledge and abilities based on specific job requirements. Questions are designed to elicit enough data for us to determine an applicant's abilities to successfully perform the job for which she/he is applying.

ILLUSTRATION 14-3

Handwritten Sample Application Form

Jackson Memorial Hospital
the health team that cares.
Application for Employment

INSTRUCTIONS. This application must be filled out personally. Use black or blue ink. False or misleading statements are cause for rejection. All statements are subject to investigation. Answer all questions accurately and completely. PLEASE PRINT CLEARLY.

Position(s) applied for: **Medical Secretary** **Medical Transcriber**

LAST NAME (Print in full): **McMeekin** First Name: **Scott** Middle/Maiden Name: Social Security Number **263-74-3859**

Present Address **8090 Southwest Eighty-fifth Street** City: **Miami** State: **Florida** Zip **33128** Residence Telephone **(305) 555-7122** Business Telephone **555-9482** Other phone number where you may be contacted

Are you a citizen of the U.S.? Yes ☒ No ☐ If no, do you have a legal right to remain and work in the United States? Yes ☐ No ☐

EDUCATION - TRAINING Foreign Language Proficiency - Print the word "Good", "Fair", or "Poor" in the boxes titled Read, Write, Speak which best describes your ability to use this language.

Place "X" in column indicating highest grade completed

	Language	Read	Write	Speak
5 6 7 8 9 10 11 12 GED College **A.S.X**	**Spanish**	**Good**	**Good**	**Good**

	Name and Location	Dates From 19 To	Grad-uated?	Major & Minor Subjects	Degree	Activities or Honors
High School	**Coral Gables High School** **Coral Gables, FL**	**19-- 19--**	**yes**	**Business Education**	**diploma**	**National Honor Society; Student Council Vice President**
College	**Mitchell Wolfson New World Center Campus, Miami-Dade Community College, Miami, FL 33122-3300**	**19-- 19--**	**yes**	**Medical Transcription Major**	**A.S.**	**Asst. Editor, METROPOLIS; President, P. Theta Kappa**
College	**N/A**					
Other	**N/A**					

Occupational or professional license(s): If you have one: Type **Certificate from MDCC** Number **none** Date obtained **March, 19--** Renewal Date **N/A** If one is pending: Type **N/A** Date to be received _____

OTHER SKILLS: Typing **60** wpm Shorthand/Speedwriting **100** wpm Other: **Word Processing Equipment, Knowledge of Medical Terminology, Medical Transcription**

Have you ever been a member of the Armed Services? ☐ Yes ☒ No Dates: From **N/A** To _____ Type of discharge: ☐ Honorable ☐ Other (Explain) **N/A** Date of Discharge Month / Day / Year **N/A**

V. Health Record Do you have any reason that precludes you from performing any part of the job for which you are being considered? **Has excellent health**

Since your 16th birthday, have you ever been convicted of a felonious offense? ☐ Yes ☒ No If "Yes", state the court, nature of offense, disposition of case and date. **N/A**

Prior to employment, your fingerprints will be taken for routine check by the F.B.I. and other agencies.

Employment Record

Have you been previously employed by Jackson Memorial Hospital? Yes ☐ No ☒ If "Yes", state department and dates **N/A**

List in order, starting with present or last employer.

Month Year	Company	Street	City	State	Zip	Telephone
From: **April 19--** To: **Present**	**BAPTIST HOSPITAL**	**8900 S.W. 89 Street**	**Miami**	**FL**		**555-8076** Supervisor **Dr. Carol Bryant**
	Job Title **Volunteer** Department **Volunteer Service**					Reason for leaving **Still a volunteer**
	Major Duties **filing, delivering goods/magazine cart, word processing equipment**					
	Starting Salary $ **N/A** Per **Day** Final Salary $ **N/A** Per					

From: **August 19--** To: **Present**	**CHICKEN SHACK**	**11905 S.W. 88 Street**	**Miami**	**FL**		**555-1131** Supervisor **Mr. Louis Marron**
	Job Title **Cook** Department **Kitchen**					Reason for leaving **Still working**
	Major Duties **Food Preparation**					
	Starting Salary $ **3.35** Per **Hour** Final Salary $ **3.70** Per **Hour**					

From: To:	**N/A**	Street	City	State	Zip	Telephone Supervisor
	Job Title Department					Reason for leaving
	Major Duties					
	Starting Salary $ Per Final Salary $ Per					

From: To:	**N/A**	Street	City	State	Zip	Telephone Supervisor
	Job Title Department					Reason for leaving
	Major Duties					
	Starting Salary $ Per Final Salary $ Per					

From: To:	**N/A**	Street	City	State	Zip	Telephone Supervisor
	Job Title Department					Reason for leaving
	Major Duties					
	Starting Salary $ Per Final Salary $ Per					

CERTIFICATION: I hereby certify that all statements made on this form are true to the best of my knowledge. I fully realize that should an investigation disclose any misrepresentation, I will be subject to immediate dismissal.

Date: **6/29/--** Signature: **Scott McMeekin**

We are an Equal Opportunity Employer and participate in Affirmative Action Programs. Our application forms are designed to obtain an applicant's skills, knowledge and abilities based on specific job requirements. Questions are designed to elicit enough data for us to determine an applicant's abilities to successfully perform the job for which she / he is applying.

1405.3   **Provide a salary range.** If asked what salary you desire, provide a salary range rather than a specific amount. Doing so will leave this subject open for later discussion during the interview.

1405.4   **Review the form carefully.** When you have completed the application form, review it carefully to make certain you have completely filled out each line with the information requested.

1405.5   **Attach a copy of your resume.** Finally, attach a copy of your resume to your completed application form before submitting both to the employer.

1406   # Employment Test

Employment tests are given to obtain additional information regarding each applicant. Scores from these tests are considered in selection of employees. Most often you have only one opportunity to be tested; however, sometimes the exam can be repeated to improve your performance.

Employment tests may cover typing, shorthand, business terminology, general intelligence, personality, or math. If you have received certificates of proficiency in any of these areas, take them with you to the employment office. A number of offices will accept such credentials and excuse you from the employment test covering similar skills.

Things to remember if you are asked to take an employment test:

- **Relax** as much as possible.

- **Read all instructions carefully.** If you are being given a timed test, request a moment to read instructions before the clock is started. Ask questions if you do not understand any directions.

- **Use your time wisely.** Divide your allotted time so that you know how long you have for each section of the test. Don't waste time on one particular question. Skip the troublesome questions and come back to them later, if you have the opportunity.

- **Look for answers** to harder questions in other parts of the test. You will be surprised how many hints you may find.

- **Write clearly and neatly** so that your answers can be read.

1407   # The Resume

Your **resume** should always be neatly typed. It provides a written picture of you—your experience, your skills, and your abilities (see Illustration 14-4, page 317). It is sometimes referred to as a **personal data sheet.**

If you type your cover letter on light-colored stationery, you should type your resume on the same kind of paper. Putting the cover letter and resume on colored paper can make your application stand out from the rest.

Your resume will consist of the following general sections:

1407.1   **Personal information**—Include your name, address, and telephone number. Review this information for accuracy. Once, information such as height, weight, marital status, number of children, birth date, social security number, health, and birthplace were included in the resume. However, recent laws preventing discrimination in hiring have made these items optional.

1407.2   **Education**—Include the degrees you have earned (most recent first), dates you attended each school, institution (high school, college, or university) where degree was awarded, location of school (city and state), educational major (minor optional), and month/year degree was awarded.

1407.3   **Work experience**—Include the dates of employment (most recent first), position title, company name, and location (city and state). Optional items in this category include name and title of your direct supervisor, actual job duties, and responsibilities. If you do not have much paid work experience, list volunteer work in this category, clearly indicating that you were a *volunteer worker.*

1407.4   **Special skills**—Information in this category includes specific courses taken or skills mastered that are relevant to the job you seek.

1407.5   **Other categories**—While the categories above are always included on a resume, the following categories are optional, allowing you to choose among them to present your "written picture" in the best light possible.

- **High school or college activities**—List any organizations or clubs of which you were a member; indicate offices you held, years of membership, any special activities you organized, and so forth.

- **Special honors or awards**—List any special honors or awards you have received. This category helps your resume to stand out from the rest.

- **Service to the community**—Include any community activities, professional memberships, and the like.

- **Military service**—Include the branch of service, rank, muster dates, military occupation or specialty, and any awards or honors.

- **Hobbies or special interests**

- **References**—Obtain permission from all individuals listed to use their names as a reference. You should feel certain that each one will know how to stress your particular skills. Indicate name, position, place of employment, business address, and telephone number for each reference.

Although each resume contains similar categories, you may vary the contents of your resume depending upon the position for which you are applying. For example, a position in an accounting office would call for stressing math, bookkeeping, and electronic calculator operation skills. A

ILLUSTRATION 14-4

Resume

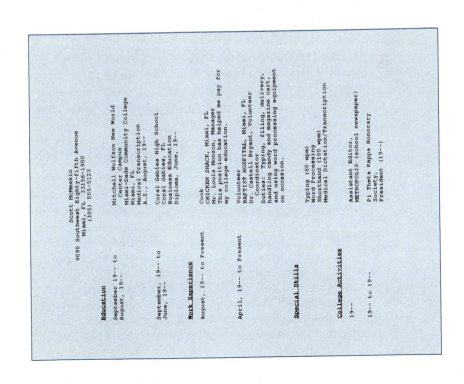

Scott McMeekin
9090 Southwest Eighty-fifth Avenue
Miami, FL 33156-1900
(305) 555-5123

Education

September, 19-- to   Mitchell Wolfson New World
August, 19--   Center Campus
                          Miami-Dade Community College
                          Miami, FL
                          Medical Transcription
                          A.S., August, 19--

September, 19-- to   Coral Gables High School
June, 19--   Coral Gables, FL
                          Business Education
                          Diploma, June, 19--

Work Experience

August, 19-- to Present   Cook
                           CHICKEN SHACK, Miami, FL
                           Mr. Louis Monzon, Manager
                           This position has helped me pay for
                           my college education.

April, 19-- to Present   Volunteer
                           BAPTIST HOSPITAL, Miami, FL
                           Dr. Castell Bryant, Volunteer
                           Coordinator
                           Duties: Typing, filing, delivery,
                           handling candy and magazine cart,
                           and using word processing equipment
                           on occasion.

Special Skills

                           Typing (60 wpm)
                           Word Processing
                           Shorthand (100 wpm)
                           Medical Dictation/Transcription

College Activities

19--   Assistant Editor,
                           METROPOLIS (school newspaper)

19-- to 19--   Pi Theta Kappa Honorary
                           Society,
                           President (19--)

Scott McMeekin
Page 2

Special Awards

19--   Silver Knight Winner,
                           Business
                           THE MIAMI HERALD

References

Castell Bryant, M.D.   Mr. Louis Monzon
Volunteer Coordinator   Manager
Baptist Hospital   Chicken Shack
8900 Southwest Eighty-ninth Street   11905 Southwest Eighty-eighth
Miami, FL 33156-8900   Street
(305) 555-8076   Miami, FL 33176-1109
                                      (305) 555-1191

Mr. Lynn Forrester
Department Chairperson
Office Technology Department
Mitchell Wolfson New World Center Campus
Miami-Dade Community College
300 Northeast Second Avenue
Miami, FL 33132-3300
(305) 555-6800

position at the reception desk would call for stressing human relations skills and good telephone techniques. Put yourself in the position of the employer reading your resume; make certain that you have answered all the questions he or she may have. As your work experience and activities continue over the years, your resume will grow; however, remember to maintain a brief and concise format (see Illustration 14-4, page 317).

1408 Application Letter

The application letter introduces the resume to the prospective employer. It points out your special skills and abilities and requests an interview.

Illustration 14-1 (on page 312) is a job inquiry/application letter; this type of letter is written to determine if there are *any* employment openings that will fit your skills. Illustration 14-5 is a letter you might send to a prospective employer when you know of a *specific* position that is vacant (see ad in Illustration 14-6). The application letter must get the reader's attention. You want yours to be outstanding. Look at the first paragraph in Illustrations 14-1 and 14-5 for attention-getting ideas. Let your creativity flow in attracting attention to YOU.

Highlight your special qualifications and special skills, education, or experience that make you the best candidate for the position you seek. Elaborate on specific items in your resume.

Ask for immediate action in the final paragraph of your application letter. Your request should be appropriate to the position for which you are applying. Such suggestions as "You can reach me during..." or "I could come for an interview on Friday" are good action phrases.

1409 The Interview

The very best chance you have to convince a potential employer to hire you is during the interview. You have the opportunity to sit down and describe in detail how your skills can assist an employer. Also, the employer has a chance to evaluate your personality, attitudes, personal appearance, enthusiasm, and ability to communicate.

Furthermore, you should recognize that the interview provides you with an opportunity to evaluate the open position. You need to make certain that this office is one in which you would be happy.

1409.1

Prepare first. Before you go to the interview, learn all you can about the employer. Ask questions of your teachers and friends about the normal skill requirements for such jobs, and make sure you are qualified. Inquire about current salaries of similar positions within the same area so that you will know what to expect or what to answer if you are asked. Be aware of fringe benefits provided by similar employers and rank their importance to you. Ask family and friends for possible interview questions so that you can begin to practice good answers. Think about and write down questions you want to ask the interviewer about the position; arrange these questions in order of priority in case you do not have time to ask them all.

ILLUSTRATION 14-5

Application Letter

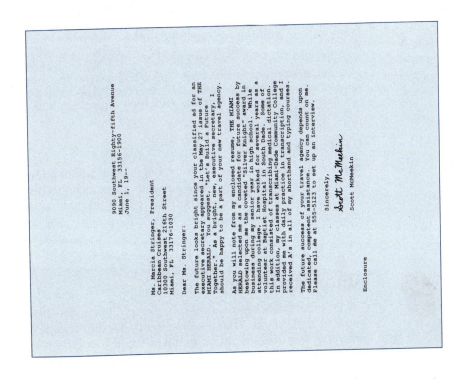

9090 Southwest Eighty-fifth Avenue
Miami, FL 33156-1900
June 1, 19—

Ms. Marcia Stringer, President
Caribbean Cruises
10300 Southwest 216th Street
Miami, FL 33176-1030

Dear Ms. Stringer:

The future looks bright since your classified ad for an
executive secretary appeared in the May 27 issue of THE
MIAMI HERALD. You suggest, "Let's Build a Future
Together." As a bright, new, executive secretary, I
should be happy to be a part of your new travel agency.

As you will note from my enclosed resume, THE MIAMI
HERALD selected me as a candidate for future success by
bestowing upon me the coveted "Silver Knight" award in
business during my senior year in high school. While
attending college, I have worked for several years as a
volunteer at Baptist Hospital in South Dade. Some of
this work consisted of transcribing medical dictation.
In addition, my classes at Miami-Dade Community College
provided me with daily practice in transcription, and I
received A's in all of my shorthand and typing courses.

The future success of your travel agency depends upon
dedicated, competent assistance. You can count on me.
Please call me at 555-5123 to set up an interview.

Sincerely,

Scott McMeekin

Scott McMeekin

Enclosure

ILLUSTRATION 14-6

Sample Job Advertisement

EXECUTIVE SECRETARY

LET'S BUILD A FUTURE
TOGETHER!

Good human relations skills,
60+ wpm, top pay,
Caribbean Cruises

Call 555-9277

1409.2 **Look your best.** Since this is the first opportunity the employer will have to judge your appearance, make sure you look your best. Decide in advance what to wear. Dress in your best business attire. Make certain your clothes are clean and wrinkle-free. Most importantly—remember to wear a smile!

1409.3 **Going to the interview.** Allow yourself plenty of time to dress and get to the interview. Call to find out exact directions before leaving home.

1409.4 **During the interview.** Try to appear relaxed. Although, everyone is somewhat nervous during an interview, try not to show your anxiety by moving often in your chair. Usually, an interview lasts approximately half an hour.

1409.5 **Focus on the interviewer.** He or she will take charge with the first question. Listen to all questions carefully and ask for clarification if you are confused. Reply honestly and briefly, but provide more than "yes" or "no" answers. Look the interviewer in the eye while speaking, and smile often.

1409.6 **Remember you are there to sell yourself.** Think about all of your skills and interests; discuss them in relation to the job requirements. Save your questions about the position and the employer until the end of the interview. Although pay and benefits are important concerns, you should not focus all of your questions on salary, vacations, and bonuses.

1409.7 **Avoid any criticism about past work experience, teachers, or family members.** Keep the situation positive and expectant. Watch for indications that the interview is nearing an end. If you are interested in working for this office, close the interview by letting the employer know.

> "Ms. Stringer, you've been very kind to take time from your busy schedule to talk with me. The information you have provided about the position has been helpful. You can count on my dedication if I have an opportunity to work with you."

1410 ## Check Back

Write a brief thank-you letter to the interviewer within a few days. Doing so will bring you and your qualifications once again to his or her attention. The interviewer should be thanked for the time and courtesy expended. You should repeat your interest in the position. See Illustration 14-7.

AFTER EMPLOYMENT

1411 ## Automated Office

Once you actually begin a new job, there will be many things you do not know or understand. Take the time to ask questions, and check carefully regarding instructions. Admit mistakes readily. Approach your employer with the discovered error and discuss frankly how to solve the problem.

Also, assure your employer what steps you will take to avoid making the same mistakes in the future.

You will also find more and more technological advances within the modern office. Present-day word processing software allows the easy revision and reorganization of typed material, checks the spelling, and performs some simple mathematical computations. The word processing software of tomorrow will provide even more advanced features.

ILLUSTRATION 14-7

Thank-You Letter

```
                                    9090 S.W. 85th Avenue
                                    Miami, FL  33156-1900
                                    June 5, 19--


          Ms. Marcia Stringer, President
          Caribbean Cruises
          10300 S.W. 216th Street
          Miami, FL  33176-1030

          Dear Ms. Stringer:

          Thank you very much for taking the time from
          your busy schedule to meet with me last
          Wednesday.  Your description of the job was
          quite comprehensive and very informative.

          I am most interested in working in an office
          such as you described.  If you decide to give
          me the opportunity, I shall strive to be
          always accurate and dependable.

                              Sincerely,

                              Scott McMeekin

                              Scott McMeekin
```

You should be aware that the word processing and data processing environments are moving closer and closer together. Microprocessors function as both word processors and minicomputers, when equipped with special software programs.

Telephonics (transmission via telephone) is expanding, with computerized telephones that allow easy transmission of data via regular telephone lines. These same phones will allow access to a large mainframe computer so that information may be withdrawn and added to the text of a letter or report.

Office technology is changing so rapidly that we all must stay abreast of the latest developments. Machines can make the modern office environment more efficient, thus allowing more time for working with customers and staff. (See Unit 8 for more information on office automation.)

1412   How to Advance

Although your first years on the job will be for learning and perfecting your performance, you should also begin to consider future goals. Sometimes it helps to think of more advanced positions you might like to be promoted to within the same organization. Other times, upward movement requires changing employers. It is important to keep constantly in mind the goals you are working toward.

Good advice for those who wish to advance is to dress and act for a position they aspire to, rather than for the position they now have.

1412.1   Continue learning.

If you are to advance within your profession, you must continue to improve and expand your knowledge. Because of their own dedication to the pursuit of knowledge in the field, most employers believe firmly in continuing education. The modern office worker should show a willingness to learn, even on weekends and "off" time. For instance, you should read as much as possible about recent developments in your field.

Bring any notices of pertinent seminars offered to the attention of your supervisor. Continued interest in learning new techniques highlights you as a possible candidate for a higher position or pay schedule. Frequently, employers will offer to pay tuition costs for seminars or classes. Depending upon what you need to learn, local adult basic education programs, community colleges, universities, and professional organizations all offer continuing education in the most recently identified skills required.

1412.2   Professional organizations.

Join the professional organizations most related to your new position. Many such organizations publish a periodic magazine with interesting articles on recent developments. Professional organizations also hold regular local, regional, and national meetings with expert speakers on particular topics. You will also have a chance to interact with others and share experiences.

1412.3   Move ahead with the organization.

As your organization grows, it will become more professional, more up-to-date, and more polished. It is important that you grow with your company. Sometimes this requires considering new ideas or new possibilities.

1412.4 **Join the office team.** Complete all tasks by the deadlines assigned, even if it means working later than usual. Be positive and cheerful in your dealings with other office workers. Volunteer to assist co-workers on high-priority projects. In times of stress, remain courteous.

1412.5 **Demonstrate your ability for working independently.** Look for ways to prevent problems in advance; take the initiative to follow each task through to completion; and organize your work in a way to allow speedy completion.

1412.6 **Always keep in mind your future goals.** Remember to model your actions, your behavior, your work, and your dress on those currently holding the position you want to achieve.

Follow these suggestions and you'll soon find yourself advancing up the career ladder. Always do the best you can on each task, and your efforts will be recognized. Best of luck!

Unit XV   References

1500 Neither this book nor any other single source can possibly answer all the questions that arise in the typical office. The following references will enable you to identify and locate a wealth of additional information. Many of these publications (and others equally as useful) may be found in your school or community library.

1501 Almanacs

Almanacs are usually published on an annual basis. They contain a variety of general information; the emphasis is on statistical information for the previous year, athletic events and records, the names of government officials, memorable dates and holidays, events of historical significance, and the like.

> *Information Please Almanac, Atlas, and Yearbook.* New York: Simon & Schuster, Inc.
> *The Official Associated Press Almanac.* Maplewood, NJ: Hammond, Inc.
> *The World Almanac and Book of Facts.* New York: Newspaper Enterprise Association, Inc.

1502 Bibliography

The publications listed below contain brief biographical notes on prominent persons. More detailed biographical information, when available, is obtained by looking up the person's name in the card file of your library.

> *Current Biography.* New York: The H. W. Wilson Company.
> *Dictionary of American Biography.* New York: Charles Scribner's Sons.
> *International Who's Who.* London: Europa Publications.
> *Official Congressional Directory.* Washington, DC: United States Government Printing Office.
> *Webster's American Biographies.* Ed. Charles Van Doren. Springfield, MA: Merriam-Webster, Inc.
> *Who Was Who: Companion to Who's Who.* New York: St. Martin's Press, Inc.
> *Who Was Who in America.* Chicago: Marquis Who's Who, Inc.
> *Who's Who.* New York: St. Martin's Press, Inc.
> *Who's Who in America*: Chicago, Marquis Who's Who, Inc.

15

1503 # Comprehensive Lists of Publications in Print

Virtually all books and periodicals in print can be found in one or more of the sources listed below.

Ayer Directory of Publications. Philadelphia: Ayer Press.

Bell, Marion V., and Eleanor A. Swidan. *Reference Books: A Brief Guide.* Baltimore: Enoch Pratt Free Library.

Books in Print, U.S.A.: An Index to the Publishers Trade List Annual. New York: R. R. Bowker Company.

British Books in Print: The Reference Catalogue of Current Literature. New York: R. R. Bowker Company.

Business Periodicals Index. New York: The H. W. Wilson Company.

Cumulative Book Index. New York: The H. W. Wilson Company.

Education Index. New York: The H. W. Wilson Company.

Gates, Jean Key. *Guide to the Use of Libraries and Information Sources.* New York: McGraw-Hill Book Company.

The New York Times Index. New York: The New York Times.

The Publishers' Trade List Annual. New York: R. R. Bowker Company.

Reader's Guide to Periodical Literature. New York: The H. W. Wilson Company.

Sheehy, Eugene P. *Guide to Reference Books.* Chicago: American Library Association.

Ulrich's International Periodicals Directory: A Classified Guide to Current Periodicals, Foreign and Domestic. New York: R. R. Bowker Company.

1504 # Dictionaries, Spellers, Thesauri, and Word Division Manuals

Unabridged dictionaries (the large ones, usually found in libraries) contain most of the words in the language. **Abridged** (shortened) **dictionaries**, typically about the size of a textbook, contain most of the *more common* words in the language.

Spellers contain lists of words spelled correctly—and sometimes divided into syllables.

Thesauri are books containing lists of synonyms and near synonyms arranged by subject. This arrangement allows the thesaurus user to select the very best word for the purpose intended.

Word division manuals list words correctly spelled and provide indications of the points at which each word may properly be divided.

12,000 Words, A Supplement to Webster's Third New International Dictionary. Springfield, MA: Merriam-Webster, Inc.

The American College Dictionary. New York: Random House, Inc.

The American Heritage Dictionary of the English Language. Boston: American Heritage Publishing Co., Inc. and Houghton-Mifflin Company.

Anderson, Ruth I., Lura Lynn Straub, and E. Dana Gibson. *Word Finder.* Englewood Cliffs, NJ: Prentice-Hall.

Brown, Alvin R. *Spelling: A Mnemonics Approach.* Cincinnati: South-Western Publishing Co.

Byers, Edward E. *10,000 Medical Words.* New York: Gregg Division/McGraw-Hill Book Company.

Funk & Wagnalls' Standard College Dictionary. New York: Harcourt Brace Jovanovich, Inc.

15

How and Where to Look It Up. New York: McGraw-Hill Book Company.

Kahn, Gilbert, and Donald J. D. Mulkerne. *The Word Book.* Beverly Hills: Glencoe Press.

Kurtz, Margaret A. *10,000 Legal Words.* New York: Gregg Division/McGraw-Hill Book Company.

Lamb, Marion M., and Devern J. Perry. *Word Studies.* Cincinnati: South-Western Publishing Co.

Leslie, Louis A. *20,000 Words.* New York: McGraw-Hill Book Company.

The Original Roget's Thesaurus of English Words and Phrases. New York: St. Martin's Press, Inc.

Perry, Devern J., and J. E. Silverthorn. *Word Division Manual.* Cincinnati: South-Western Publishing Co.

The Random House Dictionary of the English Language. New York: Random House, Inc.

Roget's International Thesaurus. New York: Harper & Row, Publishers.

Sisson, A. F. *Sisson's Word and Expression Locator.* West Nyack, NY: Parker Publishing Company.

Webster's Collegiate Thesaurus. Springfield, MA: Merriam-Webster, Inc.

Webster's Instant Word Guide. Springfield, MA: Merriam-Webster, Inc.

Webster's New Dictionary of Synonyms. Springfield, MA: Merriam-Webster, Inc.

Webster's New World Dictionary of the American Language. New York: Warner Books, Inc.

Webster's Ninth New Collegiate Dictionary. Springfield, MA: Merriam-Webster, Inc.

Webster's Third New International Dictionary, Unabridged: The Great Library of the English Language. Springfield, MA: Merriam-Webster, Inc.

1505 Directories

Just as the telephone directory for your community lists most of the telephone subscribers, other **directories** list people and organizations in other categories (manufacturers, banks, physicians, attorneys, and so on) on a national basis. Some directories concentrate on a specific kind of information — credit ratings, the ratings of bonds, and so forth.

American Medical Directory. Chicago: American Medical Association.

The Directory of Directories. Detroit, MI: Gale Research Co.

Dun & Bradstreet Ratings and Reports. New York: Dun & Bradstreet, Inc.

Encyclopedia of Associations. Detroit: Gale Research Co.

Fortune Directory. New York: *Fortune* Magazine.

The Martindale-Hubbell Law Directory. Summit, NJ: Martindale-Hubbell, Inc.

Polk's World Bank Directory, North American Edition. Nashville: R. L. Polk & Co.

Rand McNally International Bankers Directory. Chicago: Rand McNally & Company.

Standard Corporation Records. New York: Standard & Poor's Corp.

Thomas Register of American Manufacturers. New York: Thomas Publishing Company.

1506 Encyclopedias

An **encyclopedia** is usually an entire set of books explaining (usually in an introductory, general manner) virtually all branches of knowledge. Encyclopedias are arranged alphabetically by subject.

Although there are specialized encyclopedias that treat a single branch of knowledge in greater depth, the encyclopedias listed below are general purpose references that explain virtually all branches of knowledge.

Academic American Encyclopedia. Danbury, CT: Grolier, Inc.
Collier's Encyclopedia. New York: MacMillan.
Encyclopedia Americana. New York: Americana Corporation.
Lincoln Library of Essential Information. Buffalo: Frontier Press Company.
New Book of Knowledge. Danbury, CT: Grolier, Inc.
The New Columbia Encyclopedia. New York: Columbia University Press.
The New Encyclopaedia Britannica. Chicago: Encyclopaedia Britannica, Inc.
The New York Times Encyclopedic Almanac. New York: The New York Times Co.
World Book Encyclopedia. Chicago: World Book.

1507   Geography, Mail Service, Shipping, and Travel

The following references provide information on the movement of documents, goods, and people that is necessary to the transaction of business.

Address Abbreviations. Washington, DC: U.S. Postal Service Publication No. 59, U.S. Government Printing Office.
Ambassador World Atlas. Maplewood, NJ: Hammond.
Bullinger's Postal and Shippers Guide for the United States, Canada, and Newfoundland. Westwood, NJ: Bullinger's Guides, Inc.
Customs Regulations of the United States. Washington, DC: U.S. Government Printing Office.
Hotel and Motel Red Book. New York: American Hotel and Motel Association.
National Geographic Atlas of the World. Washington, DC: National Geographic Society.
National ZIP Code Directory. Washington, DC: U.S. Government Printing Office.
New International Atlas. Chicago: Rand McNally & Company.
Official Airline Guide. Sausalito, CA: Official Airline Guide.
The Postal Manual. Washington, DC: U.S. Government Printing Office.
Rand McNally Commercial Atlas and Marketing Guide. Chicago: Rand McNally & Company.
Vacations U.S.A. — Getting the Most for Your Travel Dollar. Washington, DC: Kiplinger Washington Editors.
Webster's New Geographical Dictionary. Springfield, MA: Merriam-Webster, Inc.

1508   Information Processing

This section contains references on computers, information processing, data processing, and word processing.

Bohl, Marilyn. *Essentials of Information Processing.* Chicago: Science Research Associates, Inc.
Cecil, Paula B. *Office Automation: Concepts and Application.* Menlo Park, CA: Benjamin-Cummings.
Clark, James F., and Kathy H. White. *Computer Confidence — A Challenge for Today.* Cincinnati: South-Western Publishing Co.
Crawford, et al. *Century 21 Keyboarding, Formatting, and Document Processing.* Cincinnati: South-Western Publishing Co.
Davis, Gordon B. *Computers and Information Processing.* New York: McGraw-Hill Book Company.

Fuori, William M., and Lawrence J. Aufiero. *Computers and Information Processing*. Englewood Cliffs, NJ: Prentice-Hall.

Gore, Marvin R., and John W. Stubbe. *Computers and Information Systems*. New York: McGraw-Hill Book Company.

Hardgrave, Terry et al. Eds. *Database Concepts*. Cincinnati: South-Western Publishing Co.

Harrison, William L. *Computers and Information Processing: An Introduction*. St. Paul, MN: West Publishing Company.

Long, Harry. *Introduction to Computers and Information Processing*. Englewood Cliffs, NJ: Prentice-Hall.

Mason, Jennie. *Introduction to Word Processing*. Indianapolis, IN: Bobbs-Merrill.

Rosen, Arnold, and Rosemary Freiden. *Word Processing*. Englewood Cliffs, NJ: Prentice-Hall.

Stern, Robert A., and Nancy Stern. *Introduction to Computers and Information Processing*. New York: Wiley.

1509 Finding a Job

A search for a new position can be conducted more effectively if it is planned well. Information from the following sources will be helpful in that planning process.

Dictionary of Occupational Titles. Washington, DC: U.S. Government Printing Office.

Figgins, Ross. *Techniques of Job Search*. San Francisco: Canfield Press.

Goble, Dorothy Y. *How to Get a Job and Keep It*. Austin: Steck-Vaughn Company.

Molloy, John T. *Dress for Success*. New York: Warner Books, Inc.

_____. *The Woman's Dress for Success Book*. New York: Warner Books, Inc.

Pivar, William H. *Work Experience Handbook*. San Francisco: Canfield Press.

Resume Service. *Resumes That Get Jobs*. New York: Arco Publishing Co., Inc.

Walter, Tim, and Al Siebert. *Student Success*. New York: Holt, Rinehart & Winston.

1510 Personal and Social Development

Appropriate personal manners and appearance will be helpful to you — whether you are seeking a new position or want to be more effective in your present position.

The Amy Vanderbilt Complete Book of Etiquette. Rev. ed. Letitia Baldrige. Garden City, NY: Doubleday and Co., Inc.

Eggland, Steven A., and John W. Williams. *Human Relations at Work*. Cincinnati: South-Western Publishing Co.

Letitia Baldrige's Complete Guide to Executive Manners. New York: Rawson Associates.

Post, Elizabeth L. *Emily Post's Etiquette*. New York: Harper & Row, Publishers.

Reynolds, Caroline. *Dimensions in Professional Development*. Cincinnati: South-Western Publishing Co.

1511 Quotations

A good quotation is seldom out of place. It can be used to strengthen an argument, provide a change of pace, or improve text simply because someone has expressed an idea so well that there is no better way to say it.

Bartlett, John. *Familiar Quotations*. Boston: Little, Brown & Company.

The Oxford Dictionary of Quotations. New York: Oxford University Press.

Sisson, A. F. *Sisson's Word and Expression Locator*. West Nyack, NY: Parker Publishing Company.

Stevenson, Burton. *Home Book of Quotations: Classical and Modern*. New York: Dodd, Mead.

1512 Secretarial Handbooks

For relatively brief but comprehensive coverage of the topics most useful in the office, consult a secretarial handbook.

Anderson, Ruth I., Dorothy E. Lee, Allien A. Russon, Jacquelyn A. Wentzell, and Helen M. S. Horack. *The Administrative Secretary: Resource*. New York: Gregg Division/McGraw-Hill Book Company.

Association of Records Managers and Administrators. *Rules for Alphabetical Filing*. Chicago: Association of Records Managers and Administrators.

Becker, Esther R., and Evelyn Anders. *The Successful Secretary's Handbook*. New York: Harper & Row, Publishers.

Clark, James L., Jr., and Lyn R. Clark. *How 2: A Handbook for Office Workers*. Belmont, CA: Wadsworth Publishing Co., Inc.

Crawford, et al. *Century 21 Typewriting*. Cincinnati: South-Western Publishing Co.

Doris, Lillian, and Besse May Miller. *Complete Secretary's Handbook*. Englewood Cliffs, NJ: Prentice-Hall.

Engel, Pauline. *Executive Secretary's Handbook*. Englewood Cliffs, NJ: Prentice-Hall.

Flynn, Patricia. *The Complete Secretary*. Belmont, CA: Fearon-Pitman Publishers, Inc.

Goodman, David G., Joseph S. Fosegan, and Ernest D. Bassett. *Business Records Control*. Cincinnati: South-Western Publishing Co.

Hutchinson, Lois Irene. *Standard Handbook for Secretaries*. New York: Gregg Division/McGraw-Hill Book Company.

Janis, J. Harold, and Margaret H. Thompson. *New Standard Reference for Secretaries and Administrative Assistants*. New York: Macmillan, Inc.

Johnson, Mina M., and Norman F. Kallaus. *Records Management*. Cincinnati: South-Western Publishing Co.

Kabbe, E. *Medical Secretary's Guide*. Englewood Cliffs, NJ: Prentice-Hall.

Kahn, Gilbert, Theodore Yerian, and Jeffrey R. Stewart, Jr., *Filing Systems and Records Management*. New York: McGraw-Hill Book Company.

Miller, Besse May. *Legal Secretary's Complete Handbook*. Englewood Cliffs, NJ: Prentice-Hall.

Parker Publishing Company Editorial Staff. *155 Office Shortcuts and Time Savers for the Secretary*. West Nyack, NY: Parker Publishing Company.

_____. *Secretary's Desk Book*. West Nyack, NY: Parker Publishing Company.

_____. *The Successful Secretary*. West Nyack, NY: Parker Publishing Company.

Sabin, William A. *The Gregg Reference Manual*. New York: McGraw-Hill Book Company.

Sletwold, E. *Sletwold's Manual of Documents and Forms for the Legal Secretary*. Englewood Cliffs, NJ: Prentice-Hall.

Taintor, Sarah, and Kate M. Monroe. *Secretary's Handbook*. New York: Macmillan, Inc.

Tilton, Rita S., J. Howard Jackson, and The Late Estelle L. Popham. *Secretarial Procedures and Administration*. Cincinnati: South-Western Publishing Co.

Whalen, Doris H. *The Secretary's Handbook*. New York: Harcourt Brace Jovanovich, Inc.

1513   Written Communication

Questions of grammar, style, punctuation, capitalization, abbreviation, and the like, arise from time to time in every office. The sources identified below contain answers to most of these questions.

Brown, Leland. *Communicating Facts and Ideas in Business.* Englewood Cliffs, NJ: Prentice-Hall.

_____. *Effective Business Report Writing.* Englewood Cliffs, NJ: Prentice-Hall.

Brusaw, Charles T., et al. *Handbook of Technical Writing.* New York: St. Martin's Press, Inc.

Burtness, Paul S., and Jack E. Hulbert. *Effective Business Communication.* Cincinnati: South-Western Publishing Co.

Campbell, William Giles. *Form and Style in Thesis Writing.* Boston: Houghton-Mifflin Company.

The Chicago Manual of Style. Chicago: The University of Chicago Press.

Frailey, L. E. *Handbook of Business Letters.* New York: Prentice-Hall.

Hodges, John C., and Mary E. Whitten. *Harbrace College Handbook.* New York: Harcourt Brace Jovanovich, Inc.

Keithley, Erwin M., and Margaret H. Thompson. *English for Modern Business.* Homewood, IL: Richard D. Irwin, Inc.

Lewis, David V. *Secrets of Successful Writing, Speaking, and Listening.* New York: American Management Association.

Perkins, W. E. *Punctuation: A Programmed Approach.* Cincinnati: South-Western Publishing Co.

Perrin, Porter G. *Writer's Guide and Index to English.* Chicago: Scott, Foresman & Company.

Schachter, Norman, and Alfred T. Clark, Jr. *Basic English Review.* Cincinnati: South-Western Publishing Co.

Schwartz, Robert J. *The Complete Dictionary of Abbreviations.* New York: Thomas Y. Crowell Company, Publishers.

Sigband, Norman B., and Arthur H. Bell. *Communication for Management and Business.* Chicago: Scott, Foresman & Company.

Style Manual. Washington, DC: U.S. Government Printing Office.

Turabian, Kate L. *A Manual for Writers of Term Papers, Theses, and Dissertations.* Chicago: The University of Chicago Press.

Wolf, Morris P., and Shirley Kuiper. *Effective Communication in Business.* Cincinnati: South-Western Publishing Co.

Page Index

Numbers refer to page numbers

P

Q

NOTES

Contents

By matching up the guides at the edge of this page with the marks opposite them along the edge of the book, you can quickly turn to the unit containing the material you want.